Human Resource Management in Europe

Human Resource Management in Europe

Edited by
Shaun Tyson
Peter Lawrence
Philippe Poirson
Luigi Manzolini
Ceferi Soler Vicente

KOGAN
PAGE

First published in 1993

Kogan Page Limited
120 Pentonville Road
London N1 9JN

© Shaun Tyson, Peter Lawrence, Philippe Poirson, Luigi Manzolini, Ceferi Soler Vicente 1993

British Library Cataloguing in Publication Data

A CIP record for this book is available from the British Library.

ISBN 0 7494 0362 4 (Hbk)
ISBN 0 7494 1311 5 (Pbk)

Typeset by DP Photosetting, Aylesbury, Bucks
Printed in England by Clays Ltd., St Ives plc.

Contents

Part 2: France

Part 3: Italy

Part 4: Spain

Part 5: United Kingdom

Contributors

Daniele Boldizzoni is Professor of Organisational Behaviour at the Istituto Studi Direzionali (ISTUD) in Stresa, Italy.

Donna Burnett is a Teaching Fellow at Cranfield School of Management.

Enrico Castagnolli is Assistant Professor of Operations at the Istituto Studi Direzionali (ISTUD) in Stresa, Italy.

Joan Cornudella is a Professor at ESADE in Barcelona. He is also a business consultant.

Samuel Husenman is a Professor at ESADE in Barcelona. He is also a business consultant.

Peter Lawrence is Professor of Comparative Management at the University of Loughborough Business School.

Yves-Frederic Livian is a Professor at Groupe ESC in Lyon.

Luigi Manzolini is Professor of Human Resource Management at the Universita Luigi Bocconi in Milan.

Manuel Marcet is Human Resources Director at Bimbo, the largest baking company in Spain. He also teaches at ESADE in Barcelona.

Francesco Paoletti is a Lecturer in Organisational Theory at the Universita Luigi Bocconi in Milan.

Philippe Poirson is Professor of Human Resource Management and Director of Human Resources at Groupe ESC in Lyon.

Godfrey Smith is Group Employee Relations Executive at Coats Viyella Plc.

Carlo Turati is a Lecturer in Organisational Theory at the Universita Luigi Bocconi in Milan.

Shaun Tyson is Professor of Human Resource Management and Director of the Human Resource Research Centre at Cranfield School of Management.

Ceferi Soler Vicente is a Director of Human Resource Management and Business Administration and Management at ESADE in Barcelona.

Carol Ward is Director of Human Resources Europe for the Avon Corporation.

Acknowledgements

We wish to thank the many companies and organisations described in this text for their permission to use the cases. We are also indebted to the case writers and to all the managers who allowed our authors to interview them and observe what was happening in their organisations.

Finally, we wish to thank Ann Davies and Dorothy Rogers for their final preparation of the manuscript.

Introduction

Europe is on the brink of integration, moving through the long and painful process of creating union. The management of people is a critical feature of the emerging Community. The creation of this massive new economic trading bloc has raised awareness among managers, academics, politicians, trade unionists and workers of the differences between the major economies in Europe: differences which are exposed most vividly in the way human resource management is conducted.

Our book seeks to explain the characteristic features of the management of people within Germany, France, Italy, Spain and the United Kingdom. For each of these countries we describe the main management features. Not just the basic statistical data and institutional facts – but how it feels to be a manager in those countries, what are the traditions for employees and what within organisations are the key European issues.

Much has been written about Euromanagers and a European style, but we believe that as European-wide management becomes common, understanding the distinctions between different countries with varying organisation structures and national cultures becomes important. In spite of institutional convergence, we expect these cultural differences to remain significant for some time.

We believe there are many levels of analysis which reveal the necessary understanding of human resource management, whether undertaken by personnel specialists or by line managers. At the societal level, the political, legal and institutional arrangements are the backdrop to the specific cultural traditions in each country. There are common activities for managers wherever they are located. How to manage may be different according to cultural differences, but human resource strategies must address common questions about how employees respond to new policies, how people feel about their work, what behavioural consequences will follow from actions and all the related motivational and attitudinal issues. There is also an 'action' level of analysis therefore, where managers act out their roles. Managers work in organisations, and we must therefore explain what is happening typically within organisations as a third level of analysis.

As experienced managers are aware, the 'devil is in the detail'. It is in organisations where actions occur, where societal influences are acted out, and where the problems and issues are addressed. For this reason, we present here a series of chapters explaining the cultural background with case studies which demonstrate the reality of management in organisations.

The case studies come from the main economies in Europe, with the exception of the newly united Germany. The bringing together of two existing contrary systems poses problems for a text of this kind. This is especially true where a highly formalised system changes. Flexible, voluntary systems with few legal controls are perhaps more adaptive and used to evolutionary change. We have therefore not included German cases in the present book, because we do not believe the lessons learned could be applied or would signify the organisations to be found in the future in Germany, but we hope that by the time we produce a further edition the situation will be more stable.

Case studies have been chosen as the best method to convey the experience of managing in different cultures. Case histories of organisations use the values, traditions and beliefs of organisation members as the context where human resource policies are pursued. By taking up the story in each case, we can see how managers act, and we can bring together the societal level, the level of social action for individuals and groups, and the organisation level of policies and human resource strategies.

Many of the cases centre on change management. Throughout Europe it seems we encounter the need to manage the processes of adjustment to structural and business change. Whole industries have been disappearing, new technology has been introduced, alliances and collaborative ventures formed and new management approaches demanded. There are also highly important local issues described in each case: how to formulate a new industrial relations strategy, how to involve trade unions in a change programme, how to manage a conflict, how to create cooperation and so on. This recognises the 'contingent' nature of organisational life – that what happens in organisations is dependent upon a range of variables, such as the history of the company, its size, structure and markets.

One of the benefits we can derive from comparative study is the possibility it offers for seeing what is different and what is the same. Surprisingly in all these different, contrasting cultures, many of the issues are the same: although our book concerns managers, we are describing the human condition. The problems faced by managers are as eternal as the human problems we all face. Whether it be the travel-stained Odysseus returning home, fierce Roland and wise Oliver standing together in adversity at Roncevaux or Mozart, struggling against ill health and debt, writing his last opera in the stage coach to Prague, we can see fortitude, persistence and the willpower of individuals acting in spite of fate and mischance. The universality of the human condition and the central problems of existence are common to art and literature. They are also the common denominators in all human resource policies, wherever such policies are enacted.

The chief value of comparative studies is to reveal not just what is the same – but to control for what is common, and to reveal cultural, institutional and political differences. In our book we discuss the traditions and characteristics in each country. From our case studies we draw on key issues and personnel policy responses at the organisational level of analysis, where social action takes place. We anticipate that when drawing comparisons the reader will consider the differences between countries. The case studies have been selected so comparisons can also be made at the organisational level. In each country there are two cases which are written about human resource management in that country, and one case concerning a company with a European business strategy. The structure of our book is therefore intended to facilitate comparisons both between countries and between organisations.

We have assumed a wide audience: undergraduates, graduates (including MBA students), managers and human resource specialists should each find material appropriate to their needs in this text. The focus shifts for each particular audience, as indeed does the extent of the coverage. We also see how a variety of methods of analysis can be utilized. We do expect that the professors who teach from our book will provide their own appropriate models and specific questions.

When readers examine the focus, coverage and analytical methods found in this book, the table below should be helpful.

Table 0.1 *Benefits of the text for different readers*

	Extent of coverage	Focus	Methods of analysis
Undergraduates	Understanding the facts	Discover differences	Description of main issues
Graduates	Interpretation of the facts	Contingency approach	Case study analysis
Line managers	How to manage in different countries	Pragmatic	Solutions and implementation plans
HRM managers	In-depth understanding of cultural differences and HRM situations in different countries	Major strategic issues	Diagnosis
Top managers	Implications of running businesses in Europe	Broad overview	Sifting and rapid intuitive understanding

The cases themselves have been written to reveal specific teaching points. Quite naturally, we anticipate some readers will wish to go beyond our simple rubric for each case and delve deeper into the hidden meanings to be found. Explicitly, the cases reproduced here are attempting to focus on the issues listed under each country heading.

France

Merlin Gerin

To describe to what extent it is difficult to modify a traditional French pattern of management, and to show how such a change is possible.

CDP

To explain the problems which require the organisation of a new management development programme. In particular, the case discusses how to involve union leaders and line managers in a process of modernisation.

Chloride

To show how a newly created European company can operate and the difficulties experienced.

Italy

SIP

How to cope with change and how to challenge an industrial relations system.

Telespazio

Managing HRM in a high-tech company. How to manage technicians and highly skilled professionals:

Valma Industries

How to manage HRM in a strategic alliance.

Spain

Sociedad de Servicios

How to develop a cooperation process and an efficient decision-making process from a business point of view between two strong units with separate cultural identities.

Edicli

How to manage conflict in a company which has a low level of profitability. The legal framework and industrial relations in Spain.

Bimbo

Analysis of the relationship between general strategies and the industrial relations system.

United Kingdom

Coats Viyella

Changes in collective bargaining and the move to productivity bargaining at local level.

British Telecom

How to develop women managers, the different options and the significance of gender in management.

Square D

How to create organisational structures and management systems in a European organisation, especially the HRM implications.

Common themes

Throughout the book common themes in strategic human resource management emerge which readers will encounter in the descriptions and case studies drawn from the different countries.

All countries in Europe are experiencing rapid and fundamental change. The turbulent environment which characterises our modern lives has arisen from the collapse of the Soviet Union, the new democracies in the East, the world role for the USA, the growing economic and political union of the European Community and the increasingly global nature of business. These and other trends in our

every-day understanding of events puts us into a 'continuous change' mode. Change is thrust upon change. From the international to the national and local level come new business opportunities, threats and economic conditions. New technologies and changing living standards among the newly industrialised nations put pressure on the older industrial countries, with a constant requirement to improve productivity.

These political and institutional changes are but one indicator of new values and new issues emerging. In addition the ageing population in Europe, unemployment in all EC countries, the EC fight against inflation through the exchange rate mechanism, all provide a common series of challenges to the human resource function. New product markets are quickly created, with a diminishing life cycle for most consumer products. Technological innovation is now almost expected to generate new production methods, and new ways of conducting our commercial existence are constantly to be seen.

With the rapidity of these business changes it is easy to lose sight of the changes to society which are also taking place. Our organisations are changing, so are our occupations. We now employ more technical specialists and professionals, and there are more women employed than ever before, in more senior positions. Managing in the new environment requires new competences – not least of which are flexibility and the capacity to work with ambiguity. The old rationalities – economies of scale, large production units, long production runs – are no longer applicable in our modern world, where head offices have shrunk in size, new trading partners are quickly found and where alliances are changed. In this 'post-modernist' state, there is a coincidence of interests between employee development and the demand for change. We need new ways of understanding, and the capacity to change our own roles to suit rapidly changing situations.

As one might anticipate, it is the industrial relations systems in all the countries in Europe which demonstrate the new institutional realities. We need to understand the existing industrial relations traditions within Europe, therefore, in order to appreciate what is changing. Trade union membership is changing, trade unions are themselves looking towards European collaboration. The social dimension to the EC gives it a central position within those changes. The question now raised is whether there will be EC-wide minimum standards, with a role for trade unions in the regulation of work, and this is the subject of a major debate in EC countries. Institutional changes made over the next decade will produce a new pattern on which much of the future in employee relations will depend.

Human resource strategies are the link between the societal and industrial relations changes mentioned above and the organisation level where new structures, new priorities and new business strategies are acted out. It is the purpose of our book to examine the changes and the human resources and industrial relations strategies which are found in the main European economies. The cases we believe illustrate these strategies, based as they are on the actual histories of companies which are implementing the changes and creating the new Europe from the old.

Part 1
Germany

1

Human Resource Management in Germany

Peter Lawrence

It has to be said straight away that at the time of writing (May 1992) several problems arise in any attempt at a rational discussion of the human resource function in Germany. The first and overriding problem is that it is only a year and a half since German reunification (3 October 1990) and still less than two years since currency union (1 July 1990). While the two Germanys have been united, they have not been integrated; or to put it another way, West Germany is far from having 'digested' East Germany. Second, the question of unification has 'knock-on' effects for the availability of statistics. Either the statistics one would like to have are not available, because 'the show has not been on the road long enough', or where they are available they are semi-meaningless. Take as an example unemployment. One can get an overall unemployment rate for unified Germany from the *Bundesanstalt für Arbeit* (federal labour office) in Nürnberg, but it will not be particularly revealing, being an 'average' of the lowish West German rate and the very high East German rate, the latter having quite separate and remarkable causes attendant on reunification. This is hopefully not a permanent state of affairs.

Or if unemployment seems too obvious and sensational an issue, consider trade union membership. It might be possible to produce a unionisation rate for Germany, but what would it be worth? In the late 1980s West Germany, in round figures, had a meaningful unionisation rate of 38 per cent, while East Germany had a meaning-less (ie circumstantially constrained) rate of 98 per cent of workers belonging to unions affiliated to the state sponsored trade union umbrella organisation ADGB. With unification ADGB and its affiliates were abolished and the political pressures to be a member of a union ceased; East German employees could choose to join 'West German' unions, or not, according to personal wish. But whatever they have done, as of the spring of 1992, will be no more than transitional; stable behaviour in such matters has yet to arrive.

The third problem concerns the West German reaction to the East German burden. Since reunification in the autumn of 1990 West Germans have paid, *inter alia*, higher petrol prices, higher telephone charges, and from the spring of 1991 a *Solidaritätszulage* (solidarity payment), all in support of their East German cousins. Now in the spring of 1992 they are being asked to moderate their wage demands because the federal Government is bowed down with the expense of rebuilding East Germany and in particular with refurbishing the infra-structure. So far there have been strikes by public sector employees, and the threat of a strike by the members of IG Metall, the engineering industry workers union, by far the largest. Perhaps the end of German economic stability and industrial peace is 'just round the corner', or perhaps it will turn out to be no more than what Harold Macmillan would have termed 'little local difficulties'!

Given these uncertainties the sensible way to proceed (though not necessarily in this order) is probably to:

- outline what has been the dominant, West German reality;
- describe the systems which have become pan-German;
- note the problems and question marks;
- try to establish the key issues in personnel matters for the former East Germany, now known as *die neuen Bundesländer*, or the new federal states.

The German economy

From 1942 onwards it was clear that Germany was going to lose the Second World War, yet the country and people probably suffered more in the first three years of peace than in the three years of successive military defeats, a theme that has been explored in more detail elsewhere (Lawrence, 1980). Yet by the time the two German states were founded in the autumn of 1949 things had already started to go better for West Germany.

First the British and Americans put in relief measures in 1946 with the GARIOA (Government and Relief in Occupied Areas) scheme, which the Americans followed in 1948 with the ERP (European Recovery Programme), better known as Marshall Aid. Second the currency reform of June 1948, albeit an exercise in 'monetary rough justice', proved a huge success. In the short term it ended hoarding and barter, stimulated production and dethroned the cigarette as the unit of post war currency; in the longer term it provided in the Deutschmark one of the world's most stable currencies. The Korean War (1950–52) gave the recovering West German economy a further boost; West Germany was of course neutral in this conflict (and had not even been admitted to the United Nations) but undoubtedly benefited as a supplier to the principal western belligerent, the USA.

From the early 1950s to the early 1990s the West German economy seems to have gone from strength to strength. GNP (gross national product), trade surpluses and disposable income grew throughout the 1950s and 1960s. West Germany was a founder member of the EEC (1958) and has always been its economically dominant member. After the period of the *Wirtschaftswunder* (economic miracle) the West German economy seems to have been marked above all by relative stability. Whenever there is an oil crisis, slump, period of unemployment or burst of inflation, it never seems to be as bad in West Germany as in most of the other industrialised countries. And as indicated in the previous section this happy state of affairs seems to have lasted until the spring of 1992; this remark should not be interpreted as a prophecy of German economic doom (a piece of wishful thinking all too popular among British commentators) but for the moment at least there are question marks.

The labour force

Using pre-unification data, West Germany is the largest of the EC member states with a population in 1990 of 62.7 million representing 19 per cent of the EC's overall population (for the same year Italy is in second place with a population of 57.576 million, this being 17.8 per cent of the EC's population at that time; Britain is close behind Italy).

Reunification in the autumn of 1990 added some 16 million to West Germany's population making the new state the largest in the EC by a comfortable margin.

Again staying with 1990 pre-unification data, West Germany has a civilian labour force of 29.829 million, this being 20.6 per cent of the EC's total. There are three further civilian employment statistics which are of interest in situating West Germany. The first is the share of women in civilian employment. Taking 1989, a year in which data on all EC countries is available, women in West Germany constitute 40.3 per cent of those in civilian employment, very close to the EC average of 39.5 per cent. The 'front runners' here are Denmark (45.7 per cent) closely followed by the UK (44.1 per cent). Those countries 'bringing up the rear' are the southern European countries, Spain, Greece and Italy (though interestingly not Portugal); the Netherlands is the only northern European country with a figure below the EC average of 37.6 per cent. If this statistic puts West Germany in the middle, the next two, conveniently taken together, give that country a distinctive profile. These are that West Germany has 'less than its share' of the EC's agricultural workers, but significantly more than its share of the Community's industrial workers – in round figures, 19 per cent of EC population but over 27 per cent of its employees in industry. This strength of manufacturing in West Germany and the persistence of this sector relative to the tertiary or service sector is characteristic, in fact and in spirit. In Germany 'real men' (and a lot of real women!) work in industry. Or to put it another way, the shift from industry to services which is typically hailed as 'the shape of things to come' and viewed as a mark of progress has not gone so far in Germany and has less credence in that country.

Trade unions

Throughout the post-war period West Germany has had a strong trade union system and, as noted in the introductory section of this chapter, with reunification this system has been extended to the former East Germany. It has several key features.

First, the number of trade unions in Germany is small, essentially 16, which are affiliated to the DGB, the central umbrella organisation equivalent to the Trades Union Congress (TUC) in Britain. In addition there are two non-affiliated 'white collar' unions: the DBB civil servants' trade union, and the DAG or salaried workers' union – this last has a largely professional membership including, for example, qualified engineers. And to complete the picture there is a Christian workers' trade union, the CGB, which is also independent of the DGB (umbrella organisation) but whose membership in the late 1980s was only around 300,000. A list of the trade unions with membership figures is given in the appendix to this chapter. Most of what follows refers to the 16 affiliated trade unions, of which the largest is the metal workers' union, IG Metall, with a current membership of 3.6 million.

Second, these 16 trade unions which are the heart of the German system are *industrial* unions, as opposed to being craft, general, enterprise or professional unions. That is to say, membership of these industrial unions is open to anyone *in the given industry* who wants to join a union, whatever their particular job or skill level, blue-collar and white-collar, production worker or maintenance, supervisory or manual. A consequence of this system of industrial unions is that demarcation disputes are precluded (the disputants would all belong to the same union). Indeed there is no expression in German for 'demarcation dispute', it has to be paraphrased (though many Germans believe such disputes to be rife in Britain, and get a lot of harmless fun out of this conviction).

Third, the DGB or umbrella organisation, the German equivalent of the British TUC, is generally viewed as well resourced, well staffed, relatively more important than the British equivalent and exercising stronger leadership (and discipline) over its member unions. To this positive picture it must be added that the DGB has been rocked during the 1980s by various investment and appropriation scandals centring primarily around the *Neue Heimat*, the DGB's subsidiary home construction company. Even so, the DGB remains bigger and stronger than the TUC in Britain; it is better resourced, and does more for its members (it even runs a bank, the BfW or *Bank für Gemeinwirtschaft*).

Fourth, the trade union system in general and pay deals in particular (see next section) are all rather more legalistic, with the implication that the unions themselves take their obligations (to employers) seriously. This formal legalism shades into a more intangible reasonableness. Again with the qualification made at the start of this chapter that no one knows what the future holds for industrial relations in Germany, for the most part German employers have not taken a hostile view of the unions. For more than three or four decades the word most commonly used by employers/managers to refer to the unions is *vernünftig* – sensible, reasonable. It has also been common for both the trade unions and the codetermination system (see below) to be referred to as an *Ordnungsfaktor*, an element in national stability or public order.

Fifth, the union has been the key factor in the negotiation of pay awards, as is made clear in the next section.

Pay awards

Most companies in Germany belong to the relevant employers' association. The employers' associations are industry based, like the trade unions, and they have an umbrella organisation, the BDA, with its headquarters in Cologne. The typical pay negotiation in Germany has two parties: the relevant employers' federation and the appropriate trade union; they negotiate a deal that is binding for all non-management employees. The negotiations take place at *Land* level, that is at the level of the various *Länder* (states) that make up the Federal Republic of Germany (*Bundesrepublik Deutschland*). The level of settlement varies a little between the *Länder*, being higher in a prosperous *Land* such as Baden-Württemberg, and lower in say Schleswig-Holstein, a poorer and largely agricultural state. This process occurs in an organised, scheduled, sequential way; it does not start at random because some group of workers suddenly feels like a rise! To put it another way, everyone knows when the pay round is going to start, which industry/union will take the lead and in what order the *Länder* will negotiate.

The above remarks make it clear that the system is structurally simple, though there are one or two qualifications. First, many smaller firms do not belong to the employers' federation (the expression is being *verbandpflichtig*, or duty-bound to accept the deal struck by the association) though these smaller companies are still likely to be guided by the association. Second, at the other end of the scale some very large companies, for instance Siemens, do their own negotiations with the union direct. However the above account covers the majority of settlements. Third, on the odd occasion when employees in an industry belong to more than one trade union, and this is not common because of the industrial union system, the convention is that the larger union takes over and negotiates for both sets of employees.

Tariff Agreements

The procedure outlined in the previous section leads to the annual wages contract, which when it has been negotiated has the force of law and may be upheld in the labour courts. To put this negotiation into context, it is the second act of a two act play.

The first act is the negotiation of a higher level, longer interval, more general *Manteltarifvertrag* (something like umbrella wages contract). The *Manteltarifvertrag* specifies everything except the actual pay rates. The sort of issues dealt with here will include the duration of the working week, shift work and overtime rates (as percentage additions to basic rates), arrangements for the remuneration of part-time employees, what happens if the company has to introduce short-time working, paid breaks, special payments, holiday entitlement, bonuses and extras of various kinds again expressed in percentage terms, sickness provisions, circumstances in which a worker is entitled to time off, probationary periods for new employees, termination of the work contract and pension arrangements. This *Manteltarifvertrag* will normally last for five years and then be renegotiated.

The *Manteltarifvertrag* is the background to the annual wages contract described in the previous section. The annual contract is variously known as the *Lohnvertrag*, *Lohntarifvertrag* or *Gehaltstarifvertrag*, and in fact contains information of two kinds. First, of course, are the wage rates for the various grades of workers. To take a real life example, a fairly simple one for a low technology company employing predominantly semi-skilled workers, the wages contract specifies monthly base wage rates for 35 categories of employee based on a points system of 0–186.

This brings us to the second kind of information contained in the annual wage contract, that relating to *Eintarifung*, or fitting people into categories. For this to happen there must be some agreed method of classifying the jobs, so that worker X can be said to be occupying, for example, a senior experienced semi-skilled job carrying a group 5A salary, or whatever. Sometimes the classification of the job is straightforward, commonsense stuff, which can be easily agreed; but sometimes it is based on an elaborate analytical model where all jobs are graded in terms of several analytical criteria yielding an overall pay grade for each. In the present writer's experience, there is little dispute in Germany over differentials in the British sense, over the pay gaps corresponding to the skill differences. It is the *Eintarifung*, the fitting of people into the system, that is sometimes both complicated and controversial.

Pay and the Personnel Manager

It will be clear straight away that the role of the typical personnel manager in Germany is affected by the payment system. Firstly, the majority of personnel managers are simply not involved in the negotiation of pay, unlike their Anglo-Saxon counterparts, all this happening as we have seen at the employers' association/trade union level above the company. In short, a principal activity and dimension of professional importance is removed from most of them 'at a stroke'. Compare the German personnel manager in this matter with his or her American counterpart, where negotiation of the union contract is seen by colleagues as the ultimate act of executive *machismo*.

But secondly, although German personnel managers do not get to do the exciting and important bit, the negotiation, they do have to do the boring implementation, requiring more attention to detail. *Eintarifung* may exercise a professional appeal for some personnel managers, but it suffers from the fact that one gets blamed for getting it wrong rather than praised for getting it right.

The relationship between the payment system and personnel practice in Germany is one of several factors inclining the typical personnel manager in that country to be reactive rather than proactive. Another such factor is the codetermination system.

Industrial democracy in Germany

Before outlining the system, and a more detailed account may be found elsewhere (Lawrence, 1980), a few introductory facts may be helpful. Public companies in Germany, those with AG after their name, have 'two tier' boards. The higher-level one is the *Aufsichtsrat*, usually rendered in English as supervisory board, a non-executive board. Typically the *Aufsichtsrat* is made up of representatives of the company's bank, customers and suppliers, perhaps together with some senior executives from elsewhere. The *Aufsichtsrat* does not initiate policy, but it is concerned with the company's capitalisation, has to give its consent to any major changes in the scope and purpose of the company's business, and appoints the second of the two-tier boards, the *Vorstand* or executive committee. The *Vorstand*, of course, is composed of senior executives in the full-time employ of the company concerned. The *Vorstand* does initiate policy and runs the company. This *Aufsichtsrat* v. *Vorstand* distinction is important for understanding the operation of the codetermination system.

It should be added that codetermination or industrial democracy has existed in Germany for some time. There were some codetermination measures in the period of the First World War (1914–1918), though these were swept away when the Nazis came to power in 1933. But the early post-war codetermination legislation dates from the early 1950s, and the last major codetermination law was passed in 1976 when Helmut Schmidt was Chancellor and leader of an SPD (socialist) coalition. Different levels of codetermination apply, or have applied, at different times, in different industries, and in different legal types and sizes of companies. In short it is an intricately complicated subject and what is attempted here are a few summarising generalisations.

With this qualification, codetermination in Germany operates at three levels. First there are elected worker-representatives in the *Aufsichtsrat* or supervisory board. Depending on size of company and type of industry these worker-representatives may make up a third or a half of the *Aufsichtsrat* members. Second there is an *Arbeitsdirektor* or labour director on the *Vorstand* or executive committee. This institution of the labour director began in the *Montanindustrie* (iron, steel and coal) where the *Arbeitsdirektor* had to be confirmed by the majority of the worker-representatives on the *Aufsichtsrat*; thus the labour director was a genuine representative of workers' interests, at least in terms of the mechanics of his election. The 1976 legislation extended the labour director system to other branches of industry, but without the above electoral provision. The typical *Arbeitsdirektor* now is a career personnel manager, or sometimes even a commercial director given the 'labour brief' as a collateral duty. Even so, the 1976 Act does raise the importance and representation of personnel matters via the *Arbeitsdirektor*.

The third level at which codetermination occurs is that of the *Betriebsrat* or works council, and in the view of the writer this is by far the most important. Every place of work with more than five employees has to have an elected works council. These councils have been in existence since the early 1950s and are regarded as an

Ordnungsfaktor, an element in national stability. The elected works council has three sets of rights:

1. *Mitbestimmingsrecht* (codetermination right) or the right to give its consent to certain things: appointment of workers to new positions, internal transfers, transfers between wage groups, dismissals, setting the start and end of the working day, introducing shift working or overtime and so on.
2. *Mitwirkungsrecht* (right to be consulted): this refers particularly to planning problems, such as decisions to close plants, open new plants, investment decisions and business policy issues.
3. *Informationsrecht* (right to be given information): in practice information about the company's performance and prospects. This information right is exercised by the *Wirtschaftsausschuss* or economics committee, an organ of the works council itself.

Implications of codetermination for the personnel function

In general the codetermination system tends to generate a climate of restraint, shared information and responsibility, and perhaps more trust than is normal in the rather more adversarial system of industrial relations that has been common in Britain.

The works council in particular provides a forum for the discussion of issues that concern employees and it does so in a routine way: that is, it meets regularly in a scheduled way, not randomly in response to crisis. There are also mechanisms for it to bring its concerns to management, and get a response from management. Or again the works council negotiates agreements called *Betriebsvereinbarungen* (lit. works agreements) with management (in practice with the personnel department) on issues not already defined by the codetermination laws or the *Manteltarifvertrag* (umbrella wages contract).

Thus the works council has a temporising and on the whole defusing function. In particular, issues which it is empowered to decide cannot, as in Britain, escalate. There cannot, for instance, be the wildcat strike over tea breaks in a German company because the works council sets them!

Furthermore the information right exercised through the works council's economics committee will tend to induce a spirit of realism, and make it more difficult for either side to posture or bluff. If the company really cannot afford a rise because of the state of the order book, then the works council will know that, and the reverse.

The codetermination system also has a mildly subordinating effect on personnel managers. Not only are they in a certain sense in competition with the trade unions, as elsewhere, but there are all these other forums or representatives of the employees' interest – the *Arbeitsdirektor* on the *Vorstand*, the employee representatives on the *Aufsichtsrat* and above all the works council. In addition the works council particularly helps to cast German personnel managers in a reactive mode. They will always know when the works council is meeting, even though they do not have to attend it. The council meetings are a contingency for them, what is on its agenda will concern them, perhaps disquiet them; they will respond to its deliberations and initiatives, give explanations, collate data, may have to check out the consistency and validity of its claims, put things to it, prepare cases for its consideration and so on.

There is a further twist to the story. The argument has been developed elsewhere that in Britain most industrial relations issues not only arise in the production area but are dealt with by production managers and supervisors (Lawrence, 1984). The personnel department will typically be involved only when such issues have attained a certain critical mass and/or lend themselves to formal processing (and many do not). Now this dictum applies to Germany as well, but it is modified by the existence of the works council. That is to say, a lot of issues in the production area of German companies are fed into the works council and from there get 'dumped' on personnel managers. Thus the prerogative and proactivity of the German production manager is preserved somewhat at the expense of the personnel function. Whether or not this is judged 'a good deal' it is still an interesting difference.

The personnel function

In this summary section we would like to suggest four things concerning the personnel function in German companies, namely that it is:

- more reactive;
- more legalistic;

- less autonomously professional; and
- more concerned with training

than is the case with the personnel function in Britain.

With regard to the proactive and reactive dimension, we have already argued that both the process of pay negotiation and the codetermination system incline the personnel function to a more reactive role, one more concerned with response and implementation than with origination. This reactive tendency is also in part conditioned by the greater legalism of the German system.

The German situation is more legalistic in a quite literal sense. More of the relevant activities, that is, are defined by law, encoded in legislation. The rights and duties of the trade union, the codetermination system, the *Manteltarifvertrag* and the annual wages contract, are all legally enshrined. There is also a system of labour courts, to which German employees or their representatives may appeal, and while this may not be a daily event in the life of the German personnel manager, in doing his job (= applying the law) he will always have in mind how his actions would look if the matter came to court. Incidentally, the use of masculine pronouns in the formulation is not incidental; the personnel function in Germany seems to be much more of a male preserve than it is in Britain.

Furthermore, the German system is legalistic in what might be called a metaphorical sense. There are more rules, regulations and procedures than in Britain and they tend to be treated as though they were laws. We have shown, for example, how the pay bargaining process works – in a formal, scheduled way, between recognised institutional partners. Consider as an example at a lower level the question of overtime working. A German company that has a bursting order book cannot just institute overtime by its own authority. It needs the agreement of the works council to do this and even then it cannot engage in unlimited overtime working. Above a certain level the company is required to inform the federal office of its intentions and to have the consent of that body. Right at the bottom of the scale quite small issues between management and workforce can only be said to be 'settled' when they have been formally agreed with the works council and written down.

It will be clear that Germany is not for the most part a society in which things get done by 'a nudge and wink'; 'fudging' is not a German speciality. It is not an accident that the traditional qualification set for the German personnel manager is the *Dr Jura*, the German equivalent of an LL B plus a PhD in law, even though a small survey has shown the *de facto* spread of qualifications to be somewhat wider (Lawrence, 1982).

The approach of German personnel managers to the conventional body of personnel instruments and techniques seems to the present writer to be somewhat different from the Anglo-Saxon norm. The Germans, that is, are less likely to esteem these instruments as part of personnel practice and therefore as 'a good thing'. Their attitude is more pragmatic, conditional: if *Eintarifung* requires job descriptions or employee performance appraisal we will have to do it, but otherwise . . .

Again there is a German equivalent of the IPM (Institute of Personnel Management) but it is a rather lower profile organisation. Unlike its British equivalent, it does not offer membership grades having a qualificational significance. It is perfectly possible to meet German personnel managers in quite respectable companies who are not only not active in this organisation but who have not even heard of it!

It has often been claimed that Germany lacks formal management education. There is nothing exactly like the American or British first degree in business administration, no MBAs until very recently, no DMS (diploma in management studies), no indigenous equivalent of Harvard Business School, London Business School or INSEAD. This may all be true but it should not disguise the fact that a vast amount of training takes place in Germany *inside* companies. A lot of the training is technical rather than managerial, and it is more specific as to the level and function of those on the receiving end of it than would be the case in the UK or USA, but the provision and organisation of the training is still an important function of personnel. And as has been demonstrated elsewhere (Windolf and Wood, 1988) an incredibly high proportion of the relevant age group in Germany does an apprenticeship (over 60 per cent). Picking the apprentices is another duty for personnel, indeed German personnel officers often speak of apprentice selection as one of the most important (and proactive) things that they do. It is another country!

East meets West

With reunification all West German laws apply to East Germany, unless explicitly excepted. So then the 'new federal states', the former East Germany, have got all the labour laws, the labour courts, the West German trade unions and the West German codetermination system as described earlier in this chapter. The new federal states do not yet have the West German wage bargaining system, being still in a transitional phase in which across-the-board percentage rises are proclaimed to bring the wages of East German workers into line with those of the West by stages.

However, there are other issues that go beyond the extension of the West to cover the East. Under communism the role of personnel was somewhat attenuated, as one would expect in a command economy with so much centrally planned. But now real demands are being placed on personnel.

First, there are urgent training and education needs. The East German managers you talk to have their own lists, but three recurrent items are:

- sales and marketing;
- EDP;
- general management and business strategy.

Second, personnel decisions have to be made pretty quickly. Those East German companies that have not gone under since reunification are typically shedding manpower (against the background of the overmanning that was normal in the old GDR). This immediately presents personnel managers with problems of selection and implementation, as well as with negotiating redundancy arrangements with the new works councils. There are also issues of retraining and reallocation within former GDR companies which usually had too many people in social–political roles and too many (for free market conditions) in the purchasing function, but virtually nobody in sales and marketing, and with inadequate general management structures at manufacturing company level.

Finally the whole ethos of (surviving) East German companies is changing, not only in terms of capitalist ideology and free market practice. Management is becoming free (from the ubiquitous plan) and proactive for the first time. These managers are being paid more, are deciding more, are handling more contingencies and are being newly performance driven. Workforces are slimmer, busier and more disciplined; there is less absenteeism, less 'goofing off', shorter tea breaks, more supervision. Companies are more performance driven, less paternalist, less caring, provide less services and amenities for employees. People at all levels will tell you that the ethos now is more tense and exciting, but also more hard-bitten. Real wage differentials have arisen, the individual selfishness of the West has descended. Like the West Germans, they tell you, we don't have time to listen to each other any more.

Nostalgia for the old regime at works level has begun. What has happened to the solidarity of the old days, the endless conspiracies at works level to defeat the inefficiencies of central planning, the spirit of improvisation, the smuggling out of West Berlin of spare parts for broken down machines, the bribing of suppliers, the endless manoeuvres to show why the plan could not be fulfilled? These changes and tensions are a challenge to all, but personnel managers are in the front line.

References

Lawrence, Peter (1980) *Managers and Management in West Germany*, Croom Helm, London.

Lawrence, Peter (1982) *Personnel Management in West Germany: Portrait of a Function*, Report to the International Institute of Management, Berlin.

Lawrence, Peter (1984) *Management in Action*, Routledge & Kegan Paul, London.

Windolf, Paul and Wood, Stephen (1988) *Recruitment and Selection in the Labour Market*, Aveburg, Aldershot.

Appendix: German trade unions and their membership

Christian Workers Union (CGB), non-affiliated to DGB 1989 membership 304,741

German Salaried Employees Union (DAG), non-affiliated to DGB 1992 membership 574,000

German Civil Servants Federation (DBB) non-affiliated to DGB

German Trade Union Federation (DGB) is the umbrella organisation roughly equivalent to the TUC in Britain. Its 16 affiliated unions are:

1. German Postal Workers Union (DPG)
   1990 membership 476,763
2. Union of Railway Workers of Germany
   1992 membership 520,000
3. Trade Union Education and Science (GEW)
   1992 membership 330,000
4. Trade Union Horticulture, Agriculture and Forestry
   1992 membership 125,000
5. Trade Union Commerce Banks and Insurance
   1992 membership 360,372
6. Trade Union Wood and Plastic
   1992 membership 149,724
7. Trade Union Leather
   1992 membership 46,000
8. Trade Union Food Processing and Catering
   1992 membership 400,000
9. Trade Union Public Services and Transport
   1992 membership 1,173,525
10. Trade Union of the Police
    1992 membership 167,572
11. Trade Union Textiles and Clothing
    1992 membership 249,880
12. Industry Trade Union Building and Construction
    1992 membership 77,500
    (including 314,000 members in East Germany)
13. Industry Trade Union Mining and Energy
    1992 membership 350,000
14. Industry Trade Union Chemicals, Paper and Ceramics
    1992 membership 674,105

15. Industry Trade Union Media, Printing, Paper & Publicity (IG MEDIEN)
    1992 membership 220,000
16. Industry Trade Union Metal (IG Metall)
    1992 membership approximately 3,600,000

Part 2
France

2

The Characteristics and Dynamics of Human Resource Management in France

Philippe Poirson

Introduction

The sustained good performance of Japanese firms led American and European business practitioners and academics to look closely at the basis of their success. One of the hypotheses which has been put forward most frequently over the last few years stresses the connection between national culture and the culture of the company. Systems of values and beliefs, whether they be outside or inside the firm, are therefore seen as important elements in the policies and practices of human resource management which are liable to have a direct impact on company performance. The notion of one universal management model must therefore be called into question.

At a time when the economic integration of countries within the European Community is under way, it would appear appropriate, with this notion of national and corporate culture in mind, to consider the following questions:

- Just how do the national differences in Europe manifest themselves?
- Are there any specific areas which link national culture with that of French institutions?

- If this is the case, how are they connected to the principles and practices of management?
- To what extent can they be regarded as assets or handicaps with regard to France's competitiveness within the new European single market?

To answer these questions, the keys to understanding the 'French way of working' and what this is based on will be examined.

A number of variables influence the way organisational and national cultures interrelate. These can be set out in diagrammatic form which helps to clarify how they interact (figure 2.1).

The implication of this framework is that there are strong environmental influences which impact on the operation of an organisation. The analysis in this chapter will therefore begin by

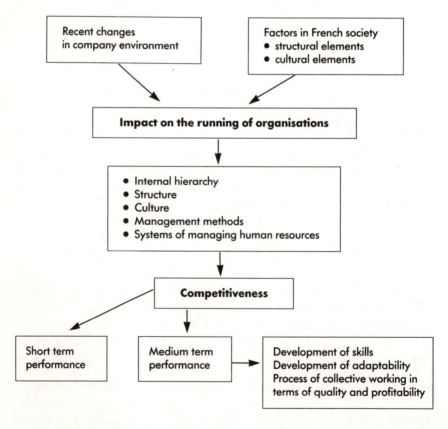

Figure 2.1 *Interrelation of organisational and national cultures*

examining the environmental factors. It will then continue by considering some of the profound trends in French society and national culture. This will enable an evaluation of the impact of these factors on the structure and running of French organisations. However, this does not signify that the running of companies is only determined by a collection of historical, sociological and cultural mechanisms. The chapter will conclude by describing the way certain go-ahead French firms have put into practice human resource policies and efficient organisational structures which take specifically French aspects into account.

In order to define more precisely the questions which were stated at the start, the principal indicators of dynamic human resource management will be underlined. Many authors would agree that the first indicator of an efficient form of human resource management and organization is the company's short-term performance. Human resource management practices should enable high levels of output to be reached regularly in terms of the quality of products and services, avoiding delays in carrying out work, the speed of reaction to market changes and, naturally, profitability.

However, other parameters which affect medium-term performance need to be taken into account. In particular, the following are influential:

- the process for developing professional skill;
- the development of adaptable people and structures;
- the systems which facilitate employee involvement.

Finally the characteristics of French society and culture will be examined to establish what room for manoeuvre they allow and how the most dynamic companies use them.

The strategic management of human resources implies putting into operation internal changes which have been made necessary by changes in the environment. However, a careful examination of the running of companies shows that strategic management greatly depends on how human resource management is applied. Therefore both aspects are considered.

This chapter is aimed primarily at European readers who are not very familiar with French realities, and it may appear somewhat schematic or superficial to French readers. It is intended to present a summary as an introduction to human resource management practices in the major European countries.

The economic, political and social environment of organisations

The context within which human resource management in France has been practised has changed considerably over the past ten years. The pages which follow aim to recall certain political, economic and social factors which influence the running of companies in France.

The economic and demographic picture

From an economic point of view, France is one of the first rank of countries. Its gross domestic product is the fourth largest in the world (after the United States, Japan and Germany). It also features as number four in the top exporting countries.

Its industrial base is characterised by a very large number of small to medium-sized firms, mainly of family origin. There are more than 24 million people economically active, but only 6,000 companies with more than 200 personnel. Moreover, in France quite a number of large industrial groups employ more than 50,000 personnel (Peugeot, Renault, Rhône-Poulenc, Péchiney, Saint-Gobain, etc). Generally flourishing concerns, they invest in Europe and in the United States. However, their size is relatively modest if compared with their major competitors.

The population of France continues to increase for two reasons:

● the natural surplus of births over deaths among the French;
● the relatively high birth rate of the immigrant population living in France (mainly Portuguese, Algerians, Moroccans and Tunisians).

The main economic data are shown in table 2.1.

Demographic figures are covered in appendix 1. Generally speaking, the economic health of the country has been satisfactory since 1988. Economic indicators such as exchange rate and inflation are favourable. On the other hand, for a number of years France has experienced two 'blackspots', the rate of unemployment and the foreign trade deficit.

The continuing high level of unemployment is due to a number of economic conditions which have a severe effect:

● an insufficient rate of economic growth over a number of years to create the necessary number of jobs;

Table 2.1 *French economic trends*

Themes	Statistics	Trends (1992-94)
Growth in the economy	(1992) 2%	↘
Rate of inflation	(1990–92) 3%	→
Gross domestic product (OECD 1990)	1,191 billion dollars	↗
Rate of unemployment	(1992) 10%	
Trade deficit in industrial products Current balance of payments (INSEE 1990)	55 billion francs 40 billion francs	(Improving) ↘
Number of jobs created in 1990 (INSEE 1990)	220,000	↘
Forecast for job creation in 1991		→

Source: INSEE (*Instutut National des Etudes Economiques*) 1991 except where stated.

- a high proportion of under-qualified personnel unable to adapt to jobs whose content has become more and more technical;
- relatively large numbers of young people seeking a first job each year.

In spite of the relatively high level of unemployment, there is a certain tension in the employment market. Qualified personnel are very much in demand. As an example, graduate engineering schools (5 years post-*baccalauréat* studies) train 14,000 students each year, whereas the overall needs of industry, taking into account replacement of staff, have been evaluated at 40,000 people.

The lack of competitiveness of certain French products stems from a number of causes. Some of them arise from deficiencies in the field of human resource management which will be considered later.

Political and social background

1981 was an important turning point in the political history of the country because it saw the arrival as the head of state of a president of the republic and a government with socialist tendencies, while the country had been ruled by conservative majorities since 1958.

The socialist government (delayed for two years by Jacques Chirac's neo-Gaullist government) modernised the country. Having been obliged to run France in full economic crisis, the government was able to help the French to understand economic logic and the links between the economic health of companies and employment. Slowly attitudes changed. The ideological debate surrounding nationalisation and privatisation has now been superseded and pragmatic management of the country is in the main well understood by the French.

Although it is not recognised for electoral reasons, there in fact exists a kind of consensus among the French in a number of areas: foreign policy, defence policy, economic policy, and European policy. However, there are major economic and social problems. It is perhaps a paradox that a socialist government should encounter several difficult social problems. Briefly, these can be summarised as follows:

- how low salaries can be increased without boosting inflation;
- how the development of social inequalities can be prevented;
- how to counter the influence of the extreme right-wing party which fed the difficulties arising from the economic crisis of the 1974/1986 period;
- how the financial balance of the social security system can be maintained.

Industrial relations in France

An overview of France, even as brief as this, would be incomplete if it did not mention industrial relations. France has a notably poor tradition of collective bargaining. For a long time relationships between the bosses and trade unionists were strained and antagonistic. Heads of companies, particularly those of small to medium-sized firms, could not accept that their authority should be called into question.

The most powerful unions, particularly the CGT (General Workers' Confederation), which in ideology is close to the French Communist Party, often took action according to a 'class struggle' form of logic.

For historical reasons, French trade unionism is supported by a minority, divided between several ideological standpoints. It was traditionally seen as a group of militants who 'fought' for an ideal of social justice (see appendix 3). France has a national social security system which guarantees the vast majority of French people against the risks of illness, accidents at work etc. The system enjoys a high level of national consensus and is financed by both employers and employees.

Social legislation has for a long time recognised the existence of several bodies of workers' representation. Among them, the works committee (*comité d'entreprise*), whose existence is mandatory for all companies or units which have more than 50 employees, has a consultative role. It should be informed and consulted concerning numerous subjects in the economic and social life of the firm (the introduction of new technology, continuing education policy, economic results etc).

In France workers' representatives and company heads have always refused all forms of joint decision making or co-management, the former, in order to conserve their power to contest, and the latter in order to safeguard their power of decision making. However the State, whose role is to guarantee social peace, has often invited them to negotiate under the threat of voting in social legislation if they were unable to reach agreement. Over the past few years, certain changes have occurred with the objective of improving relationships. Several large companies are trying to develop harmonious and constructive relations with workers' representatives. For example, BSN has put into effect what is called a 'negotiated modernisation' of its factories. It informs its social partners of its long-term development forecasts and negotiates the foreseen technical, organisational and human changes with them (opening and closure of factories, purchase of new installations and the like).

On a national level, several agreements particularly concerning professional training, unemployment benefits and social security have been signed. Social legislation has, since 1982, considerably increased both the obligation to provide information to social partners and consult with them thereby increasing the formal power of representatives. Trade unionists are better informed, better trained, and often better recognised by company management. However, at the same time the unions have recorded a significant and rapid loss in their numbers. In contrast employers have regrouped within two confederations which unite the sectors of economic activity: the *Conseil National du Patronat Français* (CNPF) and the *Confédération Générale des Petites et Moyennes Entreprises* (CGPME).

Several factors have come together to contribute to the loss of trade union influence:

- the powerlessness of the unions in the face of the 1982–86 period of lay-off plans;
- the increasing age of militant unionists;
- the disappearance or reduction in size of traditional industries (coal, steel, car industry etc);
- the emergence in French society of individualist values which are contrary to worker traditions of solidarity.

Finally, the unions are firmly implanted in the public sector and in the majority of large private firms. They are far less present in companies which employ fewer than 500 people.

Changes in values and attitudes

The development of individualism is only one aspect of the changes which have occurred in collective mentalities over the past few years. The company image and that of the head of the company have also completely changed.

Without claiming to be complete, Table 2.2 gives an idea of the changes which have taken place 'in the minds' of French managers and working people.

The weight exerted by the past: structural and historical aspects

France, like other European countries, was established over a number of centuries. More than a thousand years ago, a kingdom of France already existed in the area around Paris. The country has been strongly marked by its history which has produced particular social structures and shaped the mentalities of its people. In order to understand French management today, a short detour has to be made into the past. One aim will be to search in some of the foundations of the French social system to try to explain how French traditions are sustained. This brief analysis ought to enable a better understanding of the French management style and also certain aspects of the way it works.

Table 2.2 *Changes in mentalities and values over the past ten years*

Values	Trends	Comments
Solidarity/union influence		The percentage of union members among employees has gone from 22% to 9% in ten years in the private sector.*
Class struggle ideology		Weakening of the communist parties in France and in Europe led to a loss of influence of revolutionary ideologies.
Consensus on market economy		The socialist government enabled French salaried employees to understand the market economy.
Company image		The company is from now on considered to be a positive value linked with employment.
Individual success		The economic crisis (1974–1986) favoured the emergence of individualistic behaviour.
Image of the heads of companies		The legitimacy of heads of companies greatly increased.
Exclusion		The economic crisis marginalised part of the French population and encouraged a certain xenophobia towards immigrant workers.

* This is one of the lowest trade union membership rates among industrialised countries.

The traditional French company is a pyramid composed of a number of layers

The French company is characterised by a marked social stratification within the firm itself. Traditionally, there are four categories of salaried employees:

- senior executives;
- junior and middle management;
- employees and technicians;
- workers.

The differences between these categories of personnel arise from the role they play within the firm. These distinctions in roles, however, are to be seen in the French context in particularly marked differences in social status. Status here may be defined as the whole collection of social advantages from which a category of personnel benefits.

In industrial companies in particular, the distinctions between these different levels remain strongly marked. For example, scales for salaries and qualifications are quite distinct; this however only constitutes one of the differences.

To give an illustration of this, in the majority of large French companies an employee who benefits from having *cadre* status (junior to senior management level) has the right to specific advantages (travelling expenses and meals reimbursed at higher rates, a more advantageous retirement pension, and, depending on collective agreements, more paid holidays).

The term *cadre* originally came from military language and at the beginning of industrialisation, the hierarchy model of the firm presented strong similarities with that of the French army, corresponding to the following breakdown:

- senior officers;
- officers;
- NCOs (non-commissioned officers);
- men.

In today's French companies, being a *cadre* does not necessarily mean that one manages a team, it is simply a distinction which is recognised by all and accorded only to a certain number of employees.

In practice, those who have priority of access to this status are those who have distinguished themselves by obtaining a prestigious degree or diploma from one of the *grandes écoles* (graduate engineering and business schools). To a lesser extent, graduates who have obtained a degree from the university system (law students, economists, scientists, psychologists etc) may also have access to the status of *cadre*.

However, a further important category of *cadres* also exists, although not so well recognised socially, and that is the 'self-made' men or women, the *autodidactes*. These are people who have distinguished themselves by their dynamism and their capacity for hard work, their sense of responsibility and their behaviour. They are able to accede to this status by the company's internal evaluation process. To a certain extent they are regarded as worthy of forming a part of

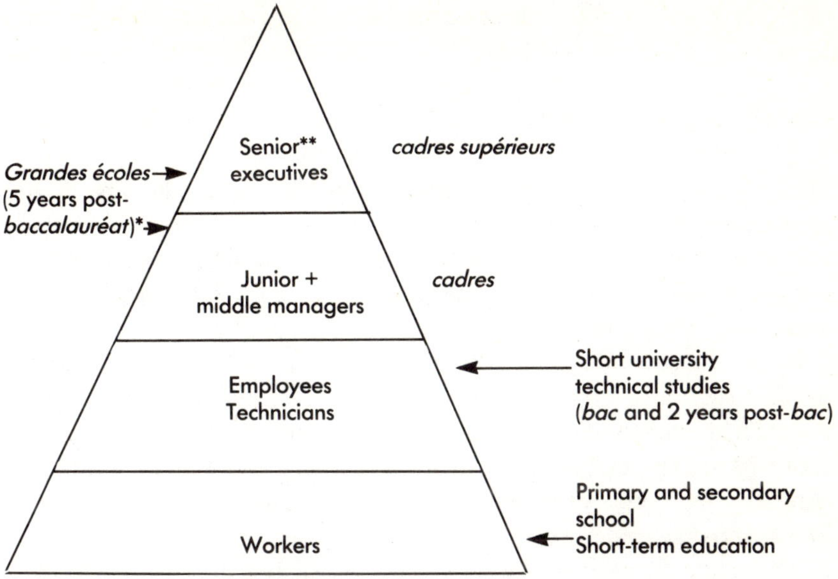
Senior**
executives
cadres supérieurs
Grandes écoles
(5 years post-
baccalauréat)*
Junior +
middle managers
cadres
Employees
Technicians
Short university
technical studies
(bac and 2 years post-bac)
Workers
Primary and secondary
school
Short-term education

* The *baccalauréat* (or *bac*) is the examination taken at the end of secondary or high school studies.
** Or senior management decision-makers.

Figure 2.2 *The French company pyramid and its connections with educational systems*

the élite of the firm, ie the group of people in whom top management places its confidence.

Belonging to this group may also mean, implicitly, that this confidence has to be earned by a high level of commitment and greater number of working hours than those invested by other members of staff. Therefore, being a *cadre* carries with it both rights and duties.

This illustration can be generalised to cover all firms. Figure 2.2 indicates how the various different layers relate to each other. Right from the beginning, education systems outside the firm strongly influence the future career paths people will follow. Indeed, vertical mobility within French firms is not very well developed. The passage from one layer to another is often difficult, particularly between *non-cadre* and *cadre*.

Continuing education programmes, although highly developed in France, are used more to encourage consolidation of the position already held than to obtain professional promotion from an increase in qualifications. In the following pages, a comparison with German firms will clarify this further.

One strong point: the diploma

When we look at the career paths and the logic used by French employees, it is striking to observe that the initial diploma plays an important role. As far as access to senior and middle management jobs are concerned, the French system of *grandes écoles* is by far the surest and most privileged way.

France has a dual system of higher education. On the one hand, the public universities train future doctors, economists, scientists, pharmacists, lawyers and graduates for literary and artistic careers. On the other hand, the majority of future engineers and a large number of company managers are trained for the five years after the *baccalauréat* in the *grandes écoles*.

These are characterised by several specific features:

- a highly demanding selection process on entry;
- a high ratio of faculty staff to students;
- the degree of care taken to ensure there is applied, relevant teaching;
- relatively low numbers of graduates each year (300–700);
- close links with the business world (through selection programmes, practical work experience in companies, meetings between students and companies and former students);
- a more and more significant development of applied research.

For more than a century the *grandes écoles* have trained the majority of future *cadres* and heads of industrial companies. (The civil service has, in part, its own system of training.)

In fact, within the French company, a degree or diploma awarded by a prestigious system of education is the surest sign of belonging to the élite. It corresponds with the deep-rooted values of the French company that were detected by the sociologist Pierre Bourdieu in *La Noblesse d'Etat* (1989). According to Bourdieu, just the fact of preparing for difficult competitions and passing exams awards the degree-holder with a form of distinction which, in a certain way, is the equivalent of a sign of nobility. In days gone by, the nobility owed its privileges to the fact that it defended the country by paying its taxes in the form of blood on the battlefield. Today this distinction operates through the

Table 2.3 *The impact of 'grandes écoles' on managerial skills*

Qualities strongly developed by the *grandes ecoles* system	Qualities less developed
Strong capacity for formulating problems	Capacity for interpersonal communication
Marked aptitude for reasoning through data given in figures	Capacity for managing people
Good capacity for planning	Capacity for implementing strategy

degree system. It would therefore appear that over the past two centuries, which have been marked by the egalitarian ideas of the revolution, France has nevertheless remained strongly imbued with the different values of the old regime. Hardly has French society abolished the old nobility than it has instituted a new form of élitism, based on a specific system of education. Still today, the diploma provides favoured access to companies and also facilitates prestigious professional career paths.

A summary of the characteristics and opinions of French senior managers

One useful way of completing this review of the underlying mechanisms of French style management is to consider what are the major characteristics of these senior managers 'produced' by the *grandes écoles* system.

Peter Lawrence (1990) compared the qualities and limitations observed most frequently among French senior managers in comparison with their European or American counterparts. The elements that he brought to light appear in Table 2.3.

To summarise, at the risk of being somewhat simplistic, the system of teaching in the *grandes écoles* encourages intellectual and rational qualities. In the Cartesian tradition, it develops the qualities of analysis and reasoning. On the other hand, it is less pertinent for training action-oriented people to achieve results.

In fact, senior managers who are 'achievers' show what they are worth 'on the job' during the first few years of their professional life. They occupy the jobs of 'managers' at different levels; and they learn operational management by 'throwing themselves into the task'. They are, most of the time, people who have an excellent professional attitude and who, through their temperament, intuition and relationship qualities, know how to compensate for the limits of the *grandes écoles* system from which they have come.

Can one succeed without prestigious diplomas?

There are examples of professional success stories in France outside the *grandes écoles* system. Men such as Georges Salomon (skiing and golfing equipment industry) or Bernard Tapie, the famous 'acquirer of ailing firms', show that enterprising people can create and develop companies without being holders of prestigious diplomas. Parallel to this, an entrepreneurial attitude has developed over the past few years, particularly in those under 30.

The perception of organisations

A second approach may give a further perspective on French managers. André Laurent has conducted research into the beliefs and opinions of managers on the subject of organisations and their operation (Joynt, P and Warner, M 1985). His aim was to get to know the mental pictures of the organisation which existed in each of the cultures of the large industrialised countries. According to his research, French senior managers distinguish themselves from the others, and from the Americans in particular, on two essential points. Firstly, they have a uni-dimensional and rational concept of the organisation. For example, they are very much attached to the unit of command and have difficulty in understanding the operation of matrix-like structures which, to the French mind deeply marked by Henri Fayol's organisation theories*, do not appear to be 'logical'.

Secondly, they do not have a clear representation of the structures of an organisation. The least formalised dimensions of these structures (the systems of coordination, for example) do not come spontaneously to mind for French managers. They have a tendency to confuse the structures of an organisation and their schematic representation by the company's organisation chart.

---

* Henri Fayol, a French engineer and contemporary of Taylor, was one of the founders of the 'rationalist' movement concerning the theory of organisations (Fayol, 1970).

Both of these research results are coherent with the system of training managers mentioned earlier. However, Laurent adds that there is also an emotional vision of the authority that is exercised within organisations. Sixty-five per cent of French senior managers consider that organisations are systems of authority, while only 30 per cent of Americans are of this opinion. Similarly, a large proportion think that business organisations are places where power is played out and that there is, more than anything else, a political dimension. They further distinguish themselves strongly from other European senior managers by stressing that authority is linked to an individual, rather than to a professional role.

Finally, French managers appear to be ambivalent, at the same time rational and sensitive to relationship phenomena. Their professional experience seems to have developed in them an individual and social concept of the exercise of authority. This point will be returned to in the following pages.

The French managerial system (*système d'encadrement*)

Each country, depending on its history, culture and social characteristics, organises the hierarchy of jobs and individuals within companies in its own way. A comparative research study of France and Germany, led by French researchers from the National Scientific Research Centre (CNRS) (Maurice *et al.*, 1982), compared the social organisation of several production areas in the metallurgical industry at the beginning of the 1980s.

This study sheds some light on how the middle line management functions. Faced with the same technological and organisational constraints, the two countries have set up specific management models which the authors call the *système d'encadrement*. One of the fundamental traits of the French supervisory system compared to that in Germany concerns the level of training of middle managers. The comparative data are in table 2.4.

It appears clear that the relationship between degrees and diplomas is reversed. Although the example concerns metal manufacturing, where 'self-made' managers are numerous, French managers are better trained if one takes the level of university studies as a reference. On the other hand, they are assisted by junior management personnel (technicians and supervisory grades) whose level of training is

Table 2.4 *French and German systemes d'encadrement compared*

	France	Germany
Proportion of industrial managers holding a higher university degree	46%	16.5%
Proportion of industrial managers holding an intermediate-level university diploma	20%	42.4%

considerably lower than that which can be seen in Germany.

This table is particularly significant at one point: the German system encourages comprehension and cohesion between the hierarchical levels because the individuals possess related qualifications. It also facilitates internal promotion. The French system, on the other hand, does not present the same flexibility because moving to a higher level supposes the two obstacles have been overcome:

- passing the *cadres* threshold which has been discussed above and which is a social barrier,
- an intensive continuing education effort to compensate for a generally lower level of theoretical training.

To sum up, the French management system is marked by the distance between the levels and by a certain rigidity, while the German model presents the reverse characteristics. Table 2.5 illustrates this and highlights the fact that the German line of hierarchy is characterised by continuity, by a common reference to technique.

The French model is more marked by the risk of 'vertical breakdown': in addition to the differences created by social structures and access to systems of education, there is the absence of a common reference between the hierarchical levels. As Maurice and his co-authors say, the French model of management 'spotlights the social distance'.

Hierarchical relationships in French bureaucracies

Michel Crozier, a French sociologist, has pointed out (Crozier, 1964) that within large French administrations there is an absence of listening to others and direct communication. The latter is made

Table 2.5 *Comparison of the systeme d'encadrement in France and Germany*

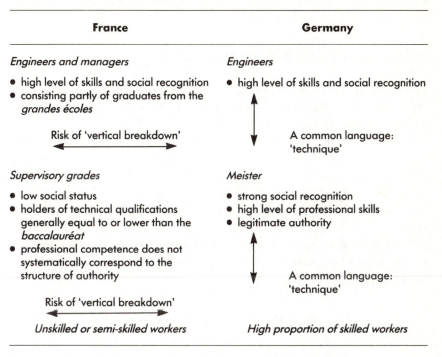

France	Germany
Engineers and managers	*Engineers*
• high level of skills and social recognition	• high level of skills and social recognition
• consisting partly of graduates from the grandes écoles	
Risk of 'vertical breakdown'	A common language: 'technique'
Supervisory grades	*Meister*
• low social status	• strong social recognition
• holders of technical qualifications generally equal to or lower than the baccalauréat	• high level of professional skills
• professional competence does not systematically correspond to the structure of authority	• legitimate authority
Risk of 'vertical breakdown'	A common language: 'technique'
Unskilled or semi-skilled workers	*High proportion of skilled workers*

Source: Maurice *et al.* (1982). Research carried out in the metal manufacturing branch.

difficult because of the weight of hierarchies and status. He describes the following features of French bureaucracy:

- The running of the organisation is based on written rules which aim to avoid despotic behaviour and the abuse of power.
- The hierarchical superior has no power of decision with regard to the individual career of his/her subordinates.

Hierarchical relationships, in such a context, are thus codified. The system is built in such a way that management by direct influence cannot exist. In practice, these regulated systems only manage to function because of informal relationships and processes.

Observations 'in the field' confirm that relationships between hierarchical levels are often formal. It is rare, for instance, for a supervisory grade to dare to use the *tu* form of address with an engineer. Hierarchical relationships also strongly depend on the sector of activity; in many service industry companies in France the hierarchical distance is not so strongly marked and the use of the *tu* form of address is widespread.

Professional qualifications of supervisory grades

The German *meister* is a training master. The role has developed from the craftsman tradition. Technical skills are fully recognised, and authority is legitimate.

In contrast, the *agent de maitrise* in France, often less well trained, possesses a legitimate position whose origin is to be found in the structure of the company. Technical skills are not always recognised by hierarchical superiors nor by workers. The role is mainly seen as one of a hierarchical authority function and its social status is not very great.

Over several years, however, in the more dynamic French companies the level of professional qualifications of supervisory grades and workers has improved considerably.

Limits to the traditional French model

It is now possible to draw together some of the strands concerning the 'spontaneous management' model in French firms, ie that which concerns current practices which may be observed throughout the country firms which have been least marked by foreign managerial influences.

The idea of management as disseminated by American companies and business schools does not correspond with French values and traditions. Historically, this country has trained an élite, capable of conceiving policies in a centralised manner and applying them in conformity with the rational principles of organisations as decreed by Fayol: plan, organise, coordinate, command and control. For a long time this model proved to be pertinent and efficient. It was coherent with its initial aims: to train senior managers for public administration and for industry. It meant, in principle, administering matters and decreeing rules which were in conformity with the public interest. Human problems and problems of organisation were considered to be secondary.

However, at a time when French companies are discovering that they need to 'mobilise all forms of intelligence', this model, inherited from the past, has been shown to have limits. The most obvious of these are:

- lack of listening properly to staff on the part of certain senior managers;
- difficulty in understanding certain problems 'on the ground';
- difficulty in vertical communication (both down and up the line).

It happens that staff do not dare to speak out because the hierarchical distance is so great. At the lowest levels in the hierarchy, they have to keep their dissatisfactions to themselves, as well as technical problems, and so they also have to develop skills in this area.

When a large number of firms are trying to implement internal changes to make the application of strategic choices possible, and at a time when the involvement of all employees is necessary in order to fulfil the demand for 'total quality', it has become clear that the French model of hierarchical relationships and human resource management needs to be revolutionised. This is precisely what several progressive companies have tried to do, as the case studies later in this chapter will describe.

How human resource management operates in France

In addition to explaining the historical and structural bases of French management, it is also important to analyse how it operates in everyday life in companies. Rather than undertake a complete descriptive analysis, the paradoxical situations which appear characteristic of French management will be underlined. This approach has been followed by other authors (Moran and Harris, 1982).

The 'vicious circle' of rules

France is a country where rules and regulations abound. In large organisations many things are regulated, which produces a multitude of memos. The French like to administer and organise things according to their conception of logic and appear to take great pleasure in decreeing detailed rules for all kinds of subjects. The mechanism is as follows:

- An anomaly is noted in relation to existing usage or rules or because a new problem turns up.

- A hierarchical or administrative authority decides on and drafts a rule.

- This rule comes up against individualism on the part of fellow citizens or employees. It may also, in certain cases, be opposed to their conception of their work and to the idea that they have of their professional conscience.

The French, in a case such as this one, will tend sometimes not to follow the rule while thinking to themselves: 'I know what I have to do, they're getting on my nerves, I'm old enough to know what I have to do'. The decreed rules, in this way, are only partially applied or simply ignored, which appears as total disorder. This then leads the one who originated the first rule to send out a reminder or to decree another one. This paradox reveals several dimensions of what Philippe d'Iribarne (1989) calls the 'French way of living together'. This stresses the importance of the written law, the weight of far-off authority which considers itself to be 'all powerful' and the game the French play with rules.

A concrete example may serve as an illustration: an American tourist in Paris notices that in the *métro* there are stickers which indicate that seats have been reserved, first of all for war-wounded, then pregnant women, then old people, but that no one respects this rule. Astonished, the tourist does not understand that none of these categories indicate that it is their right. In fact, the rules are not applied to the letter, they are always submitted to everyone's interpretation of them. What counts are the implied norms. This enables a flexible operation to be achieved. The French know how to adapt themselves to a considerable extent in everyday life. In the present case it is the rules of courtesy which are called into play. People will give up a seat in the *métro* in order to 'be kind' or because they feel that it is their duty to do so. In this case, the regulation is more or less applied because it appears reasonable to all. However, no one will bother to work out whether a war-wounded person has precedence over the others. People arrange things among themselves depending on circumstances and on goodwill and the desire to 'please'. The logic of behaviour is implicit, depends on relationships and operates beyond written rules.

This observation also applies to working relationships and to hierarchical relationships.

The paradox of control

Companies often need to adopt monitoring and control systems, whether they concern production or management. In the French context, the control is also a 'critical phenomenon'. Most of the time the French view 'control' in an administrative way, eg tax control or inspection. The word *'contrôle'* in French signifies a form of monitoring or supervising by an all-powerful boss. It is synonymous with inspection and is not immediately understood with its Anglo-Saxon meaning which signifies operating control or regulation.

As has already been mentioned, there is fear of the hierarchy in France. It is true that the traditional French hierarchy was authoritarian and often paternalistic. However, this model was strongly called into question by the events of May 1968. Following a massive strike by students, workers and employees in both public and private sectors, the symbols and traditional forms of authority were very strongly contested. The authoritarian boss has begun to be seen as not very legitimate, not to say ridiculous. However, a national culture cannot be changed in one generation.

The boss–subordinate relationship remains a delicate point. Geert Hofstede (Bollinger and Hofstede, 1987) says on this subject: 'The efficient manner in which a boss must command, depends to a large extent on the cultural conditioning of his subordinates, ie their degree of subordination, submission and dependence with regard to him.' This example also affects the sphere of 'individual autonomy' of which the French are often possessive. The reflection that one hears most often on this subject is: 'I know my job, if I'm controlled, this means that they have no confidence in me'. These remarks could lead one to believe that the French are ungovernable, but it is not quite true!

It is also worth pointing out that those phrases often uttered under one's breath, as though aimed at oneself, most often manifest a real sense of professional duty and a desire to earn confidence. Most of the time the French want to do a good job and have a sense of their professional obligations. But deep down, many would not want to account to anyone else but themselves!

The 'French social pact'

Philippe d'Iribarne, quoted above, has worked for many years on the subject of relations between national cultures and human resource management practices. His research method is close to an ethnographic approach.

He recently chose to observe the operation of production units of a large French industrial group which has companies of a similar size and technology in France, the US and Holland (d'Iribarne, 1989). The three production units operated in a satisfactory manner and obtained comparable results. By conducting lengthy interviews with workers, foremen and maintenance managers, he succeeded in reconstructing everyday operational models of these production units.

His principal hypothesis can be summed up as follows: working relations are determined by national cultures. The manner in which people and departments work together depends on cultural characteristics. Each cultural tradition favours a certain kind of operation which is efficient within a given culture. The author gives the name of 'social pact' to the often implicit norms which define the way in which people live and work together.

From this research, he endeavoured to describe three different kinds of operational logic, one for each country. In the United Staes, it is contract logic which predominates. Originally a nation of merchants, American society is highly sensitive to respecting the rules of contracts. The notions of 'fair practice' or 'fair behaviour' are strong points of reference which have shaped mentalities and working relations. The rules, as in a commercial contract, have to be strictly applied. Individuals must conform with the written rules. However, that which is not written down is left to the individual to decide.

D'Iribarne shows that in each country account is taken of its characteristic 'social pact' and, depending on national traditions, each country has its own idea of freedom, of what is permitted and of what is not. This explanatory principle ought to assist with certain aspects of the two paradoxes of French management mentioned earlier. According to d'Iribarne, the 'French social pact' may be characterised by three essential points:

- the sense of duty depending on the group to which one belongs;
- the rejection of a 'servile' form of obedience;
- the duty of moderation.

The reasoning behind the 'system of honour'

D'Iribarne points out that under the *ancien régime*, French society was composed of several social strata. At the head of the social hierarchy appeared the order of nobles, those who were inheritors of the knights of the Middle Ages. Next came the order of the bourgeoisie, then that of skilled craftsmen and finally that of the peasants.

Each of these orders had to behave according to a code of conduct so that it distinguished itself properly from the others. It was, for instance, considered to be quite normal and in full conformity with his honour that a knight and later a nobleman be in debt. On the other hand, he was expected to protect the weak and defend his country. If he attached too great an importance to money, his behaviour then came close to the values and duties of the order immediately beneath him, that of the bourgeoisie. He was not acting in conformity with his code of honour. According to the author, these forms of behaviour are again to be found in French society today and in companies. D'Iribarne shows that working relations between the maintenance department and the production department, in the French firm he was observing, correspond with this logic. Each group behaves according to the idea that it has of its duties and of its role. The maintenance department is jealous of its autonomy and of the organisation of its work. Each department works according to its own interpretation of the priorities. The maintenance department, for instance, refuses to 'obey' in a servile manner what could be considered as orders by the production department.

Generally speaking, each individual interprets the rules and the demands made in his or her own way. However, the work would be better carried out if it corresponded, as far as the person doing it were concerned, with a desire to render a service, to 'give others a hand', in short to do one's duty with honour. Nevertheless, if a serious incident were to occur, the struggle to maintain autonomy in each group would suddenly disappear and the general interest would prevail. It would not be accepted, in a case such as this, if one group tried to obtain an advantage by only taking their own interest into consideration. Reference to the usual code of conduct has to give way, under these circumstances, in the face of a stronger norm: the duty of moderation. It is the mechanism which makes the regulation of the system of human relations possible. This theory enables a better understanding of the rights and duties attached to the status of *cadre* which was mentioned earlier.

Finally, there are certain practical recommendations which can be made for those who wish to manage French workers in an efficient and harmonious manner. The best way is to:

- respect the sphere of independence which enables everyone to feel responsible;
- inform them and explain what is at stake in order to enable groups to agree about the points on which they are prepared to take action and commit themselves to;
- monitor the work carried out by each one in a flexible way (the French hate to feel 'caught up' in systems which are too quantified);
- recognise the results achieved, but also the efforts provided;
- mobilise their energy by calling on their sense of honour and their pride in work well done.

How does one modernise French firms?

Within Europe, France is recognised for the modern nature of her technology, whether developed alone or with other partners. These mainly concern aeronautics, telecommunications, nuclear power and space technology. On the other hand, and following on from what has just been presented in the preceding pages, it would appear that the strategic management of human resources is not a point of excellence, inasmuch as the country remains quite marked by certain unfavourable elements in the past.

In order to avoid any hasty judgement, there follows (Table 2.6) a synthesis of the strong points and weak points which come from the history and the national cultures described.

The rest of this section will examine how companies try to exploit their 'strong points' and minimise the handicaps which have been underlined.

The search for excellence

A recent study was carried out in French companies which were selected for their performance based on conventional criteria (profit-

Table 2.6 *Strengths and weaknesses determined by French national culture*

More assets	Major handicaps
Pride felt in a job well done.	Lack of cohesion and synergy.
Frequent desire to do well and to contribute.	Difficulties with communication both up and down the hierarchy.
Strong capacity for commitment in case of difficulties or exceptional events.	Risk of barriers being put up between departments.
Expectation of autonomy and frequent capacity for using it.	Risk of resistance to the implementation of changes (both hierarchical and those concerning categories).
Individual capacity for judgement.	
Operating flexibility.	Individual interpretation of norms (or standards).
Adaptability in the face of unforeseen situations.	

ability, economic growth), as well as on their capacity to become internationalised and to hold their positions as leaders in markets or market segments on a world scale (Page *et al.*, 1988).

Only eleven firms were eventually chosen. They carry out business in highly varied fields (the agri-food industry, cement works, services, hi-tech industry etc) and they employ between 10,000 and 70,000 people.

The research considered several points, in particular:

- strategic decisions;
- financial aspects;
- market conquests;
- organisation;
- human resource management.

There were eleven common elements which the researchers considered should have been able to explain the success of these firms. Seven of these directly concerned strategic management of human resources. These fall under the following five headings.

Decision making
Important decisions for the life and the development of the company are highly centralised within a small senior manage-

69

ment group who are solidly behind a leader who has a considerable presence.

These companies are blessed with a strong capacity for strategic
reflection. They call upon the services of small observation and
advisory cells which have been placed in the immediate environment of the leader.

The running of these companies demands a remarkable circulation of information which has been designed as a decision-making
instrument and not as an instrument of power. The spoken word
has the edge over the written word.

Organisation

These firms have defined a flexible and adaptable organisation.
Operational tasks have been decentralised. The company has
been structured in such a way that its units are human in size.

The commitment of the leader to employees

In spite of the importance of the financial factors, the men and
women are considered to be the real riches of the company.

The leader commits himself or herself thoroughly to the
company. The amount of presence and the longevity of the
leaders ensures a form of continuation and coherence in the
development of the firm which are part and parcel of the
conditions for its success.

The company culture

The coherence of the company is based on a system of values lived
daily and which gives an important place to the quality of the
product and the service rendered. But it also gives credit for the
capacity for initiative and the capacity for team-work.

These companies are aware of their social responsibilities, they
are particularly conscious of safeguarding the employment of
their employees.

Motivation

Go-ahead French companies are committed to strongly motivating their personnel by a variety of means: profit-sharing schemes,
value added systems, internal communication, training and

according responsibility to individuals within the framework of decentralization.

Principles for strategic human resource management

Many of the ideas presented here could be applied universally. It may be useful in conclusion to describe certain essential aspects which feature in this study and which correspond to frequently observed company practices. The aim is to offer a kind of final synthesis which supplies managers with several reference points for future action. This stresses the principles and applications which appear to be adapted to specific French situations and may naturally be applied to French companies and, to a certain extent, to the subsidiaries of foreign companies in France.

Six strategic management principles for human resources feature in Table 2.7.

The implementation of these principles should enable support to be gained from the favourable elements in the culture and the most unfavourable aspects mentioned above to be minimised.

However, in the French context, the implementation of a strategic form of human resource management apparently demands a 'large dose' of energy and restraint, even more so than in other countries blessed with a stronger form of social cohesion, as well as a sense of communication and of negotiation at all levels in the managerial framework.

Human resource management practices of foreign subsidiaries in France

It is naturally quite impossible to define general rules in the absence of any thorough research on the subject. It seems, however, that there are several models for combining the cultures of parent companies and those of the French subsidiaries, depending on a number of parameters: degree of capital-sharing, size, technology, the existence of multinational senior management teams, the 'strength' of company cultures and the degree of decentralisation etc.

Several models of French culture developed by American or Japanese multinational firms appear to be quite effective (Dow

Table 2.7 *Six principles of strategic human resources management adapted to the French managerial context*

Action	Means of implementation	Comments
Ensure management cohesion and coherence.	• involvement of head of company • involvement and training of middle management • values which are lived with daily	The French context is not very favourable to cohesion and synergy. These may be obtained by the commitment of the leaders, practising appropriate values and applying operational action plans (total quality etc).
Explain, convince, motivate with regard to changes to be made.	Senior management and middle management inform and explain the strategic stakes involved and their consequences.	The French (as well as others) like to understand and judge for themselves, they need to adhere to a principle intellectually before committing themselves to changes.
Demand and compensate equitably.	• human resource management systems (promotion, remuneration) • daily actions of middle management	French employees are ready to commit themselves if they have 'adopted' the aims to be reached, they are generally sensitive to the social responsibility of the firm.
Develop action to break down the barriers.	• project groups • problem-solving groups • total quality plans, plans for interdepartmental improvements	This is all the more necessary since the French cultural context can encourage the formation of 'clans' by departments or divisions.
Encourage initiatives, in individual responsibilities and proposals.	• decentralisation • involvement of middle management • working groups • delegation • management based on negotiation	The old middle management hierarchy is sometimes attached to the concept of its role based on status and the prerogatives of the boss which makes it not very inclined to delegate or negotiate.
Maintenance and preservation of changes.	Well selected senior management staff who carry out the same responsibilities for a long time.	The French are generally more sensitive to people and their style of management than to systems and rules. They respect strong leaders if they regard them as being competent and committed.

Chemical, Sony, etc). There have been no in-depth studies of relationships between European firms. It could well be instructive to examine, for instance, how human resource management models are practised and lived by the French, as well as how such models arise in other cultures.

Conclusion

In conclusion, this chapter has endeavoured to show to what extent, and in what way, French national culture is composed of formal and informal elements, by examinining how the state, the institutions and companies have historically shared common values and to what extent the latter have influenced their method of operation. This having been said, the integration of European economies is already beginning to call into question the traditional French model in companies.

Many companies are discovering the weight exerted by belonging to a particular nation and its specific implications for management practices and managerial behaviour. More than ever, such companies will have to develop their capacity for listening to and understanding their employees and their European partners.

Appendix 1: The employment market in France

- Total active population: 24.1 million (1989).
- Annual growth: 150,000/year.

Distribution of the creation of new jobs (1985–89)

• Commercial services to companies	+ 6.9%
• Commercial services other than temporary staff	+ 4.8%
• Industry	– 2%
• Agriculture	– 1.5%

Female employment levels

25–29 years old	78%
30–34 years old	74%
35–39 years old	72%
40–44 years old	68%
45–49 years old	65%

17% growth on average over past 13 years.

Source: INSEE, Social Statistics 1990

Other trends

1. *Changes in the types of employment*
From 1982 to 1988:

● Part-time jobs	+600,000
● Temporary status/fixed term jobs	+600,000

2. *Lengthening of the number of years of study*
Entry into professional life takes place between 20 and 24 years old in the majority of cases.

3. *Lowering of the retirement age*
Numerous pre-retirement schemes at 55 years old.

4. *Shortage of qualified personnel*

Appendix 2: The demographic situation

	1992	Trends (1992–95)
Total population (mainland France)	57.4 million	→
Population of foreign residents	4.4 million	→
Birth rate	14 per 1,000	→
Mortality rate	10 per 1,000	→

Appendix 3: The French trade unions

Name	Major characteristics	Major demands	Estimated number of members
CGT	• Many of its leaders are members of the French Communist Party. • Strong presence in public services. • Strong shop-floor worker presence in traditional industries.	• Purchasing power. • Guaranteed employment.	1,100,000
CFDT	• Trade union supporting the Left but non-communist. • Favourable to the development of industrial democracy.	• Struggle for employment and training. • Purchasing power.	950,000
FO	• Trade union favourable to the development of contractual policies. • Strong presence with public services employees.	• Strengthening the Social Security system. • Collective agreements which guarantee social status.	1,100,000
CFTC	• Trade union which is close to the Catholic Church's social doctrine.	• Agreements on employment and working conditions.	220,000
CGC/ CFE	• Trade union which represents the interests of middle managers.	• Defence of production management. • Retirement pensions, social benefits.	250,000

Appendix 4: An International comparison of French national culture

Research conducted by Geert Hofstede (Bollinger, D and Hofstede, G 1987) has now become a classic work. He endeavoured to highlight the characteristics specific to national cultures. In a long and comprehensive study, involving a large number of people of about 40 different nationalities in an American multinational firm which is present in numerous countries, he isolated distinctive national culture traits by factor analysis methods.

Hofstede defines national culture as a 'collective programming of the human mind which enables one category of men to be distinguished from another'. The cultural traits which he defined are situated around four axes:

1. Individualism _____ Collectivism
2. Masculinity _____ Feminity
3. High or low level of tolerance towards uncertainty
4. High or low level of power distance

The last three factors require some explanation.

National cultures are called 'masculine' where there is a strong accent on competition, performance, self-assuredness, valuing money and success. Cultures called 'feminine' are more geared towards conviviality, the underprivileged and the quality of life.

Tolerance to uncertainty is similar to the acceptance of ambiguity. There exist cultures in which fear of the future and uncertainty is high. They tend, according to Hofstede, to find protection by having recourse to rules, to technologies or to the moral protection of religion.

Power distance measures the psychological distance which exists between bosses and their subordinates depending on the culture. There are cultures where the boss is feared and has to show strength. These cultures encourage tyrannical and paternalistic relationships in the hierarchy. On the other hand, in other cultures the boss is spontaneously regarded as one who brings together energy, a coordinator, almost as an equal, by staff.

French characteristics, often close to those in Italy, are strongly distinctive from the specific cultural traits in the UK and in Germany, as indicated in Table 2.8.

Three points merit comment, as they confirm the analyses developed in the rest of the chapter.

- French culture is considered to be more 'feminine' than that in Germany and the UK. It is true that compared to Germany, for instance, French culture places more stress on the quality of living than on competition or success!
- The high degree of power distance appears to be coherent with the French social structures and élitism mentioned earlier. Again it would be necessary to examine in which way the authority of the hierarchy is exercised in the every-day life of companies. There are some considerable variations depending on the sectors of activity and the different generations!
- The low degree of tolerance to uncertainty corresponds with the well

Table 2.8 *Characteristics of national cultures*

	France	Germany	UK	Italy
Power distance	68	35	35	60
Tendency to avoid uncertainty	86	65	35	75
Individualism	71	87	89	76
Masculinity/femininity	43	66	66	70

known formality of the French and their Cartesian and rational vision of organisations.

Appendix 5: Acronyms and abbreviations

BSN: Bournois-Souchon-Neuvesel, large French company in the agro-food industry
CGPME: Confédération Générale des Petites et Moyennes Entreprises
CNPF: Conseil National du Patronat Français
CGC/CFE: Confédération Générale des Cadres/Confédération Française de l'Encadrement.
CFDT: Confédération Française Démocratique du Travail
FO: Force Ouvrière
CGT: Confédération Générale du Travail
INSEE: Institut National des Statistiques et des Etudes Economiques
CFTC: Confédération Française des Travailleurs Chrétiens

References

Bollinger, D and Hofstede, G (1987) *Les différences culturelles dans le management*, Les Editions d'Organisation, Paris.

Bourdieu, P (1989) *La noblesse d'Etat*, Editions de Minuit, Paris.

Crozier, M (1984) *Le phénomène bureaucratique*, Seuil, Paris.

Fayol, H (1970) *Administration industrielle et générale*, Dunod, Paris.

d'Iribarne, P (1989) *La logique de l'honneur*, Seuil, Paris.

Joynt, P and Warner, M (1985) *Managing in different cultures*, Universität Tsforlaget, London.

Lawrence, P (1990) *Management in France*, Cassel, London.

Maurice, Sellier, F and Silvestre, JJ (1982), *Politique industrielle et éducation*, PUF, Paris.

Moran, R and Harris, PR (1982) *Managing cultural cynergy*, Gulf Publishing, New York.

Page, JP, Turcq, D, Bailly, M and Foldes, G (1988) *La recherche de l'excellence en France*, Dunod, Paris.

Données sociales (1990) INSEE, Paris.

THE CHOICE OF CASE STUDIES

The preceding pages have dealt with certain essential French characteristics in the field of human resource management. They have emphasised influential elements and 'blockages to change' bound up with sociological factors and historical and cultural traditions.

The case studies in the following pages illustrate different situations found in French firms. They have, however, one point in common: these firms, to remain competitive, have been forced to develop radically, to change their work methods, to become more responsive and more efficient.

How can they succeed in facing these economic challenges? What are the problems they must deal with? What kind of action should be taken? These are the three basic questions concerning these three situations.

From a teaching point of view, these case studies should throw light on several aspects:

- certain details of the French national context;
- characteristics of French culture;
- French institutions;
- culture of the various firms concerned;
- structure of these firms.

Case Study 1

The DGS (Merlin Gerin) case illustrates particularly an overall cultural change. Within an industrial enterprise, technical and organisational changes have proved necessary to ensure better competitiveness. The case study emphasises the cultural conception of the manager's role and new working methods which encourage large numbers of employees to become involved.

Case Study 2

The second case study is focused on the problem area created by technical change. The main questions raised concern the organisation and anticipation of change.

CDP is a service company organised in networks throughout French territory. This firm, close to its customers, enjoys a number of assets. However, it runs into coordination difficulties. Furthermore, it is particularly focused on short-term requirements.

What are the efficiency factors that stem from the cultural patterns, their structural origin? What are their limits? How can this firm cope with fresh challenges in its economic, social and cultural context? These are some of the questions that arise from this case study.

Case Study 3

The third case study concerns yet another type of change: internationalisation.

A firm of British origin, Chloride has a subsidiary in France and another in Italy. It decides to reorganise itself into transnational business units. This involves at one and the same time a change at the structural level as well as English, French and Italian managers having to work and cooperate together.

This case brings out the positive aspects but also the difficulties encountered during the first year of this new, genuinely European structure. The main points dealt with are the problems of power, of the common working language and the factors of synergy or conflict which appear between managers coming from three different countries who are working together.

3

DGS:
The Implementation of Complex Changes Within a Manufacturing Unit

Philippe Poirson

Introduction to DGS

The DGS manufacturing unit, located in Grenoble, forms part of the Merlin Gerin group of companies, a well-known manufacturer of industrial electrical equipment. This unit comes under the control of the Logistics and Sourcing Management Department (DLA).

Merlin Gerin has a workforce of 25,000 and achieved a total turnover of 15 billion FF in 1989. Its main shareholder is Schneider, a French group of companies.

The initials DGS stand for the technologies which are used by this production unit: metal cutting, galvanising, soldering – or in French *découpe, galvanoplastie, soudure* (the type of soldering involved in brazing).

DGS has a three-fold purpose or mission:

1. To help design and manufacture strategically important components intended for the entire group within a critical size unit.
2. To maintain and develop the various different skills which are useful to Merlin Gerin.
3. To help production transfers and to advise the production units outside Grenoble.

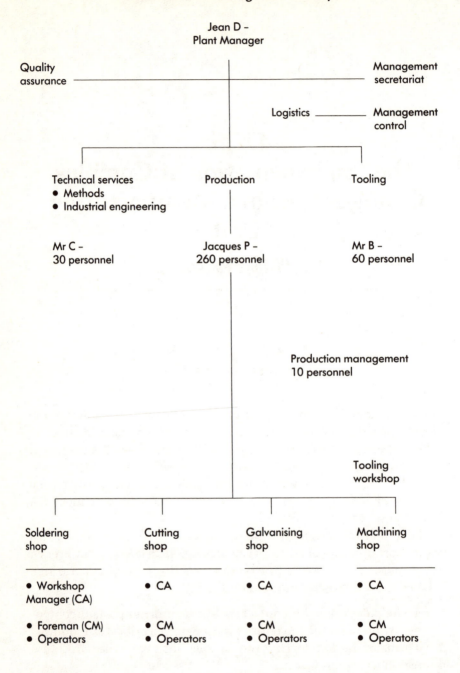

Figure 3.1 *DGS organisation chart*

DGS is a production unit where technical skills are high. During the past few years several patents for production processes and manufactured products were filed for in the major industrialised countries. It is also a production unit which has, for several years, benefited from large investments linked to new production processes. The organisation chart is shown in Figure 3.1.

The unit only deals with internal customers. Briefly, its major characteristics are the following:

- a total staff of 360 (11 engineers, 15 foremen and equivalent grades, 49 technicians and draughtsmen, 11 similar employees and 274 shop-floor workers);
- 200 million FF turnover (achieved with no profit margin: complete cost price = sales price);
- a manufactured product catalogue containing 4,000 references.

The personnel have an average age of 38. A quarter of them are women. Their qualifications are as follows:

- 12 per cent of the workers are unskilled;
- 49 per cent are classified as OP1 or OP2 (semi-skilled and skilled). In the latter case they hold a Professional Certificate (CAP) in one of the mechanical engineering trades;
- 17 per cent are OP3s (highly skilled workers);
- 14 per cent are production area technicians*;
- 8 per cent are manufacturing technicians.

There is a high proportion of highly skilled workers (OP3 and above) which can be explained by the presence in DGS of a tooling workshop which produces moulds intended for manufacturing Merlin Gerin plastic enclosures as well as cutting tools.

Among the shop-floor workers, 10 per cent are recently hired young people who hold the *baccalauréat* in an electrotechnical discipline.

Concerning the salaried workers' representatives, the results of the professional trade union elections were as follows: CGT 70 per cent, CFDT 30 per cent.

The working atmosphere in the production area is generally good.

The older workers have over the last few years become conscious of the necessity for them to requalify. They were therefore able to take

---

* Their positions correspond to the coefficient 255 in the Metallurgical Industry ratings.

advantage of an ambitious training policy on the part of the firm: the 1,000 for 1,000 project. This involved offering 1,000 workers the chance to take part in long-term training programmes in order to help them meet technological changes in the manufacturing processes.

They currently benefit from a modular basic training system (this training represents an equivalent of a full-time personnel of 12).

The product and the technical process

The products which are manufactured are parts intended for use on all sizes and ratings of circuit breakers. They ensure conduction and breaking of the electric current and the operation of internal mechanisms of these pieces of equipment.

At the risk of oversimplification, it is possible to describe the technical process in this production unit as follows:

- **Raw material stocks**
  1,400 references for the raw material exists in two forms, extruded bars (or rods) and rolls. Each year DGS uses 2,000 tonnes of copper, 500 tonnes of aluminium and 15 tonnes of silver.
- **Cutting**
  At this stage, the bars are cut up into sections in preparation for later machining.
- **Metal cutting**
  Some parts are manufactured, most frequently on presses, directly from rolls of raw material.
- **Soldering**
  In the soldering shop, the essential production operations for the contact function are carried out. The machines which are used have, for the most part, been adapted to specific Merlin Gerin production needs.
- **Tooling**
  Both the metal cutting shop and the soldering shop use specific tools which have been prepared by a tooling section. The tooling shop is equipped with machines normally found in a metallurgical workshop (lathes, milling machines etc). A specific area for spark-erosion machines has been developed.
- **Galvanising**
  Protection of the metal surface intended to avoid corrosion of the

Figure 3.2 *The manufacturing process*

metal parts and to improve on the electrical contact, is ensured by an electrochemical process known as galvanising. The parts being treated are plunged into baths and submitted to various different electrolysis processes. The technical process can be summarised in figure 3.2 above.

In addition to the tooling shop, there are other services which are part of the production process: maintenance, stores, quality assurance and management control.

There is also a methods and industrial engineering department, which defines processes and working methods, and a production management department whose role it is to plan for purchasing requirements and production scheduling. Generally speaking, the workstations in the workshop are individual and the workers work on a fixed shift system. 70 per cent of the posts, particularly those in the soldering section, are sedentary or semi-sedentary posts. 30 per cent of the posts require the worker to stand, particularly those which concern machining equipment.

The organisation of labour and the 'human function'

In 1986, when he took over the management of DGS, Jean D–, 35 years old, an engineer who graduated from the *Arts et Métiers* School of Engineering, was struck by a number of characteristics of this production unit. He observed that, generally speaking, the operators took very few initiatives in carrying out their work. Moreover, the dialogue between workers and foremen was almost non-existent. Further, he noted a certain 'them and us' attitude between the different departments at DGS; whenever a problem arose, 'it was always the other's fault'.

Work was organised conventionally, that is it was based on the principles of 'Taylorism'. At many workstations work cycles for the operators were about one minute in length. The workshop sectors were organised in homogeneous sections, so that identical machines (lathes, presses, milling machines etc) were all grouped together. The workers had to produce a certain quantity of parts per hour on workstations whose content was, more often than not, rather poor.

Work preparation (definition of the product ranges and operating methods) was carried out in the industrial engineering department. The parts to be produced were planned in the production management department. Machined parts were inspected by sampling by quality inspectors.

As a general rule, there were three levels of managerial staff (workshop manager, foreman and group leaders). Jean D– also noted that most of the works management were over 50 years old, were of CAP level (a trade or professional certificate) and had worked at DGS for over 20 years.

His first contacts with the foremen, the union delegates and the operators enabled him to gather some more qualitative data. First of all, there was a system of common references, even values, which were proper to the trades connected with mechanical engineering: rigour, accuracy and a rational approach to problems. This state of mind was shared by the engineers, technicians, foremen and most of the workers.

He also noted that 'the people were attached to their job'. They were proud to work for the tooling shop or the soldering shop at DGS of Merlin Gerin. It was frequently admitted that DGS was a good 'springboard' for a career in the Merlin Gerin group. Jean D– remembered that his predecessor told him once: 'Here the working environment is that of a mine, but we are on the look-out for potential and that serves as an incubator.'

Finally, he noted that in comparison with other assembly shops in the company, the working rhythm was different.

As he wanted to 'make a few changes' in this plant, he felt that there were a number of 'strong points' that he hoped he could count on. However, he had also noted a number of operating 'symptoms' which did not really surprise him in view of his experience as an operator in the field, but which nevertheless consisted of some really serious obstacles to be overcome. From the first few weeks of taking up his post, he had been able to note that a kind of 'negative equation' applied to this production unit as with many others he had known in other firms.

Work organised according to the Taylor model, the pyramid-shaped hierarchy and the feeling of security which comes with belonging to a large group of companies often lead to a rather passive working behaviour. In addition to this, at DGS there was a working context in which the customer's demands were never heard.

Moreover, even if Jean D– acknowledged the role of the counter-balance of power held by the unions within the company, he noticed that the attitude of the trade union leaders could also be a drawback to efficiency. With each effort asked of them, there had to be a corresponding salary increase or increase in the promotion opportunities. The basic principle was 'If you want more from me, you have to give me even more'.

The management context

Jean D– was responsible to Mr B–, also a graduate engineer from the *Arts et Métiers* Engineering School. For a number of years, Mr B– had tried to rely on human resource management to increase the efficiency and competitiveness of his division. In addition to technical competence, he expected from his managers what he called certain 'human skills'. In particular, he placed emphasis on the following:

- managerial staff should play the role of 'active teachers', they should make efforts to help their staff to progress;
- they should listen to and respect others;
- they should be rigorous in their actions and control the way in which their staff carry out their assignments.

He set up an effective information system for himself, both up and down the hierarchical ladder. In this way he tried to develop communication by the operators and set an example himself. Thus once a month he organised working lunches, where exchanges of views were possible with the foremen and operators in an open manner.

When Jean D– took over his post, at the beginning of 1986, Mr B– made the following points clear to him: 'From this year onwards, the Group are asking us to function as if we were an autonomous unit. We shall be progressively placed in competition with outside firms. We shall have to look into establishing an industrial project.'

In just a few weeks, such a project had been set up by senior management. It was aimed at 'serving our internal customers better than the competition can'. There were three essential aims:

1. technical quality: to reduce the number of rejects both at DGS and at their customers;
2. quality of service: to increase the proportion of orders delivered complete and on time;
3. reduction of production lead time: cutting the number of days between receipt of an order and its delivery to the customer.

In parallel with this, the question of the reduction in production costs was all the more important since hourly wages rates, representing 35 per cent of the product cost price, were on average 20 per cent above those of the competition.

These new rules to be applied to DGS demanded some really important changes.

The process of change

At the beginning of 1986, Mr V–, the managing director, encouraged production units to organise a 'global drive' aimed at mobilising all personnel on the following objectives:

- to enable each person to contribute his/her 'active intelligence';
- to motivate management so that they become the driving force behind the changes to be introduced;
- to resolve simple industrial operating problems rapidly.

An outside consultant, working in several units within the group, proposed action based on the following assumptions:

- it is essential to allow all personnel to express themselves and make proposals;
- middle management often constitutes a brake on the company's development. This has to be recognised, but top managers should not hesitate to talk directly with the shop floor if middle managers are tending to block the necessary changes.

Each unit was then invited to develop a 'collective mobilisation' process. A large amount of autonomy was allowed in the way this was accomplished. The general aim was to 'bring the customer into the company' and to give personnel an active part in the relationship with the customer.

This idea, which might appear quite banal, nevertheless strongly calls into question operating the company according to the pyramid model. If personnel are first of all there to serve the customers, the hierarchy must therefore assist the staff by creating the conditions required for them to be efficient. This means looking at the problem from the opposite angle. Hierarchical status has little importance, the main point is that everyone, in their place, contributes to customer satisfaction.

The senior managers at DGS then decided to put specific steps into action. Mr B– and Mr D–, in particular, did not accept the idea that since the ends justified the means, it would be possible to bypass line management. For both ethical and practical reasons, this did not appear to be desirable because unless the managers were convinced of the necessity of making the changes, they would 'put a brake' on them. The senior managers therefore decided to act, but not precipitously. With the intention of changing existing mentalities by using concrete problems, they decided to develop an industrial project to provide some stimulation.

They were in fact conscious that any action aimed at changing mentalities was a long and complex process which could take several years. They also considered that if they were successful in changing day to day behaviour at work, then they should be able to change the corporate state of mind at DGS, little by little. The first objective was to make the supervisory grades and managers of the workshops and production departments the 'players' in carrying out the changes. The second stage was to enable these changes to be disseminated to all personnel in the company.

Senior management at DGS wanted to link this process of stimulation to other changes in the organisation of work within the workshops. This last point merits additional explanation. Indeed, in parallel with the steps taken to motivate the staff, but also as a result of them, the following areas were given priority in order to lower production costs and increase operating flexibility:

- the development of individual self-monitoring systems;

• the setting up of a 'just in time' production management system.

Self-monitoring consisted in giving each operator the entire responsibility for the quality of the products which he/she makes. This meant that the parts manufactured would be delivered directly to the customer without any other form of checking by the company. It involved progressive delegation to each operator of responsibility for the quality of the parts made. In practice, and after a certain time when the work carried out would still be checked, all external quality control would be eliminated.

Setting up a 'just in time' system of production management aims to decrease stocks of work in progress. This means assigning part of the production planning to the operators. A chart with three different coloured areas was installed in the workshop, indicating the parts which were in danger of running short according to delivery schedules to customers. By referring to this chart, the operators themselves chose what they had to do; in short, they managed a part of the production, process.

In both cases, the changes consisted of a process for the operators of learning to assume responsibility and of having a certain autonomy and for learning to delegate on the part of the foremen. Through these working methods, workshop managers were encouraged to exercise less control, to explain more, to train on the spot and to advise. They used their authority differently.

Moreover, for some years an important change had affected workshop management: the removal of the first level of supervisory grades in several production areas had facilitated the delegation of responsibility and reduced production costs. In order to encourage flexibility in production, other changes were made.

These particularly involved implementing a new way of installing the machines: in-line installation. This consisted of setting machines with quite different technologies 'side by side': presses, soldering machines, machines for turning large quantities of parts in small batches. This enabled a considerable reduction in the machining cycle and thereby faster delivery to customers.

Overall motivation

Whenever Jean D– raised the subject of 'overall motivation', he could talk convincingly about it at length. He pointed out that:

Historically, human resource management has been based on small numbers of people. In the 1970s, we were mainly concerned with the 10 per cent who were trade union members, then in 1980 we tried to concentrate on the most dynamic 20 per cent. At that period, 'project' groups were formed and later we had quality circles which, most of the time, only involved a minority. What we wanted to do at Merlin Gerin and particularly here at DGS, was to involve and try to concern everyone, the entire workforce, the 80 per cent that remains the silent majority, neither opponents nor enthusiasts. But we could not use the catastrophe scenario – the firm is in poor shape, we all need to stick together – because Merlin Gerin was making profits at that time. Neither did we want to use belligerent, drum-beating language which often runs along the lines: 'We are at war, economically speaking, with the Japanese'. The message we tried to get across was: 'It could still be even better, even if things are rather good at the moment.'

To summarise, the main stages of the process were as follows:

Stage I – Diagnosis

The aim was to lay out the entire problem in front of the managers and supervisory grades.

For a number of months the foremen carried out research with customers and competitors of DGS. This enabled the problem to be formulated as follows:

- teamwork at DGS was not sufficiently effective;
- customers were dissatisfied with quality and delivery times;
- there was a risk of losing customers.

During this stage, several meetings with the workshop management enabled the action to be put into perspective:

- by encouraging a collective consciousness and cohesion among the management of workshops and other departments;
- by choosing together a motivating theme of industrial competition and a symbol, that of the Olympic Games.

The central message was the following: 'Let us always be well prepared so that we win the future competition'. The accent was therefore placed on a permanent process of improvement and vigilance in relation to competitors' performance.

Stage II – Mobilisation

Mobilising all the workforce aimed at bringing out and promoting a collective form of energy. The starting point was naturally the emergence of a form of common consciousness. All personnel were therefore assembled in a conference hall.

The managerial staff who had carried out the research then outlined the main remarks made by the customers. They also presented the main factors about the competition. At the end of this meeting the process for participation was then explained. Everyone was asked to contribute towards improving the product and the service provided by DGS by supplying their ideas, proposals and suggestions in working groups.

A 'committee of twelve' was set up which brought together workers, employees and foremen. A third of this committee was replaced every nine months, and its role was to guide the entire process. It was particularly set the task of facilitating the launch of the working groups, to help with implementing the suggestions adopted and to propose specific action for motivating personnel.

The managerial staff were set the task of permanently keeping an eye on the relationship between the actions undertaken and the results obtained. It was also their job to identify problems which were common to several groups and which revealed deep underlying problems with the way the company operated. The role of this group was to anticipate how the process would evolve. More than 200 working groups of between four and six people operated for two years during working hours and three hundred proposals for improvements were studied and implemented. Indeed, the groups operated according to the basic rule that: 'Each time someone raises a problem, he or she must try to find a solution to it'. The work of the groups therefore consisted in recording the problems and discussing the proposed solutions.

Stage III – Application

After each solution had been proposed, it was agreed by the management of the sector of the workshop concerned, then implemented in liaison with the industrial engineering and production management departments.

Some indications of the results

The outcome of this project can be seen in several ways. On the industrial side, the results recorded were as follows:

- Technical quality: the rate of rejects, following the overall motivation stage, was reduced from 8 per cent to 1 per cent per year.
- Quality of service: the proportion of complete orders delivered on time rose from 45 per cent to 72 per cent.
- Average production cycle: this was reduced from 41 days to 22 days.

Jean D– and Jacques P– also noted the following additional effects:

- a lowering of the barriers between workshops and technical departments;
- the personnel as a whole became more flexible in the face of such changes;
- the process of passing information up the line and down the line in the hierarchy became more structured (for example, demands for 'corrective action' according to remarks by customers worked well);
- motivation concerning individual training increased;
- finally, operators had a better understanding of how the Merlin Gerin group operated.

The 'strong points' as perceived by the salaried staff in the latest opinion poll were as follows:

- circulation of information;
- responsibility;
- job interest;
- autonomy;
- quality of team working;
- organisation within workshops.

On the other hand, they thought that the situation had deteriorated on three points:

- personal contact;

- quality of cooperation between colleagues;
- motivation at work.

Two further points are worth making:

- The tendency for union claims, which was always prominent on previous occasions, had very considerably decreased.
- The union delegates themselves had agreed the principle of meeting the customer's demands.

On the other hand, despite the fact that pay was already much higher than in neighbouring companies, the operators at DGS still considered that their salaries were much too low. Is this why they said they were less motivated than before?

The managerial staff themselves were uneasy about this question. They were afraid of losing the confidence shown by the personnel. Some of them felt that it would be a good thing to allow personnel to benefit from a profit-sharing linked to manufacturing results, such as already existed in certain subsidiaries.

Questions

1. List the major changes that were made at DGS.
    - What type of changes were they?
    - Who was the actors involved?

2. What are the main motivating mechanisms?
    - What assumptions do they make?
    - What are their limitations?

3. Do you notice any specific points of French management style? How can you explain them?

4

CDP:
The Training and Development
of Managers

Philippe Poirson

The company, its organisation and its culture

The CDP Company – *Centre de Distribution Pharmaceutique* – has as its main mission the delivery and distribution of medicines between manufacturing laboratories and the pharmacies which sell them. CDP was set up in Nantes in 1924 by three pharmacists who owned several small medical warehouses scattered around several districts of the town. Although provincial in origin, CDP quickly became a nation-wide concern. A Lyon branch was established in 1929. Nowadays, CDP employs 4,500 personnel in over 70 provincial offices, a large branch in Paris which has 450 staff and the head office near the Paris branch.

CDP is the leader in the fiercely competitive French market (with 36 per cent of market share). Its rather dense network of branches spread throughout the country is a valuable asset to the firm. This network structure gives the advantage of offering close proximity between CDP and its customers, while encouraging autonomy within the branches; however, it makes defining and implementing policies difficult on a company-wide basis. This is why an intermediate level of coordinators was set up in 1987 who were given the task of defining and implementing company policies on a regional basis.

CDP has a strong culture. The fact of belonging to a chain of firms within the health industry gives special significance to their work in the eyes of employees. In addition, the trade they carry out means many of them can maintain regular contacts with their customers. Telephonists and drivers, for instance, are recognised by their customers, the pharmacists, on the same level as the sales staff. This contact with the customers gives value to their work.

The branches have for a long time been run on the model of a small to medium-sized family business, the branch managers considering themselves to be 'company heads'. Relationships between the personnel of each branch are therefore characterised by a certain form of 'demanding paternalism'. Their principal task is to be able to respond quickly to the demands of their customers, which sometimes leads those responsible for the day to day running of the firm to be rather brusque. However, when there is a panic on, the branch managers do not hesitate to 'roll up their sleeves and get on with it'.

Finally, there is a strong sense of belonging to the company. As a general rule, people are proud to work for CDP. From 1960 to 1980, the firm was managed by Mr C–, a man with a great deal of charisma and authority. He developed the company considerably and this model left its mark on the executives. CDP, depending on the health industry, grew well over the past 40 years. The firm was spared the widespread restructuring which struck French industry between 1983 and 1986.

The job of distributor

CDP is a large-scale distributor. Its turnover is high but profit margins are low. The most important problems to be resolved concern stock management, rationalising storage in the shops and the organisation of the drivers' delivery rounds. The key competitive requirement is control over distribution costs at all levels.

A second dimension of the business is service. If the company knows how to adapt to customers' demands or to offer them useful service, it increases its chances of satisfying them and thereby being able to count on their continued custom. For a number of years, CDP has shown a certain creativity in this field.

For example, the company created jobs in their establishments for what they call *'pharmaliens'*, who have the task of informing and advising pharmacists on special products, especially those sold over the counter in the retail trade (ie cosmetics etc). In addition CDP offers its services to pharmacists when they are fitting out their shops: market analysis, definition of financial needs, advice on stocking products etc. In France overall 85 per cent of medicines produced are distributed by companies such as CDP, 10 per cent are sold directly to hospitals without any intermediary and 5 per cent are distributed directly to pharmacies by pharmaceutical laboratories (this particularly involves homeopathic medicines).

The French health industry and the challenge faced by CDP

CDP operates within a rather specific context which it will be useful to examine. In France, health spending increases by 10 per cent a year. This is one of the causes of the regular large deficits experienced by French social security. The reasons for this excessive expenditure are many and varied. One of them stems from a system of protection against illness which is particularly advantageous for its beneficiaries.

In comparison with their European neighbours, the French do not often use self-medication. They nevertheless consume twice as many medicines, the cost of which is reimbursed by social security. This arises from the fact that doctors, who are paid a high rate for their consultations, prescribe a large quantity of medicines, the price of which is reimbursed at about 70 per cent as a general rule. The French are very attached to this form of social protection which is defended by workers' trade unions and representative bodies, who manage the system with representatives from employers and the government.

During the last few years, successive governments have taken authoritative measures in order to avoid having to make up the social security deficit by dipping in to public finances. However, the cost of medicines only represents 7 per cent of total health spending.

Because of concern about the price of medicines, pharmacists were obliged to reduce their profit margins. Feeling that they were being 'attacked' for carrying out their profession, they have sometimes considered CDP as a very large firm, an enormous distributor, far removed from their own preoccupations. In order to avoid a certain resentment being built up against it, the company chose to demonstrate that it was on the side of its customers.

In the area of health spending, there is a complex situation concerning the monopoly over the sale of pharmaceutical products.

Supermarkets would be only too willing to sell a large number of medicines, thus placing CDP and the pharmacists in a position of direct competition. CDP chose its own camp, that of the pharmacists. The firm uses the slogan: 'The pharmacy, for your health's sake it's irreplaceable'. In this context, the company managers and their staff daily try to show that they are not only at the pharmacists' service but also 'by their side'. They are conscious that their customers, who have seen their own profit margins dwindling, have become more and more demanding as far as prices and the quality of service are concerned.

The structure and operation of a branch

CDP has branches ranging in size from 20 to 250 salaried personnel, with the exception of the Paris branch.

Each of them groups together the same job functions and working roles (see Appendix):

- a manager and a secretary;
- telephone operators who record customers' requests;
- personnel in charge of sourcing who pass orders to suppliers, to the office in Paris or to nearby branches;
- stores assistants whose job is to arrange the medicines carefully in the special bins or shelves and retrieve them when required to make up the pharmacists' daily orders;
- delivery staff who carry out several delivery rounds per day, at precise times.

The majority of employees are women, both in the stores and telephone operators. The supervisory grades and managerial staff in the stores are mostly men. They include chargehands and production foremen who oversee the stores personnel, telephonists and drivers. A large proportion of the jobs are unskilled or semi-skilled and in addition the work in the stores is rather hard.

The day is marked by periods of intense activity when the pharmacists send in their orders, particularly about 11 o'clock in the morning and at 4 o'clock in the afternoon. Following these 'rush hours' the working rhythm is a lot calmer and in each store the employees carry out the tasks of stocking and rearranging the shelves.

Over the past few years, a process of technical modernisation has been taking place in some branches. This has involved, in particular, the installation of automatic telephone systems between the pharmacies and the stores and mobile shelf storage and automatic machines for preparing orders in the CDP stores. This means that, as in other parts of industry, jobs which are often rather hard and difficult and which offer little satisfaction are becoming more and more automated. The use of part-time and short-term employment contracts is increasing. Each time an automatic installation is set up, certain employment problems have to be solved.

Policies and practices in human resource management

In view of the structure of the firm, a large part of the personnel management is decentralised. This means, for example, that the branch managers and the supervisory grades are given authority to hire personnel who report directly to them, with the exception of the *cadres* (managers/executives) who are recruited and looked after by head office. When recruiting, branch managers apply salary scales and personnel status as defined by the personnel management.

The large majority of employees, those who are unqualified, are more 'administered' than managed. This means that after having been recruited, the development of their abilities and skills is only considered in the restricted area of the branch where they work. On a centralised level, the personnel manager regularly conducts negotiations with the union representatives. All trade unions are represented within the company. Their position and influence is particularly strong in the Paris area and in several large provincial branches.

Over the past few years, negotiations have particularly been about salaries, social status and working hours. Personnel managers have also been careful to develop communication within the company. In addition to conventional methods such as in-house news journals etc, personnel management has recently taken the initiative of organising a meeting of fifteen members of management and employee representatives from CDP. In the opinion of all concerned, this two-day seminar turned out to be very fruitful. The result was a report to the company's top management.

There is a department known as 'executive management' which is attached to the company's personnel management and which manages branch managers, supervisory grades and head office executives. Its mission is to define and implement policies for the recruitment, training, remuneration and development of management.

Over the past few years, Mr D–, director of executive management, has been careful to use a management by objectives approach. In concrete terms, this means that with the aid of head office specialists, who report directly to Mr D–, branch managers have undertaken the job of clarifying the missions and jobs carried out by executives and supervisors. This has enabled them, little by little, to identify negotiable objectives to be reached by their teams. This approach was then completed by the setting up of appraisal interviews, of which one dimension was annual objectives. Mr D– is in the process of progressively applying a policy of individually negotiating executives' salaries. The executive management department also has the task of managing the way executives move between the various different branches.

Manager training

During a number of years, the head of executive management and the training manager have developed a policy of management training, particularly aimed at operational and branch managers.

The first stage in this policy consisted of providing the executives with the benefit of some general training concerning the company environment, its strategic choices and its general management procedures.

However, in 1987 a number of issues surfaced which required attention:

- There were few general directives in existence about the whole company.
- The various branches were geared towards immediate production.
- Working methods were, more often than not, by rule of thumb, impulsive and too closely linked to the people involved.

In a company which had a strong tradition of decentralisation, many branch managers behaved like leaders with strong personalities, often possessive of their independence. It was difficult to apply general policies to them. Several actions were taken to coordinate and bring the various branches into a federal system. The training activities set up at this time were set within this context. Beyond individual manager training, it then was a question of an opportunity to create a common language and common references for all of the company's branches.

With the help of Groupe ESC Lyon (a French business school), an internal 'management school' was set up. The seminars were aimed at two different types of people:

- branch managers;
- operational managers.

Finally, after undertaking a study of what the company needed, the following seminars were offered:

- Team Management (lasting 5 days);
- Individual Leadership (lasting 3 days);
- Conducting the Annual Appraisal Interview (lasting 3 days).

These seminars appeared in CDP's national catalogue and managers who wished to undergo training could enrol on them, with the agreement of their superior and if they felt they needed them, whenever they wished. In general, these training activities were appreciated as they corresponded well with the participants' needs.

Current problems

CDP now finds itself confronted with two significant problems:

- the relocation of the Paris site;
- the management of technical modernisation.

The Paris branch, situated within the inner city, seems to be too large and badly placed with difficult access. Transport problems in the Paris area are becoming more and more acute and feature heavily in the cost of overheads. It has been decided to move the current branch to the inner suburbs in the north-east of Paris. A reduction in the number of employees is anticipated. How should this be managed?

In general, to keep its costs down in the face of competition, the firm has to look for productivity gains. Since their numbers are increasing, the pharmacists are able to take advantage of automatic call systems. Certain branches have set up robot collection in the stores. Eventually the least qualified jobs will disappear.

These problems deeply affect certain branches when they have to proceed with reorganisation or where they are setting up new investments. Many managers have tried to anticipate these problems by relying on temporary personnel (by using fixed-term contracts or temporary staff).

However this is a general problem which concerns the entire company. Mrs M–, the training manager, pointed out:

> Managers have benefited from training activities, they have become more at ease about operational management; however, the actions that we are taking are less and less credible because they do not attck the real problems. We will need to be able to help them get to grips with technical modernisation and handle the problems of overmanning.
>
> In my opinion, we have to be able to reply to the following questions:
>
> - What are our technical choices and organisations in the medium term?
> - What will the target organizations and target posts in the branches be in the next three years?
> - What consequences are foreseeable as far as employment is concerned?
> - How can we prepare to manage the loss of personnel?
> - How does one help management to carry out productivity gains while still handling employment problems in the best way possible?

She regularly brings these questions up with her director. They envisage negotiating a framework agreement with the firm's union representatives nationwide, about modernisation and employment problems. For her part, she is trying to lend her support to the branch managers, who themselves have to bring about the reorganisations in reality. She sometimes has to bring up these questions informally with certain employee representatives. She wants to help managers achieve these changes and to be able to formulate general conclusions to be used in future. In fact, she has observed that, up to now, the question of overmanning has not been met head on.

The productivity gains expected from future investments risk being strongly compromised if, in the absence of a clear definition of the problem, the excess personnel is kept on while the firm is still investing.

Appendix: Simplified layout of a CDP branch

```
Entrance

                                                          D
                                                          i
                                                          s
Telephone                                                 p
service                                                   a
(telephone          Stores department                     t
operators)                                                c
                                                          h
                 (Operational management, employees
Management       who deal with stocks and collect medicines  s
                       from the storage areas)            e
                                                          r
Secretariat                                               v
                                                          i
                                                          c
                                                          e

                                                       (Drivers)


Buying
department                                               Garage

(Buyers)
```

Questions

1. What are the assets and handicaps of this company in relation to the projected changes?

2. The company's management committee asks you to organise an initiative for management development in this context:
   - What steps would you recommend? Why?

Case analysis

This case study should enable participants to play counselling roles on the subject of developing executives. It is about making a company face up to difficult changes, particularly when these changes create work problems among the staff.

The basic questions to be dealt with seem to be the following:

- How can all the people affected by these problems be enabled to work together?
- What work procedure (or training programme) should be set up so that distribution unit managers feel strongly involved in the 'real challenges', present and future?

Answer to Question 1:

The main advantages and drawbacks the firm has at its disposal to bring about these changes are the following:

- *A fairly widespread anxiety within the company about how the employment problem is analysed and dealt with.*

  CDP is characterised by its paternalist tradition. It has not experienced large-scale restructuring problems until now. Most managers feel guilty about making redundant employees they have known for a long time.

- *A tradition of decentralisation.*

  Distribution unit managers behave more like heads of small to medium-sized companies than executives who must respect policies. This tradition also has certain positive aspects. In particular, it encourages managers to become strongly involved in the life of the firm since they really feel responsible for it.

- *Work habits based on the short-term approach.*

  The whole of CDP is influenced by the necessity to meet delivery dates given to the customer. This means not only delivering on the agreed date but also being willing to be of service to the client, to 'get him out of a fix' (which French firms generally like doing). This sense of service is, of course, very positive. But it often does mean that distribution unit managers have a short-term perspective.

Not enough of them devote sufficient time to thinking about the medium term. Finally, decentralisation makes cooperation difficult between head office functional departments and executives in charge of the distribution units. However, new problems are arising which require specific answers because they are general, national problems. These are all the more difficult to resolve as they concern poorly qualified workers, unable to move easily from one firm to another (indeed, it is often female staff with heavy family responsibilities).

Comments on Question 2

There are, of course, several scenarios that could answer this question. The following seems perhaps the most relevant:

- a meeting with the managerial team to outline the general procedure;
- the setting up of a project group to study a number of modernisation procedures adopted by other firms (distribution units), taking into account their environment, their size and their background.

This group should, over several months, analyse the technical, organisational, budgetary and human problems associated with technical changes introduced to increase productivity gains. Their aim should be to work out recommendations about modernisation procedures:

- under what conditions are they worthwhile?
- what kind of distribution units should be dealt with first?
- what are the different possible approaches?
- what are the variables involved?

These recommendations should be presented to the managing directors in such a way that it clearly advocates or warns against certain trends.

At this stage it should be possible to write case studies dealing with the modernisation procedure adopted by various types of distribution units. At a later stage, short seminars (each lasting two non-consecutive days, for example) could bring together different distribution unit managers in small groups. During these seminars, a time should be set aside for discussion with the original project group.

In this way, the managers could benefit from knowledge at three levels:

- a method for diagnosing the problem and relevant elements to be included;
- a framework of general attitudes towards policies;
- an opportunity to discuss their particular concerns.

This group could comprise the operational director, the training programme manager and the heads of three distribution units.

5

Chloride:
Organisation Change in a Multicultural Context

*Yves-Frédéric Livian**

The company

Historical background

The Chloride Group of companies originated in Chloride Electrical Storage Ltd, which was founded in Great Britain in 1891. Its activity was the production of batteries, according to a patent taken out by a French inventor.

Nowadays, the Chloride Group employs about 10,000 people throughout the world and is composed of five divisions:

- Power Electronics;
- Power Supplies;
- Emergency Lighting;
- Fixed Site Batteries;
- Exide International;

plus a further two miscellaneous divisions which cover, for instance, solar applications and new materials (lithium etc).

---

* This paper was specially written and is based on a study report which was drafted by F Walbaum and F Gozlan.

The Power Electronics division, which is the one with which this case deals, comprises four production plants:

- Chloride, situated in Eastleigh in the UK, employs 145 people.
- Silectron, situated near Bologna in Italy, was founded in 1967. It was bought by Chloride in 1988 and employs about 150 people.
- Coredel France, based near Lyon and founded in 1969. It was bought by Chloride in 1977. Its activity has been growing by 10–15 per cent per year over the past ten years and it employs about 150 people.
- Clean Line Thailand, bought in 1989.

The Division achieved a turnover (total sales) of 350 million FF (£35 million) during 1989–90.

The Chloride Group was known as very dynamic right up until the early 1980s. It was experiencing a very fast worldwide expansion, and employed about 15,000 people. However this particular coin also has another side to it: the group was well represented in countries from which it could not repatriate the profits (in India, for example). Obliged to reinvest in the same country, it was able to develop flourishing companies (Chloride India is currently the largest firm in the group and employs nearly a third of the total number of staff).

Unfortunately, these profits were unable to be used to set off the losses which the European companies started to accumulate at the beginning of the 1980s. The group therefore experienced a period of financial difficulties up until 1987. The management decided to sell investments and to abandon part of the group's original production know-how, in order to recentre the activity on electronics.

The Power Electronics division followed a parallel evolution to that of the group. During the difficult period, in 1984, a decision was taken to merge Coredel with Chloride France in order to encourage greater sales and marketing synergy, take advantage of complementary products and simplify company structures. Coredel benefited from having a very good reputation and its products were able to keep their brand names. With the purchase of Silectron in 1988, the problem arose of deciding on the most rational way to organise three companies whose products were sometimes in competition with one another and which were fully independent although they all belonged to one division. Moreover, the profits from Lyon and from Bologna were insufficient to cover the losses at Eastleigh, whose products appeared to be technologically out of date.

During the time of the financial problems faced by the division in the early 80s, there was a first attempt made at rationalisation and it was decided to centralise the division around Eastleigh. This turned out to be a failure: Coredel was then only given an executive function. The division's objectives were very badly distributed and this led to the departure of a considerable number of managers.

In fact, the site at Eastleigh at that time was shared between two divisions, Power Electronics and Emergency Lighting. These activities were different in nature, as were the outlets they were aimed at. Emergency Lighting was protected by very strict regulations and was quite profitable. It therefore tended to mask the lack of dynamism on the part of the electronics activity. In 1987, the group decided to move the Emergency Lighting division and Eastleigh found itself with an activity which resulted in chronic losses. Its products were too heavy, too big, too noisy and technologically outdated. Eastleigh was unable to take advantage of its complete range of products (special and standard models). In relation to Coredel, Eastleigh played the part of an intermediary within the group. This site was therefore the dominant one within the division.

Silectron and Coredel had a similar past in certain respects. Both were small to medium-sized family businesses, very well placed within their own markets and they had a very good reputation in their respective countries. Their products were modern and offered a good quality/price ratio, although their product ranges were incomplete. Both companies had always known a good level of profitability. Each attempted to complete its range: Coredel only produced special products and Silectron tried to develop medium to low voltage products. For both of them the new organisation meant a waste of time, money and production skills.

Particularly as far as Silectron was concerned, its integration into the Division was quite recent. For 20 years it had been run by its founder, who died in 1989. A charismatic man, he made the majority of the decisions, was kept informed of everything which concerned his company and knew every one of his workers.

Following the intervention of a firm of international consultants, the decision was made to set up, as from 1 January 1989, a product-by-product structure covering the three sites: the strategic business unit (SBU). Since complementarity between the three sites was a question of survival, their respective product ranges were remodelled and maximum effort was made to rationalise all the division's functional and operational activities.

The products

The products made by the Power Electronics division are UPS systems: uninterruptible power supplies. These consist of power electronic appliances which ensure electrical current conversion in various different forms.

More than just a product, this in fact includes a service: avoiding power supply cuts. AC current cannot be stored. It is therefore converted into DC current, which can be stored in accumulator batteries and eventually reconverted back again to AC. The rectifier transforms the AC current into DC form and the current converter does just the opposite.

The electrical current frequency can also be varied in order to reduce the noise emanating from the installations (low frequencies are rather unpleasant for the human ear to put up with).

The customer is not interested in the product itself, nor its technology. Often he knows nothing about it at all. He is only interested in its applications and therefore the concept of a service.

The division's products are classified into four groups according to their power:

- High power heavy equipment: from 30 to 2,000 KVA (kilovolt amperes). Now quite commonplace, they can be easily adapted to the industrial customer's needs.
- Medium power equipment: from 5 to 30 KVA, particularly used in data processing applications; these are also now quite commonplace.
- Low power equipment which is highly standardised: under 5 KVA, these are particularly aimed at the microcomputer protection market.
- Special equipment which is manufactured to customer's requirements, often part of large engineering contracts. This represents almost a third of overall turnover (sales).

The smaller the products are, the shorter their life cycle tends to be. The distinction made between standard and special products is essential because there are very significant differences in manufacturing, marketing, distribution and delivery times.

Chloride

The markets and customers

The products of the Power Electronics division belong to the market for emergency power supplies. There are three types of outlets which correspond to the various ratings of the products:

- small products: office equipment;
- medium-sized products: data processing;
- large products: industry, hospitals, engineering projects.

The customers are industrial: Chloride Power Electronics has several thousands of customers. In this type of market a new generation of products appears about every five years. Certain customers use the product directly themselves; others tend to be installation outfits which resell the product to the final customer.

Engineering contracts are always large and important affairs. In France, for instance, customers such as SPIE-Batignolles, Alsthom etc integrate Coredel products into their electrical installations. This mainly involves special systems. It is very difficult to negotiate with such customers, because they impose technical specifications in line with their own: they too have to respect their customer's budget and lead times. The division's customers are spread across the world and Chloride Power Electronics uses a network of distributors.

An indication of Chloride's position in its major markets is given below:

- In France: Merlin Gerin   50%
                  Emerson   17%
                  Coredel   10%
                  Socomec   8%
- In Italy: Sice (Emerson Group)   15%
                  Silectron   13%
- In the UK: Chloride is the leader with 28% of the market.
- In Europe: Chloride is number three after Merlin Gerin and Emerson with 10% of the market.
- In the US: Chloride only holds 2% of the market, which nevertheless represents 50% of the world market.

The most important key success factor in Chloride's market is reputation. This is why Coredel and Silectron have kept their trade names and are not also called Chloride. Chloride's worldwide market position is not yet sufficiently strong for them to build on the reputation of their own name. Their major competitors on a world scale are Merlin Gerin and Emerson. Merlin Gerin, which produces standard products, are also customers of Chloride for special systems from time to time.

The new structure

The structure which has been sent up is based on main functions, managing the same teams in each of the three production units (see the simplified organisation chart in Appendix 1).

The director of the SBU is a Frenchman, Mr Martin, who has taken over from a British national. The personnel function is led by an Englishman who is directly responsible for the Eastleigh personnel. The production manager is French and he has direct responsibility over the French plant. The marketing manager is British, as is also the quality assurance manager and the financial manager. The research and development manager is Italian and the sales manager is French.

It should be pointed out that in one year, several changes in manpower have already taken place. In the revised organisation chart which was published six months after the first one, the nationality breakdown of the 29 names which appear on it is as follows:

- British: 12
- French: 9
- Italian: 8

Eight of these are the top managers of the SBU (three British, three French and two Italians).

At each site, one of the managers is considered as head of the unit and looks after the every-day management, 'solving every-day problems and waving the national flag'. The 'vertical' line management structure, as far as it is involved, is responsible for strategy, decisions, methods and control. Each national company keeps its own legal personality, while waiting, as one of the company managers said, for the eventual appearance of a legal system governing a European company.

The structure, according to the company plant managers, answers certain strategic objectives. In the first place, the integration of the three sites into one structure should enable them to benefit considerably from the effects of volume:

- Purchasing: collective purchasing for the three sites enables economies of scale to be achieved (in fact, this mainly concerns the components which are used in standard products, ie production at Eastleigh and Bologna. As it produces specific one-off types of equipment, the Lyon plant benefits less from this advantage).
- Sales: each site will be able to sell any and all of Chloride's range of products. The hope is that the sales capacity will thereby be increased.

Secondly, the structure satisfies the demand for a truly European division if the three sites of Bologna, Lyon and Eastleigh are taken into account, if not an international one with the foothold in Thailand. Thus it is hoped that efforts made to attract new customers and to capture market shares will be multiplied.

According to the plant managers, the importance of the division in Europe on the eve of 1993 has to be quite considerable. Chloride enjoys, because of its privileged market position in large European markets, a strategic position and a competitive advantage over its rivals. In fact the latter are still poorly prepared for the opening up of the European Single Market.

Moreover, the structure of the Power Engineering division guarantees better proximity to its customers in the various different markets and therefore a better knowledge of national requirements.

In addition, according to the company managers, there are numerous points in common between the three sites:

- the customers and the product applications are identical;
- the competitors are the same;
- the three companies share the same opportunities and the same risks;
- finally, the last objective in the setting up of the SBU is connected with production. This has to be perfectly coordinated in order to ensure the complementarity of the range. This assumes the exclusion of all redundancy between production at the various different sites and creates a real industrial synergy within the division.

According to Mr Martin, the conditions for the success of such an enterprise are mainly that everyone wants (and, of course, that it is possible) to go beyond the culture barrier, to build up efficient multicultural teams and, in order to do this, 'to renounce the use of egotistical nationalism'.

Shortly after their appointment, about 20 senior managers from the SBU got together for a weekend seminar in the Alps, to discuss the implementation of the unit's structure and to fix the annual objectives. Mr Martin then explained the new structure to them and there were relatively few questions. A large part of the seminar was therefore given over to the annual objectives.

The position of certain functions can be briefly summed up as follows:

Marketing

Marketing is located at Eastleigh and only takes account of standard products. This is a recently introduced function which has the objective of developing technical communication and information for all standard products in all markets.

Certain countries react more favourably to one form of communication than another. For instance, advertising in the industrial press goes down well in the UK, but not in France. Trade fairs and exhibitions represent 80 per cent of the communication budget in Germany. In Italy and Spain, Christmas presents have to be a lot more expensive than in France or the UK.

Some problems arise, particularly in the drafting of technical data sheets which have to be written in the customer's language: trips to Lyon and Bologna have to be made to study the products which are made there and the corresponding text must be written.

Sales

Each salesperson in the division sells all of the products from the three sites. Whenever a British salesperson sells a French product in the UK, Lyon invoices Eastleigh for the product with a very low margin, not the customer directly.

This enables the salesperson to achieve a good profit margin, even for products which are not manufactured on site. 'We are trying to optimise the margin per product; the different sites are not profit centres.'

- In France there is one sales manager for standard products and nine salespeople operating from five sales offices.
- In Italy there is one sales manager and three sales offices. Silectron achieves 80 per cent of its total turnover in Italy and only sells standard products. 65 per cent of its sales are direct, the remainder go through distributors.
- In the UK there is one sales manager and seven salespeople for standard products (supervised by the French Manager who is responsible for special systems). 50 per cent of sales are direct and 50 per cent go through distributors.

There is a sales manager for each site in the division, all supervised by the SBU sales director.

As far as strategy is concerned, Chloride used to play the 'nationalist' game: customers bought a product manufactured in their own country. Henceforth, as all the products come quite indifferently from Eastleigh, Bologna or Lyon, stress is placed on the lead taken by Chloride in European integration. Chloride has anticipated 1993 and will not suffer any backlash from the unification of the European market, its top managers have declared.

After-sales service

After-sales service still differs greatly according to the site. The strategy is quite different in Italy and the UK.

In Italy and France, at Silectron for example, stress is placed on the speed of after-sales service. The aim is to be at the customer's plant within two hours of a call. At present, the delay is four hours. To achieve this, there is a direct and an indirect structure.

- Direct: each sales office has its own after-sales service technicians.
- Indirect: there are exclusive after-sales centres for Silectron products, but they may also intervene in other areas of activity (data processing for example).

In the majority of cases, the defective part is replaced and no attempt is made to repair the machine, because this is the quicker way.

In the UK response time is guaranteed. They repair the product: this requires more time and much better qualifications than those held by Italian technicians who only change the part, but it is less costly.

The overall strategy of the division is moving towards the

Franco–Italian system which is faster. They are trying to standardise procedures and technical literature.

Financial system

Chloride's financial year runs from 1 April to 31 March, which is in accordance with the British financial year. Each country keeps its own official accounting system and in parallel has to produce other figures according to the chloride standard form, for consolidation purposes. This often causes problems in France and Italy because the codes are different and the information is not processed in the same way. Administration managers therefore have to prepare their tables each month in two different ways.

Research and development

R&D is mainly concerned with technology and not the basic physical principles. 3 per cent of total turnover is devoted to it. There is applied research which is linked to marketing, and there is an R&D team at each site.

Attempts are currently being made to rationalise this activity within the framework of the SBU and to coordinate the three research teams. Before resolving a problem, a teacher tries to question the other sites which multiplies informal contacts.

Personnel

The personnel function is the one which has for the moment received the least attention regarding standardisation between the three sites. Some company managers say that they cannot see what can be done in this area, since in fact each production unit has to continue to operate according to the legal regulations and salary systems specific to each country.

Certain characteristics of the personnel remain quite distinct: the plants in Lyon and around Bologna employ personnel who face short home-to-work transport times. Their relationships are characteristic of average size production units which have not known any serious economic problems and have a low staff turnover. The British factory has always been part of a large group of companies and has itself known serious financial difficulties. The rate of staff turnover is higher. Some technicians and managerial staff are currently spending long periods of time in other production units in order to be trained in and to study specific problems. For instance, at the moment there is an engineer from Eastleigh working in Bologna for 18 months.

The first year of operation

Attitudes in the face of change

The common factor affecting the three sites, as far as the SBU is concerned, was a strong feeling of suspicion.

Eastleigh doubted the possibility of efficient cooperation with the Italians. Intuitively, they felt them to be rather close to the French and therefore felt somewhat anxious about this. They also had doubts about the management of the division: as we have said, this is carried out by a Frenchman, who took over from an Englishman who had not been in the job for long. This could be a sign of instability, which worried the British.

In addition, certain British workers were afraid that the re-organisation would lead to decisions unfavourable to them, based on the memory of past financial difficulties.

The problem faced by Coredel was different. Some of the French feared that the English would benefit from the SBU by maintaining a certain domination over the rest of the division, as was the case beforehand. However, Coredel did not fear re-organisation of production because its activities were mainly geared towards special products and it was not in direct competition with the other sites.

Finally, at Silectron, there was a general atmosphere of concern. Without doubt integration would lead to significant changes whose nature they still did not know. The Italians would have preferred to have been bought out by an Italian group of companies (Olivetti for instance) and not by a British group: this would not have caused any problem of cultural integration.

They were ready to fight against the British 'invader' if the latter had begun exercising too strong a domination. However, one of the Italians declared: 'It was not a colonisation, but a form of cooperation!'

Broadly speaking, some of the managerial staff appear to hold a very positive view of the Europeanisation of the firm, in terms of the opening up of and the development of careers. This is particularly the case for certain salespeople. On the other hand, some people, particularly those in technical functions, are more reticent, or at any rate more prudent.

Whatever happens, the general environment of the company is marked by a strong orientation towards results and a desire for rigorous management, in view of the difficulties lived through in the past. 'Many executives felt that they had been placed in the hot seat.'

In any case, the new unit appeared to be more of an organisation in the process of being built, the 'live' units to which individuals referred remaining the local companies, especially for the French and the Italians. The majority of the employees and workers appeared to be little concerned by the change.

Choices about production

One of the most tangible signs of the change was a series of decisions leading to industrial rationalisation. The 'special products' activity, which previously had been dispersed, was then concentrated at the French production unit. The transfer of this activity, even if it had been carried out without fear for the overall employment situation of the production unit, nevertheless caused a considerable amount of regret in the British factory. The issue was raised of its influence on the nature of the work on the shopfloor, in the sense of an increase in standardisation and less recourse to technical skills. One of the British factory's production managers saw the change as a complete turn-round, leading to a restructuring of the workers' tasks so as to increase their autonomy and compensate for the change. Some 15 skilled workers left Eastleigh at that time.

In Italy a production line was shut down without any jobs being lost. 'It was not easy to get the personnel to accept the changes,' one of the Italian managers said.

Overall, it appears that the technical reliability of the products was widely recognised throughout the three sites. Large-scale quality assurance campaigns were carried out, but the central quality function of the SBU was eliminated.

Communication

For engineers and managerial staff, the time spent on business travel has become considerable, especially as there are no direct flights between the three towns. Meetings are held alternately at one or the other of the sites. The SBU has no real headquarters and Mr Martin travels between the three sites and has his own office in each. A great deal of time is also spent on the telephone. 'Communication is now made via business trips,' an executive said. Travelling a great deal appears to be both the sign of belonging to a group of decision makers, but also a considerable constraint.

What strikes everyone as an obstacle to communication is the difference in working hours. 'After 1700 there is no way you can contact anyone in England,' say the French and Italians. On the other hand, the British complain of having difficulty contacting the French and Italians between 1230 and 1400. Nevertheless, the British say that they are struck by the quantity of work and motivation of their colleagues on the continent and tend to be a little self-critical: 'Too much pay for too little work to do (in the UK),' said one of them.

Beneath the managerial group, at the employee level, the differences in initial organisation are still very noticeable. They point out to you that the precise functions are very different, even for the same titles on the organisation chart. 'If I call someone on the telephone at one of the other companies (even after having checked her function), I am never sure of what she really does,' complained a secretary.

The working language used during meetings within the SBU is English. Linguistic capabilities in English are unevenly distributed: some French and Italian managers remain relatively silent during meetings, even if they really have something to say. An Italian manager did not get the position that certain people envisaged for him in the SBU organisation chart because of his poor English. English tuition is organised in France and in Italy. The British feel to a lesser extent of course, that they are obliged to be capable of expressing themselves in the other languages. One of them said that he was always irritated during meetings if the French sometimes spoke in French among themselves and he was unable to understand what was going on (the same thing applies to the Italians). He added that the British, among themselves, can also speak fast and use English slang expressions whenever they do not want to be understood. French lessons are organised at Eastleigh.

The first sales director of the new structure, an Englishman, was quickly replaced, we were told, because of his inability to work with foreigners.

The eight senior executives come together every month for a day's working meeting. A few months ago, there was a meeting which concentrated on sales: all of the salespeople and distributors met together at Nice to discuss sales objectives and methods. Following this, the main managers of the SBU tried to analyse and set objectives to satisfy market needs as much as possible.

Working methods and attitudes

No one discussed this subject without some reticence, no doubt for fear of underlining differences between the countries which, for good reasons, they want to avoid.

The British see the French and Italians as hard workers and turned more and more towards Europe. The French, and to a great extent the Italians as well, judge the English as rather slow, sticklers for detail and not having muich 'get up and go'. For them, procedures must always be respected. Whenever a technical change is indicated on a fax from England to France, the French have to send back a memo acknowledging receipt. In France this practice is considered to be quite useless and unnecessarily formal.

The attitude with regard to a special request from a customer is also cited as representing the usual differences in behaviour. The British salesperson will tend to redirect the customer to an existing piece of equipment or advise him that it is impossible to meet the request. An Italian or French salesperson will accept the order and then consider how to satisfy the requirement.

The Italians are seen by the French as being fast and hardworking, but sometimes 'less than reliable'. 'With them it's the haziness of the soft-focus effect,' said one engineer.

Generally speaking, care is taken not to express generalised opinions about colleagues from other countries. While weighing up the results of this first year of operation, several managers underlined the importance of the personal role played by Mr Martin in bringing the various points of view closer together and overcoming the cultural differences (see Appendix 3 on p 123).

Appendix 1: Simplified organisation chart

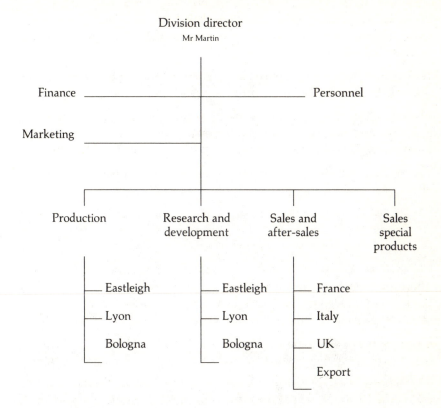

Division director
Mr Martin

Finance

Personnel

Marketing

Production

Research and development

Sales and after-sales

Sales special products

— Eastleigh

— Lyon

Bologna

— Eastleigh

— Lyon

Bologna

— France

— Italy

— UK

Export

Appendix 2: Extracts from interviews with managers

At the beginning there was a certain mobility of the organisation . . . it was necessary to find competent people, some people were under a good deal of stress . . . those who did not speak English began to ask themselves some hard questions.

There is the problem of distances involved, this does not help matters, a lot of coming and going . . . fortunately the director of the SBU speaks five languages and travels very frequently . . . but it is difficult to see people regularly and with the proper follow-up.

It's harder to work in a company which operates on an international scale, but it's more exciting.

We ought to set up a database on human resources in such a way that we can tell who is who and be able to guide people within the group . . . We should also set up a teleconference system.

Key posts are missing: business analysts should be operating in each country, there is no control over stocks, it would be better to link up the data processing systems.

We wondered whether there could be a form of equality between the three sites and if everyone had the same interests.

There should be development in the exchanges of personnel at all levels of the hierarchy and not just at top management level . . . not all of us think European: that is of rather more concern to the managers and engineers.

The SBU is good but the structure is too heavy in comparison to the number of persons involved and the total turnover: it is very expensive.

We had to change the sales approach since the integration. Before that, we were proud to sell British products, it was a good sales pitch. Now, we speak about the Europe of 1992 and we are already ahead of time!

It is not really a problem of nationality, it all depends on the persons involved. There are more relationship problems . . . the employees who carry out the tasks do not understand very well the necessity to specialise the sites . . . It's up to the manager to inform his team about the life of the group.

We grew in size much too quickly: the functions, the structures and quality have not yet been redefined, it's all still a bit of a mess, we are wasting time.

The company does not have the right to make [commercial] decisions without asking the advice of each of the other countries and getting them involved. Each country has a margin for discussion, for each market is quite specific.

The organisation changes every month . . . We are trying to attain the ideal form of organisation . . . things are improving step by step.

Appendix 3: How managers of different nationalities perceive each other

	British	French	Italians
As seen by: British	• not very hard working	• executives very motivated • very hard working • long hours of work • conscious of Europe	• a 'family business' mentality • conscious of Europe
As seen by: French	• rather slow, cautious • concerned with their leisure time activities • not hard working • not rigorous • not very much initiative	• rapid, 'even rushed'	• rapid • easier to work with than the British • a bit 'head in the clouds' • not very reliable
As seen by: Italians	• we work more than they do, but are we more efficient? • orderly and organised • lacking imagination • slow	• hard working	

Questions

1. Describe and evaluate the moves made in the setting up of the new structure.

2. Analyse the attitudes of the staff towards the new structure and towards integration within a European group.

3. Analyse the potential organisational problems that this firm will have to solve.

4. Identify the cultural differences, as they are perceived in this company, and compare them with the results of other studies into intercultural management.

5. Mr Martin, the director of the SBU, would like to launch some initiatives aimed at improving internal communication and the integration of the production units. What would you advise him to do?

Case analysis

This case gives rise to a discussion on the establishment of a new structure in a European firm. The analysis should follow two paths.

- It should examine the setting up of a new organisational structure and its attendant problems.
- It should examine the intercultural management aspect.

Before attempting to reply to the questions above, certain facts about the past development of the firm should be mentioned:

- the group is reorientating towards the electronics sector and is keen to promote worldwide sales.
- Eastleigh products were already out of date.
- Giving the UK direct responsibility for running the French subsidiary before the new structure was in place had not proved to be a success.
- The French and Italian companies are efficient, small to medium-sized firms, whereas the Chloride Group is a large group with a record of economic difficulties.

Comments on Question 1

An SBU is an organisational unit based on a sector of strategic activity. In this case the different legal structures remain the same (pending a European status for the firm).

Comment on the organisation chart, emphasising the creation of new functions at the level of the SBU (marketing, research and development etc). Notice the nomination for each function of one of the people already in post in the three companies (which means his ex-colleagues will be responsible to him!)

Steps taken:

- no head office;
- seminars;
- varied nationalities;
- the attempt at communication is not convincing.

Comments on Question 2

There was suspicion at the beginning, and different attitudes within the various groups:

- managers: lots of travelling;
- executives: rather motivated.

The interests at stake were not the same:

- Salespeople: opportunities for career development;
- production: more reticent.

Because the change had altered the distribution of work internationally, the Italians had to close down one production line and the British were anxious about the standardisation of their production. There was a general fear of loss of autonomy.

Differences also became apparent in professional identities (eg British after-sales technicians etc).

Were other groups apprehensive or indifferent?

Comments on Question 3

Potential general problems:

- identity, the SBU image is not clear enough;

- availability of managers (there were very few real international managers);
  - the managing director of the division;
  - 'local people' with an international perspective;
- links between general and local strategy;
- setting up common procedures.

Functional problems:

- Production:
  - rationalisation of production lines and synergy between factories;
  - staffing problems;
  - responsibilities for certain products.
- Marketing:
  - recently established;
  - how to establish it everywhere;
  - developing common technical information;
  - design and advertising;
  - policy for special products.
- Sales:
  - sound knowledge of all products by all sales staff;
  - standardisation of distribution channels.
- After-sales:
  - should it be standardised?
- Accounting system:
  - should it be based on the British system?
- Research and development:
  - local adaptation or else centralisation.
- Human resource management:
  - develop exchanges and contacts.

Comments on Question 4:

The most striking differences:

- Language: even if English is the official language, the varying levels of people's competence in it create differences and represent a form of power.
- Working hours: mutual criticisms of the two-hour lunch break in France and the British 5 o'clock closing time.
- National stereotypes: conforming to a large extent to Hofstede's studies (see Chapter 2).

Comments on Question 5

- Develop and reinforce the managerial team (team-building, common projects, etc).
- Develop exchanges and communication at all levels including employees (house magazines, factory visits, etc).
- Better utilisation of available means of communication (teleconferencing, computer networks etc).
- Make rapid progress in all common management methods (reporting above all) while maintaining local autonomy in certain fields (human resource management, research and development to a certain degree?).
- Clearly define the responsibilities of the new functions created in the SBU and the desired balance between centralisation and decentralisation.

Commentary on the French case studies

France is an old country, fashioned by the Roman Empire, moulded by one dynasty over eight centuries, marked by wars and revolutions. Fundamentally an agricultural country, it industrialised late and held fast to a distinctive social structure.

The notion of 'executive', the importance given to diplomas, the difficulties encountered in vertical communication and horizontal cooperation are a living heritage from the past. However, in present day economic competition, as much at the macroeconomic level as at the level of the firms themselves, the country is capable of change.

If managers can build on the positive aspects of French traditions and their mentalities (in particular their facility for commitment, their desire to understand, their aptitude for finding solutions), then they will be able to obtain results that live up to their expectations in quality, flexibility and productivity.

It is more at the level of internationalisation that the major obstacles are to be met. Formed as they are within a powerful cultural influence, the French still have a lot to learn and experience before being fully able to accept and understand European and international realities.

How can they frankly and openly safeguard their identity and their culture? This seems to be the major challenge that must be faced at once both within and outside the firm.

Part 3
Italy

6

Environmental Dynamics and the Organisational Innovation Process: Implications for Human Resource Management in Italy

Luigi Manzolini

In this chapter and the following case studies, we will be describing the effect changes to the economic environment and to organisations are having on Italian human resource management. The central importance of new approaches to human resource management is underlined by a description of the competences now required within specialist human resource departments. The fundamental issues raised in this debate are of general concern, beyond the Italian context. The facts and figures of Italian labour markets and industrial relations institutions are described at the end of the chapter.

If we are to succeed in dealing with the rather woolly concept of human resource strategy, questions about the different models of the human resource functions and how they relate to the economic context must be answered. This chapter is intended to provide a theoretical background and the tools to analyse the practical descriptions which follow in the case studies, where the every-day concerns of working in Italy are described.

The benefit of the more theoretical approach taken in this chapter is that generalisation is possible; the chapter also provides a counterbalance to the more pragmatic material elsewhere in the book. But it is essentially a European chapter as is demonstrated by the desire to show how institutions and society are connected to the management of human resources.

Environmental dynamics and new models of economic and company development: some premises

The situation today can be interpreted as a transitional stage between an industrial order and a new post-industrial order characterised by deep economic, technological and social transformations. Even if today it is still difficult precisely to distinguish the direction and intensity of those transformations, between the different concepts referred to as the 'new era' (a 'society at a standstill') (Crozier and Friedberg 1977), 'third wave' (Toffler, 1981) 'the age of discontinuity' (Drucker, 1970), 'a society of mature capitalism' (Offe, 1977), it is possible to find a common denominator represented by the intensive and widespread character of innovative processes.

The main factor which spurs the evolution of economic and industrial change is represented by the 'technical and scientific revolution'. This revolution determines the development of scientific and technological knowledge and ensures that the growing interaction between science and the strategies of individual companies leads to a considerable increase in the use of science in production (Vaccà, 1986). These factors of scientific development (technological push), jointly with those of the market (demand pull), as well as the institutional and cultural influences (Freeman, 1979), have generated a series of wide-ranging technological innovations which appear to be pervasive. By pervasive I mean the transferability and diffusion of intelligence (with regard to the ability of the new technologies to accumulate and process information) and of flexibility, the ability to use new technologies in both defined and different ways.

In the field of technological innovation, 'information based' technologies (aggregates of machines, applications and techniques related to the processing and distribution of data, items, texts and images) are of particular importance, as they contribute to a further evolutionary process in the economic and productive system: the growing dominance of the production of services and information over the production and processing of the physical flow of goods and materials.

The transition from an 'industrial' economy to a 'service' economy involves the continual need to raise the quality and sophistication of the service offered as an essential condition for development. So, jointly with the gradual consolidation of an advanced tertiary sector, characterised by exclusive, personalised services generally based on highly sophisticated technologies, a trend emerges to a new model of development of industrial sectors and departments, increasingly based on flexible response to the market dynamics and less and less anchored to the logic of efficiency and production, internal to companies. Therefore, it becomes important to depart from the logic of standardising mass production and rationalising production processes, in order to approach forms of decentralisation and organisational flexibility that make it possible to identify and anticipate opportunities in markets which now are increasingly volatile and segmented.

From another viewpoint, the environmental dynamics of the latest decade have shown another distinctive characteristic linked with the processes of internationalisation and globalisation of markets, which are expressed through a growing level of interdependence between companies and between economic systems in the various national contexts. Once again technological progress – and information technology in particular – reduces transport costs and makes information management processes more efficient, thus widening the possibility of communication between decision-making centres located even at great distances.

Consequently, the processes of globalisation of the economy open up to the various economic systems new opportunities for achieving higher rates of development, new and more articulated interdependencies which enable the industrial country (or the individual company) to exploit its own distinctive abililties on a large scale, integrating and developing them on the basis of the contributions which come from cooperation or competition with other economic systems and companies.

It is easy to understand how these new conditions have contributed to increasing the complexity of the environmental and strategic context in which companies operate. However, in the face of this increase in complexity and uncertainty, the desire for internationalisation has resulted in moves towards strategic and organisational innovation within companies, typically through the search for new forms of internal cooperation. As a result of increased strategic and operational interdependence between the various components of the multinational company, global strategies are characterised precisely by the establishment of a thick network of exchanges which makes possible high levels of productive, financial and technological integration. Therefore, because of new integrated structures with vertical and horizontal flows of inputs, of intermediate products, of information and of finished products and services, the source of profit is no longer only the individual operating unit but, rather, the network intertwining between the different units, constituting a flexible structure ready to take advantage of change and of the opportunities offered by the international context in which it operates.

The current strategic and organisational innovation processes require the availability of a new 'culture of change' that makes it possible to overcome the inconsistencies of the older models of analysis which were standardised, sequential and prescriptive. Therefore for companies it is a question of passing from a 'culture of crisis', in which very high attention is paid to the problems of adapting the company to environmental change to a 'culture of evolution', in which it is possible to operate actively on the environment external to the company, precisely trying to orientate its change dynamics (Di Bernardo and Rullani, 1984). Therefore, in this hypothesis, the preliminary requirements for the affirmation of a new evolutionary paradigm are created, with respect to which change is no longer considered as an element of disturbance which can be planned and programmed, but, on the contrary, as a corporate resource to be used for the development and, consequently, as an element of the physiology of the corporate organisational systems (March, 1958).

If these assumptions are accepted, at this point it is a question of identifying more specifically the organisational needs emerging in the corporate settings which are starting innovation processes and of deciding what are the most important implications connected with the new competence needs for the human resources function that are, at the different levels of the corporate organisational structure, the key factors in the change processes.

Innovation processes and induced organisational needs: the centrality of human resources in a company

The human resources in the company, the employees – which at one time were not considered in company planning processes and were relegated to the operational stages of production plans – today take on a new centrality and become the subject of new attention.

Networks of small independent firms, connected by market relationships or by agreements and strategic alliances, have developed in many sectors, as have systems of macro-enterprises based on networks of subsuppliers.

On the level of internal organisational macro-structures, matrix organisations and project organisations are widespread in production and high-tech companies. Within the scope of functional areas there is a significant evolution of logistic systems, of production planning systems correlated with sales planning systems, as well as of CAD/CAM systems (computer aided design and manufacture) which integrate research and development with the production and marketing functions.

There is now in Italy widespread use of total quality improvement programmes, interventions by consultants on productivity problems and teams of internal and external staff working to produce innovative programmes of organisational development.

On the level of job and task system planning, 'open roles', strongly oriented towards coordination and performance control are increasingly widespread and many middle managers are evolving from line controllers to managers of cross-functional processes acting as catalysts of knowledge.

A major determinant of these changes is the gradual transition of many sectors of economic activity from a logic of 'economy of scale' to a logic of 'economy of flexibility' (Chandler, 1983). This transition implies an approach to management characterised by a high degree of structural flexibility, by a reduction of the size of organisations and by the operation of structures which favour internal integration and coordination.

Consequently the stability and clarity of the structures tend to disappear, the company becomes increasingly dependent on the quality of the professional competences of the human resources involved and the decision-making processes – also more at the technical and operational levels – take on very marked forms of decentralisation.

In addition, changes to the economy as a whole, in the move to service sectors, affect all organisations. This phenomenon implies deep transformations in both the socio-professional occupations themselves, the internal labour markets in companies and the professional structure within them. All these changes require companies to develop new abilities of understanding and managing the dynamics of labour markets, as well as new skills of acquisition, management and development of human resources.

Within the Italian economy, as elsewhere, new communication and information technologies, flexible automation and robotisation, transport and handling innovations and so on, favour the removal of the traditional structural gaps between small and large companies, since today the constraints historically determined by production volumes are replaced by opportunities for flexibility in the production process, which make possible smoother and more sensitive forms of adjustment to the qualitative/quantitative variations in market demand.

Therefore, the process of diffusing the new technologies, together with the gradual move to service-based economic and production systems, inevitably leads to changes to traditional organisational models. Today organisations which are intended as 'institutions' are holding to a concept of the organisation as a 'network' (Bontadini, 1984).

The traditional models are characterised by the presence of vertical, centralised, hierarchically formal structures, in which written rules and legal authority represent the mechanisms of coordination and supervision which regulate its working. Communication and information flow from the top down, which also applies both to decision-making processes which are not very participative and the formation of areas of competence crystallised in systems of highly diffused and specialised tasks and jobs.

In contrast, the second organisational forms are based on structures of the 'adhocratic' type (Mintzberg, 1989), which are flexible, decentralised and flat. The particular character of these structures lies precisely in horizontal forms of communication and in interactions between the different levels of the structure. They are organisations based on the interconnection between organisational units, with continual exchanges of information and in which horizontal links predominate, with the minimum of hierarchical lines, with decentralised decision-making systems and more widespread employee participation.

In addition, these new approaches to structure are characterised by the same organisational logic which inspires forms of inter-firm cooperation and alliance at the macro level, giving rise to vast and articulated network structures in which the interdependences of the system become increasingly intense and frequent. Therefore, we face a new era definable as that of 'the capitalism of alliances' (Vaccà, 1986), where strategic and technological agreements, joint ventures, consortia and cartels and other forms of inter-firm cooperation will represent the real engine of the system's economic development and of a company's strategic development.

Broadening the number of protagonists and actors involved in the process of strategic and organisational innovation must necessarily be supported by the diffusion of a new corporate organisational culture. In fact, it is evident that cultural and job values focused on individual reactions and initiative represent the essential preliminary condition for the development of an innovating organisation. Corporate culture, meant as the aggregate of stable aspects shared between the members of the organisation which are expressed in the form of cognitive styles, symbols, myths, rites, principles of judgement, beliefs, values and norms of behaviour, exactly represents the essence of the corporate organisational system.

Therefore the role taken by corporate culture in either favouring or hindering innovation processes is a particularly central one. We may think, for example, of the presence of particular taboos or of values centred on economic inactivity, a rigid response to rules, the transmission of negative experiences which tend to repress the creative and innovative spirit, individual initiative and a predisposition to change, the involvement and participation of new people as part of the culture.

Consequently, it should always be remembered that organisational culture must find a specific acknowledgement as an area of intervention for new organisational needs, both from the perspective where it is the subject of the changes induced by strategic innovation processes and in the reverse perspective, according to which culture, on the contrary, is an active tool of change: that is as an essential condition for the anticipation and exploitation of potential for innovation.

Therefore, from this schematic review emerge the main categories of organisational needs which characterise innovating companies. With specific reference to the peculiarities of the Italian context, these organisational needs can be summarised as follows:

- the development of structures and organisational systems which are flexible and articulated, which make it possible to respond to the market and to anticipate the dynamics of the environmental and competitive context;
- the development of decision-making processes which are more articulated and widespread and coordination and control systems which are less hierarchical and bureaucratic so it is possible to respond to the system's need for organisational flexibility;
- the design of organisational structures and systems of tasks

oriented to the performance of those variables which have a direct influence on the most critical results and on the productivity of the organisational system, that also make possible a closer link between quality and quantity of work performance, expected results and reward systems;

- the search for new organisational forms capable of developing ways of cooperative work through forms of workers' participation and involvement in organisational processes (of communication and decision making), which is significant for supporting the competitive factors critical to the company's success.

After summarising in this way the main organisational needs to which Italian companies are giving priority in facing the decade of the 1990s, it is now a question of understanding what difficulties still seem to remain internally with regard to their ability to respond. The deep transformation in progress in companies' organisational structure and social and job structure requires, with increasing intensity, an ability to renew the strategies traditionally utilised for the management of human resources. The following pages will try to reconstruct some of the most critical historical and evolutionary aspects of the human resource function in Italy, with the objective subsequently of proposing themes and indications for human resource departments on the development and consolidation of new distinctive competences and new job values for human resource managers and specialists.

A new professional challenge for human resource departments

An analysis of the power relationships existing in corporate organisations makes it possible to note how the definition of the objectives of an organisational system is typically determined by means of an explicit or – more frequently – implicit bargaining process between individuals or groups of individuals belonging to a decision-making coalition. Therefore, within that process, the characters and qualities of the system's objectives are determined by the type of resources available to the actors, by the rationality and 'preferential functions' expressed by the actors themselves, as well as by their ability to enter into interpersonal and political relationships to be used in the development of bargaining and decision-making processes (Cyert and March, 1963).

The very assumption that the structure of the organisational objectives stems from a dynamic process in which the dimensions of 'power' and 'strategy' have a determining weight is also found in the theory of strategic contingencies (Hickson *et al.*, 1971). According to this theory, the power of the different functions or organisational units which belong to the corporate system is determined by their ability to face the uncertainty of the task assigned, by the relative importance of that task and, consequently, by the critical nature of the related results expected.

Therefore, this concept explains the power differentials existing, for example, between different corporate functions, differentials which obviously have a considerable impact on the determination of more general organisational objectives.

It is true that in Italy, at least until recently, an appeal to power theories can explain the position of the human resource function, since it controlled sources of uncertainty considered of critical strategic importance (motivations and individual satisfaction of workers, costs and relative efficiency of the labour force and so on). Nowadays, on the contrary, it is more difficult to use the same conceptual categories to interpret the power position of organisational systems such as human resource departments by reference to plans, models and objectives.

With the change of the company's response to the environmental context, with the change of corporate objectives in the face of an alteration in the critical competitive success factors for the company, there must occur corresponding changes in the power relationships within the organisation.

Now – in the so-called post-industrial era of technological revolution, of service/knowledge based economies, flexible manufacturing, of internationalisation and globalisation of markets, of the new emphasis on product and service quality and productivity, of the deep changes in job structures and of the new phenomenon of mobility in labour markets – how is it possible that human resource departments cannot draw sufficient relative advantages from the shift in priorities and from the new distribution of the sources of uncertainty? How is it possible that they cannot redefine power relationships with the other actors in the organisational system in their favour in order systematically to exploit the company's human assets? Evidently in numerous corporate environments the formulation of objectives is still a predominant characteristic of other organisational actors, who are historically better trained and familiar with the management of power and influence.

From another viewpoint, strongly complementary to the dimensions of 'power' and 'strategy' already mentioned, today in Italy human resource management strategies must respond to a growing deficit due to the non-satisfaction of the 'endless demand' for care and attention expressed by the individual and collective subjects who operate in a company and who are the most direct users and receivers of those strategies (Varchetta, 1989). Consequently, beyond the opposing distinctions between human resource strategies more or less coherent and linked with the choices of corporate strategic objectives, or more or less advanced in terms of complexity and sophistication of the management systems and techniques adopted, there remain criticisms of basic human resource strategies in Italian organisations.

In order to have the power to adopt appropriate strategies, to influence organisational culture for the development of human resources, Italian human resource departments must meet this challenge as a job challenge to be won first of all within their work. This means abandoning sterile attitudes based on feelings of identity crisis, insufficient status and inadequate organisational power (Costa, 1989a). In the past, these attitudes have often accompanied human resource strategies of the 'reactive' type, with an emphasis on doing, on productivity and efficiency recovery, as well as on the run-up – not always considered – to new and old fashions, rather than on analysis and research, on reflection and innovation (Boldizzoni, 1990). Instead, in view of this challenge, human resource departments and the other organisational factors involved in the processes of utilising human resources must develop their critical competences.

The profile of the competences of human resource departments

With a view to understanding how new needs and competences for human resource departments are being determined, the path of reasoning to be followed starts from the following statement: in Italy, after the years of social tension and strong labour conflicts (1968–1978) and of heavy restructuring and company recoveries (1978–1983), there has not been a strong revival of interest in the theme of human resource development, in particular from the late 1980s onwards. This return substantially to corporate orientations and strategies focused on a new exploitation of human resources, however, seems to have been translated – apart from ritualistic formulas and statements of principles – into a reintegration of the most classical functions and activities proper to a human resource organisational unit. In fact, as all the most recent research on the evolution of the contents and techniques of human resource functions in Italy shows (Boldizzoni, 1990; Perrone, 1989; Costa, 1990), there is not only confirmation of a strong push towards the adoption of new tools and more sophisticated management techniques, but also an integration of the activities of human resource departments within the processes of corporate strategy formation and implementation.

In other words, the emphasis is on a human resource department which has put a heavy almost exclusive accent on the content and on the specialist technical tools of different human resource management systems (recruitment, appraisal, remuneration, development and exit) according to a logic often predetermined at top management level and which can be represented as follows:

- Corporate systems must answer organisational needs described above concerned with planning, responsiveness, 'flexibility', 'productivity' and 'participation'.
- Human resource management must aim at the expression of organisational (both individual and collective) behaviours consistent with the objectives of the organisational system (planning responsiveness, flexibility, productivity and participation).
- Consequently, human resource departments must define and develop the contents and the technical tools for the achievement of these pre-set objectives.

In performing these tasks, some Italian human resource departments are encountering difficulties as they try to establish a new model of human resource development, in place of the more traditional and more widespread concept of them as concerned with human resource management (see Table 6.1).

The following difficulties have emerged, for example, in the development of complex intervention projects:

- the planning and use of human resource planning systems, appropriately integrated with systems of corporate strategic planning and directed to the expression of human resource strategies differentiated by job families;

Table 6.1 *Models of the human resource department*

Variables	Human resource management	Human resource management and development
Task	Defines human resource strategy and offers line managers the technical support to make it operational	Systematically looks for compatibility and consistency between strategic choices and human resource strategy
Focus	On management and operating problems	On strategic, management, operating and development problems
Segmentation of receivers ('clients')	Vertical (hierarchical); internal stakeholders	Vertical (hierarchical) and horizontal (job); internal and external stakeholders
Organisational position of the function	Staff or staff-line with attempts to involve the line during the stage of strategy planning and implementation	'Widespread' function, interacting with the line and the strategic level, mainly during the planning stage; strong involvement of the line in human resource management
Relationship to corporate strategy	Either residual or adaptive	Proactive: anticipation, removal of constraints and development of opportunities for both the company and the workers
Dominating criterion for assessment of performance	Ability to provide given standards of technical specialised performance; efficiency in the use of human resources	Feeding competitive advantage through the development of distinctive characteristics of human resources

Source: Costa, 1989a

- the utilisation of various forms of flexibility interrelated with the processes of technological innovation (automation, flexible specialisation and so on). Intervention in projects on organisational borders (external joint ventures, agreements and alliances) which have significant implications for human resource management have proved especially difficult for HR departments to be involved with;

- The design of variable remuneration systems, linked with the analysis, measurement and bargaining of work productivity;
- the development of processes of total quality improvement, which often involve particular requirements for intervention on human resource management systems.

However, beyond the problems of intervention on these individual themes, the commitment expressed by human resource departments to projects of variable remuneration, of total quality improvement, of human resource planning and of work flexibility, all without doubt require process abilities. Consequently these projects require, more than the specialist competences and technical tools (ie the technology of the human resource department in a narrow sense), a new marked attention to the characteristics of the organisational processes in which the human resource department is positioned: processes of internal communication, planning, coordination and integration between multiple activities and subjects, decision-making and bargaining, of influence and the management of organisational power.

In addition, these projects require from human resource departments an openness, even more marked than that found in the past, towards the environmental and strategic context in which the company as a whole operates. Therefore, it is a question of being able to discover the environmental phenomena which have significant repercussions on competitive strategies and on typical areas of corporate operations, then deducing from these phenomena the critical factors which impact on the human resource areas of acquisition, management and development. All this is achieved by taking a proactive approach, making it possible to express valuations on alternative scenarios, removing constraints and developing opportunities for both the company and the employees.

This may be a case in which interventions in the area of human resources, more than a mere linear adaptation along the chain of the relationship between environment, strategy, structure and human resources, represent, on the contrary, the engine of strategic innovating processes. They are thus able to transform a system of constraints or rigidities (economic, market, technology, regulation and so on) into a system of opportunities which feeds and consolidates corporate competitive advantage, precisely through the development of the distinctive nature of corporate human resources.

In performing new tasks, the human resource function is also called on to answer new challenges regarding the nature of the relationships with other organisational factors (top management, line management, other supporting units such as strategic planning, organisation, control, as well as the customers of human resources represented by the different populations or job families) without also overlooking the other factors external to the corporate organisation system (employers' associations, trade unions, professional associations and so on).

This means, if we consider the human resource function as one providing services rather than standardised and specialist products, taking on the following features which define the nature of its activity (Costa, 1989a):

- making its areas of competence highly pervasive, since all corporate strategies have a component which has an impact on human resources;
- a comparative despecialisation, since the management of human resources is not an exclusive competence of the function, but concerns all the corporate organisational units to a different extent.

Although these features are not absolutely original to the current evolution of the human resource function in Italy, as a whole the new frontier problems described as key to the Italian context will require a response from the human resource department.

Crucial issues for strategic management of human resources

The new frontier areas will now be summarised in a more analytical way, with a view to detailing the functions and profile of a human resource department that intends consciously to be accountable for some specific critical areas by developing specific competences.

The analysis previously performed has enabled identification of these critical areas and competences which can be represented schematically in a matrix showing a sort of 'framework of strategic control' for the positioning of the function in the organisational context (Table 6.2).

Table 6.2 *'Critical areas/competences' matrix for the human resource department*

Critical areas for the human resource function	Focus on client corporate strategy segmentation	Strategy and power of the function	Function performance
The competences of the human resource function			
General management competences			
Organisational planning competences, decision-making and bargaining skills			
Internal human resource marketing skill			

Critical areas

The 1980s show, with specific reference to the Italian environment, two new significant elements in the debate on the evolution of the human resource function in the company. The first element is the critical nature of strategic management of human resources. However, the human resource is no longer only generically determined by the characteristics of the corporate context outside the company (economic, political, labour, social and institutional), but is also induced by some specific aspects in the organisational system of the company, among which are:

- the company's new strategic behaviours, which imply new knowledge, skills and cognitive systems of human resources (Boldizzoni, 1990; Cartoccio, 1989; Costa, 1989b);
- the impact of technological innovations, of the new flexibility of work and of corporate organisational systems, as well as of the

structure of roles and job families (Butera, 1989; Turati, 1989; Vaccà, 1989);

- the consequent different forms of human resource segmentation, also determined by the use of alternative forms of managing work transactions with respect to the market/hierarchies/clan continuum (Costa, 1983; Costa, 1989b; Fabris, 1990; Manzolini, 1984a).
- the new contractual orientations (both explicit and implicit) which make wider and more articulated the traditional industrial relations system of the company (Costa, 1989b; Nacamulli, 1989).

The second element of comparative novelty is the gradual abandonment of disputes – often sterile and ritual – between 'ideological' statements on the role of human resource departments ('culture broker', 'sociopolitical operator', 'interpreter of values', 'techno-specialist staff), in favour of analyses and critical valuations on the content of functions, on the tools for an appropriate and more comprehensive integration between different human resource management systems, as well as on the nature of the relationships between the human resource function and the other key actors in the corporate organisational system (Boldizzoni, 1989).

This has made it possible to reorient many human resource functions towards an approach defined as the 'development cycle of human resources' (Devanna, Fombrun and Tichy, 1981 and 1984; Manzolini, 1984b). This approach focuses on the objective of keeping conditions of dynamic equilibrium and internal coherence between three dimensions:

- corporate strategy (the strategic and competitive framework);
- organisational structure (criteria of work division and specialisation, the working lines of the structure, delegation and control lines and so on);
- human resource management (recruitment, assessment, remuneration, development and exit systems).

In this approach, human resource functions recover organisational power vis-à-vis other factors and quality by a culture more operational and less oriented to functional specialisation.

In addition, human resource planning systems become 'control systems' for the human resource development cycle, that is, these systems tend to correlate in an explicit and formalised way the organisational needs brought about by the company's strategic and competitive framework (for example, focus on the quality of service, focus on innovating and entrepreneurial behaviour, focus on efficiency in the use of resources and so on). This means, for instance, that HR departments decide in a predetermined way to what specific and priority needs the career planning system should respond rather than, say, the remuneration strategy or performance assessment systems; it also means evaluating the quality of the results obtained in the various organisational development programmes.

This approach, which presents the undoubted advantage of having enabled, in many environments, 'intuitive' or 'technocratic' concepts of human resource strategy to be overcome, has its own limitations because of the reliance on systems and structures to influence behaviour.

The constituent elements of the strategic paradigm and the description of the strategic actions of managers in human resource functions would, together with the themes of developing corporate organisational culture, merit a close examination which is beyond the limits of this chapter. Here one final critical area of particular importance can be stressed, related to communication and the image that a human resource department typically maintains in the most advanced Italian companies – the definition of a marketing plan internal to the company and, in some cases, also directed to the outside.

However, so that this marketing plan may not turn out as an aggregate of communication tools and techniques which tend to represent by themselves just an ideally portrayed image, it is important for the human resource function to state the performance indicators for its activity. Therefore, to arrive at the measurement of expected performance from developing the activities of a human resource department, there must be precise references given to the contents of the function's marketing plan, thus also activating a virtuous circle reinforcing the opportunities for obtaining a strong commitment and an acknowledgement of status for relaunching initiatives and future interventions in the field of strategic human resource management.

The discussion of the themes referred to as the development of 'critical areas' for the human resource department will now be resumed through a more specific analysis of the classes of competences necessary for a conscious and pre-arranged activity. It is approp-

Table 6.3 *The critical areas of the 'focus on corporate strategy'*

Activities to be carried out	To analyse and anticipate the changes in corporate distinctive competences (critical competitive factors, know-how, core technology and the critical factors which impact on the processes of human resource acquisition, management and development).
Main purposes	To protect the distinctive corporate competence and consolidate the individual and collective '*savoir faire*' which enhances the competitive factors in the company's business, distinguishing them from the competitors.

Table 6.4 *The critical area of 'client segmentation'*

Activities to be carried out	To develop skills of analysis and generation of job families or groups, to which apply different strategies of: • qualitative/quantitative planning; • entrance; • evaluation; • remuneration; • labour relations/internal relations; • training and development; • career termination; • changing plans for numbers.
Main aims	To articulate and distinguish the different categories of stakeholders which have particular socio-professional characteristics and to express service strategies directed to the individual stakeholders.

Table 6.5 *The critical areas of the 'strategy and power of the function'*

Activities to be carried out	To orient sources of power in such a way that the different actors in the organisational system may express their usefulness through proper negotiations, provided by valid rules of the game, linked internally to formal processes of human resource planning.
Main aims	To exert an influence on the structure of corporate objectives and to encourage the expression of strategic behaviour throughout the organisation, so that human resources are fully utilised.

Table 6.6 *The critical area of the 'performance of the human resource department'*

Activities to be carried out	To reflect strategically on the different types of relationships the function entertains with its internal market, in order to understand the type of legitimisation required to operate (either existing or wanted) and define a job marketing plan with related communication and negotiation about the performance indicators of the function's activities.
Main purposes	To make explicit the performance indicators of the function's activities, giving precise references and contents to the internal marketing plan; to activate a 'virtuous circle' that favours the opportunity to obtain a strong commitment and an acknowledgement of status for relaunching future interventions in the field of strategic human resource management.

riate to recall the distinctive characteristics of the four 'critical areas' already identified in the matrix proposed (Tables 6.3, 6.4, 6.5, 6.6).

Competences

The most important competences which enable the critical areas to be controlled are defined by the aggregate of the general management competences which must be available to the human resource function.

As has already been pointed out, these competences favour a marked openness of the function towards the environmental and strategic context in which the company as a whole operates. Therefore it is a question of refining the use of 'selective spectacles' making possible readings of the environmental phenomena which have critical repercussions on competitive strategies, such as commercial strategies, process and product technologies, distribution and logistics systems, research and development processes.

The predictable scenario of the 1990s includes the opening up of European markets and the Europeanisation process and strategic and organisational repercussions for individual companies. A central competence is now an ability to read and anticipate the possible effects. Already for some years there have been discussions about the alternative responses possible from companies; but what will happen to those human resource functions which are unable to anticipate the impact of technological innovation, the creation of networks, alliances, moves towards the elimination of organisational inefficiencies and so on, on the processes of managing human resources? And again, how will they be able to govern the new social dynamics of a European single market which foresees free circulation of workers and freedom of residence, the recognition of educational qualifications, actions supporting economic and social cohesion, the harmonisation of provisions regulating employment relationships and actions of support for research and development (Erasmus, Comett, Eurotechnet, Fondo Sociale Europeo (FSE) and so on)? What is the best way to face the new phenomena of the competitiveness on the labour market of technicians, professionals and managers and – more generally – of the redefinition of borders and mobility in the labour market?

Coming back to the 'critical areas/competences' matrix, it should be borne in mind, in short, that general management competences favour the strengthening of:

- an ability to anticipate and emphasise a focus on the definition of the distinctive competences required by the corporate strategy, thus speeding up the strategic reorientation and redefinition of the key objectives of the human resource strategy;
- an ability to negotiate and define performance indicators for the human resource department, not so much on the basis of universal standards of generic efficiency as on the basis of objectives selected, related both to the implementation of strategic choices and to adhering closely to the specific characteristics of corporate management.

The second class of competences important for the human resource department is subsequently defined by the competences of organisational planning. In fact, the development of a corporate organisational system is characterised by phenomena of change the context of which concern:

- on one hand, the nature of the organisational structure (units and organisational positions which change their location and dimension, working lines of the structure which express different degrees of centralisation/decentralisation and so on);
- on the other hand, the human resources themselves in terms of age, values, job competences, needs and experience curves (Airoldi, 1980).

It could be hypothesised that three possible different concepts exist of the relationships of dynamic equilibrium between the evolution of the organisational structure on one side and the evolution of human resources on the other side.

The first concept is one which does not recognise the need for a dynamic equilibrium in that relationship, as in those companies with outdated organisational systems, where 'to organise is to put in order' through the development of rules, regulations, procedures and mechanisms of standardising activities and tasks, combined with human resource management models strongly oriented to managing the legal and administrative aspects of labour relations.

A second concept is one which, in contrast, tends to recognise the need for that dynamic equilibrium, but in a relationship where the centre of attention is represented by the people in the organisation and by the organisational conditions in which the people operate. According to this concept, positive results can be achieved through formulas of the type: 'willing people and clear orders and objectives, people and monetary incentives, people and identification with the company, people and *esprit de corps*' and so on (Airoldi, 1986). Consequently, companies working to this concept tend, depending on the case, either to solve problems of 'adaptation of the human resources to the structure', or more typically, 'adaptation of the structure to the human resources'.

Finally, the third concept is one which fully acknowledges the need for a dynamic equilibrium between structure and people, in a relationship of proper correspondence. And it is evidently within this concept that a strong need for integration and complementarity between the organisational planning system and the human resource planning system is expressed.

In this hypothesis, the definition of an integrated system of planning of organisational and human resources will require planning criteria defined by a logical sequence which can be expressed as follows:

- Identification of the corporate strategic behaviours which take on absolute priority, consistent with the company's strategic and competitive position.
- Planning of future organisational needs and of future needs for knowledge, skills and cognitive styles of corporate human resources.
- Composition and integration of the two categories of needs (organisational and human resources) in a planned system of job families.

- Adjustment, by means of qualitative/quantitative availability, of human resources to objectives.
- Definition of the criteria and standards of human resource strategies aimed at an integrated management of all the individual components of the human resource development cycle (recruitment, evaluation, remuneration, development and exit), consistent with the objectives of the 'plan' or model.
- Periodical evaluation of the results produced by the 'plan' choices and by the human resource strategies consequently adopted and possible iterations and adaptation of the 'plan' model.

In this concept of an integrated system, planning takes on the value of a complex and articulated organisational lever. This is intended as an operating system used to face the uncertainties of the future, to decide now what to do in order to have a future. Consequently, in 'plan' models, unlike what happens in forecast models *tout court*, the planning process takes a value far more significant than the plan itself, since it allows:

- all the system's interdependences to be made explicit;
- all actors to be oriented and made responsible for given objectives;
- reorientation to be carried out with reference to the timing of planning cycles when considerable environmental changes are anticipated.

In conclusion, it is evident that the human resource department is obliged to propose itself as the key interlocutor in defining the planning process, which is also in favour of a demarcation of the borders between the typical areas of competence of line management and of the human resource function. These borders are increasingly less definite and clear.

Consequently, in a very schematic form, it should be remembered that the competences of organisational planning enable one:

- to strengthen the chain of relationships:

  structure of ———➤ strategies ———➤ tasks assigned
  corporate   and   to organisation
  objectives   critical   and human
                      resources   resource functions;
- to strengthen the expression of the rules of the game and of formal processes which clarify the different areas of autonomy and

responsibility between the different actors (top management, line, organisation and human resource functions).

The third class of competences significant for the human resource department is the one referred to as decision-making and negotiating skills.

Besides the references already made to dealing with the subject of strategic action and of the processes of distributing organisational power, the development of decision-making and negotiating skills must enable human resource departments to express conscious strategies and tactics concerning the way power is used and its sources, which can be traced back to four sources definable as follows (Piccardo, 1990):

- reframing (intervention in the system of shared meanings, basic principles, values and beliefs which orient the actions of a given social group);
- empowerment (actions directed to strengthen individual and/or group skills to make the actors able and skilful);
- political and social pressure (actions of persuasion, conviction and negotiation);
- legal and coercive authority (actions of dominance, compulsion and obligation).

Finally, it must be remembered that the use of negotiating strategies and tactics must necessarily intertwine with a careful protection of the performance indicators of the activities of human resource departments, as well as, with the development of an internal plan for professionally marketing the function.

Human resource management as a service

The analysis of the 'critical areas' or 'competences' has made it possible to develop some thoughts about the typical profile of a human resource department which is important as we are now in the decade of the 1990s, a turning point with respect to the old paradigms. The passage from old to new paradigms also requires the ability to avail oneself of metaphors and symbols capable of strengthening and exemplifying the changes in progress.

From another viewpoint, the evolutionary process of the contents and functions typical of a human resource department can also be effectively represented through the concept of a 'product strategy' as opposed to a 'service strategy'.

In order to exemplify the meaning of this transition between different concepts of a human resource strategy, it might be useful to recall the contribution of managerial theories and practices in the field of the 'strategic management of services' (Normann, 1982 and 1985, Eiglier and Langeard, 1987).

This can be expressed by referring to some easily formulated questions providing a stimulus to thoughts on the theme of human resource strategies:

- What are the distinctive elements of the strategies and the characteristics of successful service companies?
- Do these distinctive elements really differ from the ones found in manufacturing companies?
- Is it possible to describe, by way of analogy, the differences existing between human resource departments which typically provide products?

Some of the peculiarities of service management are summarised and schematised as follows by Gianfranco Piantoni in his introduction to Richard Normann's contribution on the subject of strategic service management (Normann, 1985).

A service company is a 'problem-solving' one

- A company in love with its product habitually tends to satisfy a given need and has eyes only for its product.
- The customers, the final users, appear hazy in the background and if that company orients itself to the market it merely tends to answer a question.
- A service company often starts by having nothing in its hands and, therefore, it is pushed to scrutinise the customers, to take their questions as its own.
- A service company is obliged to listen to its customers and to propose itself as a company capable of solving problems.

A service company is, by its nature, customer-oriented

- Just because they are 'problem solving', the load-bearing axle of service companies is the relationship between producer and consumer.

- The company models itself in such a way as to be able to give the best answer to the problem the customer poses; the customer strongly interacts with the company to search for a solution with it.
- At the end one often does not know whether to attribute the result to the customer or to the company and this proves that the service has worked: what matters is that the result exists, that the problem has been solved.

In a service company the moment of production and that of marketing tend to coincide to the extent of constituting one function

- The service has a very significant but material component and, usually, it cannot be shown in an effective way since it does not exist before the purchase.
- The service cannot be stored and, generally, service production and sale coincide, at time also with a coincidence of place between production, sale and consumption.
- The purchaser/customer directly takes part in the production of the service and a direct contact between customer and company, typically by means of the contact staff, is always necessary.
- Normally the service cannot be exported, but the system of supply of the service can be.

Service companies do not necessarily compete conflictually: they can also search for alliance strategies to defend the sector's status

- In services, a basic concept is that of 'status': the image, the guarantee and the esteem a certain profession enjoys in its approach to the market and to the social environment in which it operates.
- The most undesirable competitor for a service company is not so much one who operates successfully, as one who enters and operates without preparation, thus polluting the possibilities of acknowledgement of those who operate with professionalism.
- In order to contrast the disruptive invaders the best people cooperate between each other with alliances.

Service companies have their core technology in the supply of the service by means of a very close interrelation between customer, human resources and physical supports

- Absolutely crucial is the attention to the customer since the greatest quality of the supply is a guarantee of long-range profitability and a faithful (and not captive) customer is a guarantee of competitive advantages defendable over time.
- The attention to human resources is absolutely crucial which must insist on the critical dimensions of the know-how company, of specific competences and of high dependence from the customer contact people and of the complexity of problem solving in the service spread along the axis of the customer/supplier relationship.

These concise but very effective suggestions for reflection which cannot be dealt with in depth in this chapter are, however, useful for a critical debate on the conditions of success for a human resource function oriented towards the expression of 'service strategies', articulated into stages which consciously foresee:

- segmentation of the customers/receivers of the services;
- analysis of the needs of the different classes of customers/ receivers;
- explicit description of the problems and expected results;
- exploitation of the results obtained.

This critical reasoning can be developed exactly by comparing, in the experiences and in the lives of all those who are responsible for working out and managing human resource strategies at the different levels of the corporate organisational structure, the meaning of the differences between:

Focus on problem solving skills	←——→ Focus on standardisation of human resource problems
Orientation towards the customer	←——→ Orientation towards the technicalities of products of the human resource function
Close coordination between service marketing and service production	←——→ Activity focused on development of human resource systems

Core technology   ◀——▶   Few direct contacts with
focused on ways of   the user and unwillingness to
supplying the service   transfer the service supply system

Appendix*

The Labour Market (in millions)

	Males	Females	Total
Employed	14,035	7,457	21,492
Unemployed	1,100	1,510	2,610
Not belonging to the workforce	12,513	20,322	32,835
Present population	27,648	29,289	56,937

Central and Northern Italy (in millions)

	1984	1985	1986	1987	1988
Workforce	15,630	15,649	15,747	15,844	16,013
Employed	14,274	14,292	14,409	14,515	14,772
Total population	36,145	36,126	36,107	36,086	36,051

* This Appendix was compiled by Luca Solari, CRORA Bocconi, 1991.

Southern Italy (in millions)

	1984	1985	1986	1987	1988
Workforce	7,408	7,564	7,720	7,825	7,975
Employed	6,373	6,450	6,447	6,320	6,331
Total population	20,360	20,372	20,470	20,577	20,711

In Italy, as in most European countries, the birth-rate is increasingly approaching 'zero growth'.

In recent years a significant phenomenon regarding the labour market has been accentuated migratory flow from non-European countries. In connection with this phenomenon in 1990 new laws have been issued, which have extended the provision of social services to established immigrants, including the possibility of being included in employment lists.

Employment

Changes in employment %
(by industry and geographic location)

Males (1987–1988)

	Centre-North	South	Italy
Agriculture	–5.71	–3.84	–4.81
Manufacturing	1.83	2.49	1.94
Building	–0.19	–2.65	–1.19
Other	2.85	1.24	2.28
TOTAL	1.53	0.02	1.03

Human Resource Management in Italy

Females (1987–1988) %

	Centre-North	South	Italy
Agriculture	–4.86	–6.17	–5.56
Manufacturing	0.59	7.88	1.38
Building	8.70	6.67	8.33
Other	3.41	1.76	2.98
TOTAL	2.19	0.56	1.77

Employment index – Employees
(base 1988 = 100)

	Executives, monthly-paid and intermediate level	Hourly-paid workers and apprentices	Total
January–August 1989	100.5	99.9	100.1
January–August 1990	100.7	97.8	98.5

Cost of labour by unit of product in the manufacturing industry

1980–83	1983–86	1986–89
15.4	5.3	4.8

Indexes of labour cost in the manufacturing industry
(base 1988 = 100)

	Monthly-paid and intermediate level	Hourly-paid and apprentices	Total
January–August 1989	104.9	107.4	106.5
January–August 1990	113.0	112.8	113.4

The Main Italian Employers' Associations

Confindustria	(Italian Manufacturers' Federation)
Intersind	(Federation of State-controlled Industries)
ASAP	(Petrochemical Industries)
Confagricoltura	(General Federation of Landowners)
Coldiretti	(Federation of Agricultural Owner-Occupiers)
Confcommercio	(Federation of Commerce)
Confesercenti	(Federation of Tradespeople)

Confcooperative
*Associazione generale
delle cooperative italiane*   (Federations of Cooperative
Unione nazionale   Societies)
cooperative italiane

Confartigianato
*Confederazione autonoma
sindacati artigiani*   (Craftsmen's Federations)
*Confederazione nazionale
dell'artigianato*

Main Italian Trade unions

Name	Main characteristics	Membership (1988)
CGIL	• First trade union established in Italy; • leading group comes from *Partito Democratico della Sinistra* (formerly Communist Party) and from *Partito Socialista Italiano* (Socialists); • strong presence in the manufacturing industry.	4,867,406

160

CISL
- Union in which the workers of the Catholic area are represented;
- strong presence in services and particularly in public administration;
- in its leading group there is a predominance of Christian democrats.

3,288.279

UIL
- Represents workers on the socialist and lay parties area
- strong presence in services

1,398,071

Some details of the composition and evolution of membership in the three main trade unions ('confederate' unions)

Union	Total membership including officials	Subscribing membership	% variation total membership 1980–88	% variation subscribing membership 1980–1988	% variation total membership 1980–1988
CGIL	2,747,013	2,733,017	–21.4	–21.6	+5.8
CISL	2,192,865	2,018,463	–16.0	–19.5	+7.5
UIL	1,194,298	1,099,727	–5.9	–4.0	+3.8

Membership of 'confederate' unions by sector

Union	% agriculture	% manufacturing	% services
CGIL	12.3	49.5	38.1
CISL	12.0	35.7	52.3
UIL	10.0	37.1	52.9

Acronyms:

CGIL = *Confederazione generale italiana dei lavoratori*
(General Italian Workers' Federation)
CISL = *Confederazione italiana sindacati del lavoro*
(General Italian Labour Federation)
UIL = *Unione italiana lavoratori*
(Italian Workers' Union)

The scenario of the Italian trade unions is completed by considering the independent unions present at sectoral level. Particularly important are certain unions established in opposition to the 'confederate' unions, especially in the sector of education (GILDA) and of State Railways (engine-drivers' COBAS – basic committees).

Basic Glossary

Statuto dei lavoratori (workers' statute):	Law No. 300 of 1970, a consolidation Act regarding the organic regulation of employment relations.
Livello interconfederale di contrattazione (interconfederal bargaining level):	National level of the agreements regarding the aggregate regulation of employment relations (in particular as far as wages and salaries are concerned), jointly signed by the three main workers' unions.
Contratto Collettivo Nazionale di Lavoro (CCNL) (national collective labour agreement):	Agreement signed by workers' and employers' representatives in a certain sector, binding for all workers of the sector ('categoria')
Categoria (sector):	Contractual unit represented by the aggregate of all workers belonging to a sector or to a group of sectors either homogenous or treated as such.
Contratto Integrativo Aziendale (company integrating employment agreement):	Agreement signed within a company or organisation between the workers' representatives and the employer, which integrates the application of the sector's CCNL to the specific company environment within the limits of delegation fixed by the agreement of higher level.
Inquadramento unico (equal terms):	Introduced by the workers' statute, provides for a unitary system of classification of jobs for both monthly-paid (*'impiegati'*) and hourly-paid (*'operai'*) workers.

Indennità di contingenza (cost of living allowance):	Automatic mechanism of salary and wages revaluation tied to trends in the cost of living index.

Sources

For the data regarding labour market and population trends:

Bollettino mensile di statistica (Monthly Statistics Bulletin) (1990), ISTAT, a. 65, n. 12, Dec.

Rapporto '89. Lavoro e politiche dell'occupazione in Italia (Report 1989. Labour and employment strategy in Italy), *Ministero del Lavoro e della Previdenza sociale* (Ministry of Labour and Social Security).

For the data regarding the characteristics of employment and of labour cost:

Rapporto '89. Lavoro e politiche dell'occupazione in Italia (Report 1989. Labour and employment strategy in Italy), *Ministero del Lavoro e della Previdenza sociale* (Ministry of Labour and Social Security).

For the data and information regarding trade unions and employers' associations:

Le relazioni sindacali in Italia. Rapporto CESOS (Labour relations in Italy. CESOS Report), years 1984–85, 1985–86, 1986–87, 1987–88.

References

Airoldi, G (1980) *I sistemi operativi*, Giuffrè, Milano.

Airoldi, G (1986) 'La pianificazione organizzativa', *Sviluppo & Organizzazione* 97.

Boldizzoni, D (1989) 'Tendenze evolutive della direzione del personale nelle imprese italiane', *Sviluppo & Organizzazione* 113.

Boldizzoni, D (1990) *Nuovi paradigmi per la direzione del personale*, ISEDI Petrini, Torino.

Bontadini, P (1984) 'La nuova impresa e la teoria organizzativa', *Studi organizzativi* 3/4.

Butera, F (1989) *Dalle occupazioni industriali alle nuove professioni*, Franco Angeli, Milano.

Cartoccio, A (1989) 'La funzione del personale di fronte a scelte strategiche', *L'impresa* 3.

Chandler AD Jr (1983) *Scale to scope: the Dynamics of Industrial Enterprise*, Harvard University Press, Cambridge, Mass.

Costa, G (1983) 'I paradigmi organizzativi nei paradigmi economici', in Costa *et al*, *L'organizzazione nell'economia aziendale*, Atti del Convegno dell'Accademia Italiana di Economia Aziendale, Giuffrè, Milano.

Costa, G (1989a) 'La gestione delle risorse umane come servizio', *Sviluppo & Organizzazione* 113.

Costa, G (1989b) 'Le risorse umane nella sfida degli Anni Novanta', *Economia & Management* 9.

Costa, G (1990) *Economia e direzione delle risorse umane*, UTET, Torino.

Crozier, M and Friedberg, E (1977) *L'acteur e le systeme*, Editions du Seuil, Paris.

Cyert, RM and March, JG (1963) *A Behavioural Theory of the Firm*, Prentice Hall, Englewood Cliffs, NJ.

Devanna, MA, Fombrun, C and Tichy, N (1981) 'Human resource management: a strategic perspective', *Organizational Dynamics*, Winter.

Devanna, MA, Fombrun, C and Tichy, N (1984) *Strategic Human Resource Management*, Wiley & Sons, New York.

Di Bernardo, B and Rullani, E (1984) 'Evoluzione: un nuovo paradigma per la teoria dell'impresa e del cambiamento tecnologico', *Economia e politica industriale* 42.

Drucker, PF (1970) *L'era del discontinuo*, Etas Kompass, Milano.

Eiglier, P and Langeard, E (1987) *Il marketing strategico nei servizi*, McGraw-Hill Libri Italia, Milano.

Fabris, R (1990) 'Logiche e problemi di differenziazione delle politiche di gestione delle risorse umane', in Boldizzoni, D (ed) *Nuovi paradigmi per la direzione del personale*, ISEDI, Torino.

Freeman, C (1979) 'The determinants of innovation', *Futures*, June.

Hickson, DJ and Pugh, DS (1971) 'A strategic contingencies theory of interorganizational power, *Administrative Science Quarterly* 16.

Manzolini, L (1984a) *Economia e organizzazione delle transazioni di lavoro in impresa*, Giuffrè, Milano.

Manzolini, L (1984b) 'Il ciclo di sviluppo del personale in impresa', in 'Raccolte di Sviluppo & Organizzazione' 7.

March, JG (1958) *Organisations*, Wiley & Sons, New York.

Mintzberg, H (1989) *La progettazione dell'organizzazione aziendale*, Il Mulino, Bologna.

Nacamulli, RCD (1989) 'Rapporti sindacaali e relazioni interne', in Nacamulli, RCD (ed) *Relazioni sindacali e iniziativa manageriale*, Franco Angeli, Milano.

Normann, R (1982) *Le condizioni di sviluppo dell'impresa*, ETAS, Milano.

Normann, R (1985) *La gestione strategica dei servizi*, ETAS, Milano.

Offe, C (1977) *Lo stato nel capitalismo maturo*, Etas Libri, Milano.

Perrone, V (ed) (1989) *Dettagli Orizzonti & Ingrandimenti, da Osservatorio Organizzativo* (1988) CRORA–Università Bocconi, Milano.

Piccardo, C (1990) 'Il paradigma politico e la direzione del personale', in Boldizzoni, D (ed), *Nuovi paradigmi per la direzione del personale*, ISEDI, Torino.

Pilati, M (1987) 'Cambiamento e innovazione organizzativa: un approccio evolutivo', 'Raccolte di Sviluppo & Organizzazione' 10.

Toffler, A (1981) *The Third Wave*, Pan Books, New York.

Turati, C (1989) 'Flessibilità e segmentazione dei rapporti di lavoro', in Nacamulli, RCD (ed), *Relazioni sindacali e iniziativa manageriale*, Franco Angeli, Milano.

Vaccà, S (1986) 'Imprese e sistema industriale in una fase di rapida trasformazione tecnologica', in Guatri, L, *Trattato di Economia delle Aziende Industriali*, Giuffrè, Milano.

Vaccà, S (1989) *Scienza e tecnologia nell'economia delle imprese*, Franco Angeli, Milano.

Varchetta, G (1989) 'Creatività e cultura chiavi per il successo', *L'impresa* 3.

THE CHOICE OF CASE STUDIES

The SIP case (*Società Italiana per le Telecomunicazioni*) focuses its attention on the subject of the processes of strategic and organisational change. Essential to these processes, which require also a deep review of human resource strategies and management systems, is the ability to change the rules of the labour relations system, with a view to being in a position to consider the workers' unions as one of the actors involved in the change process.

Consequently, the analysis of the SIP case allows us to interpret the evolution of the Italian system of labour relations, showing how the unions are less and less oriented to claims and bluntly conflicting policies and more and more interested in being co-opted and made co-responsible in those processes which are significant to business development.

By contrast, the Telespazio case focuses its attention on the development of human resource strategies and management systems in a high-tech company and, therefore, more particularly on the management criteria of specific 'professional families' such as those of technicians and highly skilled professionals.

This case has also been chosen because in high-tech sectors and in the management of those specific 'professional families' it is possible to observe the development of more advanced human resource management systems and technical tools, which result from the research conducted in Italy on the evolution of human resource functions in the firm.

The case of Valma industries examines the human resource strategies found in the forms of inter-firm strategic alliance and, in this specific case, in the form of a joint venture. The choice of this case is motivated by two basic reasons; one is the fact that these strategic alliances are more and more frequent in Italy and represent one of the most effective levers for strategic and organisational development. The other reason for selecting the case is that in these new forms of inter-firm cooperation, new models of human resource management are used which are more advanced and aligned with the new skills and professional values of concern to human resource management which were discussed in the previous chapter.

7

SIP:
Organisational Transformation and Industrial Relations

*Daniele Boldizzoni and Enrico Castagnoli**

In December 1984, two years after the start of a deep process of change affecting strategies, structures and management mechanisms, Dr Paolo Benzoni, SIP's vice president and managing director, wrote the following letter, addressed to all the company's workers:

> The stage of renewal and transformation, lived by all inside the company during 1984, and which will continue in the coming year, is essentially directed to put our company, with its technical and human resources, among the protagonists of the further development of the country's telecommunication system.
>
> Certainly the objective is not easy; we are aware of this, but the timeliness of the intervention already planned, the engagement of everybody – according to their respective responsibilities – to respond with his recognised professionalism and competency to the users' increasingly sophisticated needs, gives us hopes for the attainment of the goal.
>
> The recent convention and the new ten-year plan for telecommunications are elements of considerable significance, which enable SIP to accelerate – according to the financial resources

* The authors gratefully acknowledge the help of *Ufficio Studi nelle Relazioni Industriali nella SIP* (Industrial Relations Research Unit of SIP).

available – those processes of modernisation of the installations and of technical innovations are indispensable for improving the overall corporate efficiency and the quality of the service offered.

The company, within the IRI-STET Group, will be massively engaged in the next few years on the investment front which, in the three-year period, will reach lire 15,000 billion: the choices and the prominent objectives, which will have to be accompanied by further improvements in productivity, concern the quality of the service, the continuing enhancement of the basic telephone infrastructures, as well as the further development of the new services, tied to the realities and prospects of IT applied to telecommunications. The employees have already participated positively and with commitment in the change of the organisational, technological and procedural context, but a renewed effort is further required for the future years.

In this perspective, with the renewal of the collective agreement, there has been an adaptation and strengthening of the employees' training and updating in order to guarantee to all the workers concerned, in addition to the new professional figures, an integrated knowledge of their work.

The engagement of all the collaborators has produced its effects on the qualitative and quantitative results of 1984 and we appreciate the value of this fact.

We feel sure that the company will face – with as much ability and certainty – 1985, a year not less challenging than 1984 for both the complete development of the company's reorganisation and the achievement of the goals concerning the quality of basic telephony and new services, whose development is tied, above all, to the incisive and efficient action of the employees of all levels.

History of the company

The establishment of SIP (1881–1925)

The first concessions for the development of the telephone service were given in April 1881 and, in that year, the first two telephone exchanges came into operation in Italy.

The initial period of the company's life (1881–1925) was characterised by modest growth over the whole national territory owing to numerous problems and uncertainties connected with the decision whether to entrust public agencies or private companies with the management of the telephone service. At the same time, other factors unrelated to telephony such as slow industrial development and low national income contributed, in the period being examined, to the restriction of the service's development.

Some years later, in 1925, the first restructuring of the national territory into five areas took place, together with the assignment of the service to as many companies, private and independent of one another, in order to avoid monopoly situations. It did not take long to reap the benefits of this reform and, in fact, already in the early 1930s the spread of the service and its technical quality advanced significantly.

1933, with the foundation of Instituto per la Ricostruzione Industriale (IRI) marked another important step in SIP's history: in fact the decision was made to create STET (*Società Torinese Esercizi Telefonici*), a company with IRI capital through which the State took a large portion of the telephone service under its control. In that year, again, IRI bought the majority shareholding of SIP (*Società Idroelettrica Piemonte*).

In spite of the war events of the subsequent decade, the development of the national telephone network never stopped. In 1957, at the expiration of the 30-year concessions and because of laws which confirmed the requirement to give new telephone concessions only to companies the majority of whose capital was held by the public, STET acquired the controlling shareholdings of all private concessionaires. In the same year there was approval of the 'national telephone planning scheme', recognised by all as the fundamental charter for the development of telecommunications in Italy.

In the early 1960s (1962–64), through the nationalisation of electric power, SIP, after assigning to Ente Nazionale Per L'Energia Elettrica (ENEL) its activities of production, transport and distribution of electric power, brought about the merger through incorporation of the five previous concessionary telephone companies (STIPEL, TELVE, TIMO, TERT, SET), thus acquiring the concessionary activity of the telephone service.

Following that decision, the national territory was subdivided into five areas corresponding to the territories where the pre-existing telephone companies operated before.

SIP's development (1964–1980)

The first years of the merger were characterised by considerable organisational and management problems, doubtless among which the most critical concerned the setting up of the new general management system. In fact it was decided that the company's management structure should be formed by drawing personnel from the various areas, with reference to the fact that, meanwhile, the company's top management team had been mostly transferred to ENEL.

The organisational solution adopted was that of 'keeping the five pre-existing structures in an autonomous form in order, on one side, to guarantee the service's operational continuity, on the other side, to be able to gradually structure and implement the general management lines, with particular reference to the immediately operating ones (technical, commercial, planning and so on.)'

Some years later, starting from 1968, SIP was engaged in the achievement of a 'direct dialling service from the user on the national level.' SIP's commitment to the achievement of direct dialling proved so significant, chiefly in financial and human resource investments, that it did not require any attention from the top management.

Consequently it was decided to put off to 'better times' the achievement of the company's reorganisation plan, by limiting the action to re-elaborating and formalising an organisation pattern 'unified for the five areas and articulated on one central level (general management) and three peripheral levels: area, region and agency.' This solution implied the creation of the levels of region or agency, previously absent in some companies.

The two basic principles by which the general management was inspired at that time were defined as follows:

1. the application of only one structure on the territory to facilitate the study and application of a subsequent stage of organisational evolution;
2. the decentralisation of operational activities from areas to regions and from regions to agencies, to make the company closer to the user and, also, with the accelerated growth of installations (from 1964 to 1978 the number of subscribers increased from 4.2 to 13.5 million), to guarantee an economic dimension to the peripheral structures by relieving the upper levels of operational activities.

In this context the areas were entrusted with such strategic tasks as the extension of general management over the territory.

By the end of the 1970s some organisational problems deriving from the still precarious structure became more evident, while the conflicts stemming from the different management systems and organisational cultures of the areas were multiplying. A corporate document described SIP as characterised by:

- **problems of structural rigidity:** the four levels stiffen relationships and make less immediate the reaction of the structure to the trends of general management or of general management to the periphery's feedback;
- **problems of structural effectiveness:** it has been noted that, of the four organisational levels, at least one seems to repeat the tasks and responsibilities of another;
- **problems of structural essentiality:** the four levels are not only an opportunity for a 'waste' of human resources, but also do not allow the various specialists to grow adequately, owing to the fragmentation of tasks and responsibilities.

Organisational change: motivations, purposes and contents

The scenario of change

At the beginning of the 1980s the fast development of electronic and engineering technologies made possible increasingly integrated solutions in the sector of telecommunications, causing considerable repercussions for the services offered which became increasingly sophisticated, complex and integrated. Jointly with the transformation of installations, with the change from electromechanical to electronic-numerical technology, the early utilisation of optical fibres began, with developments in both the field of transmission and that of communication.

At the same time the institutional framework (regulation of concessions, exclusivity of the service and so on) also began to change and there were more insistent talks about the deregulation of services.

In the same period the unions advanced, increasingly making requests to review the company's whole structure and, on the occasion of the contractual renewal of December 1980, were asking for 'a significant reorganisation of SIP that might lead to an organisation on a regional basis with the removal of the areas.'

Against this framework SIP showed some signs of fragility and weakness, chiefly on the economic–financial front, because of the growing degree of uncertainty and instability characterising relationships with the government, which was increasingly reluctant to grant adjustments in telephone rates.

In this context top management considered the need to 'rethink their activity and, in particular, their organisational structure, in order to achieve an overall improvement of the corporate system, making it more 'adequate' to the strategic choices necessary for a more marked and incisive presence on the market'. Consequently a special work group was created, composed of managers representing the various sectors of the company, with the task of studying a new organisational and functional pattern for the company.

In December 1981, after about a year of careful evaluation of the organisational choices repeatedly indicated by the work group, the company's management decided to reduce the organisational levels to three and abolish the areas.

The change in the organisational structures

In 1981–83 SIP prepared various operational reorganisation programmes, the fruit of the work performed by *ad hoc* research groups created to define and implement the new structural design.

The objectives of the reorganisation, outlined more clearly during the project stages, were defined as follows:

- **conquest of the market for new services**, jointly with the increasingly more efficient performance of the basic telephone service, with a view to increasing the company's income source. This involves a more advanced and aggressive orientation to the market, correlated with an actual decentralisation of the activity and of operational responsibility to make it adequate, in the framework of a more rigid profitable performance;
- **acceleration of the introduction of innovations**, both of a technical character (for example, numerical techniques and optical fibres) and in services (new services provided to the users with new software applications): this with a view to guaranteeing the

efficient achievement of the quality of the services requested and the economic effectiveness of the solutions proposed;

- **improvement of the system's global effectiveness**, through a smoother operation of internal relationships, to make the structure more flexible when external conditions change and allow for the identification of definite responsibilities.

These objectives constituted the inspiring guidelines of the 'new structure, whose main characteristics were two development trends'. The first, 'horizontal', led to the definition of missions and the specification of the responsibilities and borders of seven areas of activity:

- **strategic planning and information system:** this supports the company's long-term choices on the basis of knowledge and hypotheses of evolution of various factors;
- **external relations:** this is responsible for the 'company's image' in relationships with institutions and the public;
- **purchasing:** this is responsible for the acquisition of the technical means to be used;
- **marketing:** this supervises relationships with the users and includes market analysis (volumes and prices), sales and customer service;
- **network:** this supervises the arrangement and maintenance of the collective technical means for carrying out the service;
- **human resources–organisation:** this is responsible for the 'effectiveness of the structure' and for the efficient utilisation of the workforce;
- **administration and control:** this is responsible for the 'formal guarantee' of corporate behaviours and the 'economic guarantee' of SIP's activities.

In this context the definition of the powers of the network was particularly important: 'the only point of global responsibility, both technical and economic, of the installations'. The network's interface with the market was considered as 'the only interface between the company and the users to satisfy the market's needs, to optimise sales opportunities on the existing and potential market, to obtain revenues from the corporate activity'. The users were segmented by product market into major users (companies or nationwide public bodies interested in telecommunications and telematics) and user systems (companies or public bodies not belonging to major users, but of similar importance with regard to sales turnover, with demand for sophisticated products and services); users were classified as major public (professionals, small craftsmen, small cooperatives, shops, flats), public telephony (telephone installations available to the public) and traffic (special user services).

The second trend, the 'vertical' one, led to the identification of the competences, objectives and purposes of general management, regional management and agency management. In particular, specifications of competence were given:

- general management competence concerns the strategic activities which are the exclusive responsibility of the top of the company, that is strategic choices, organisation of the settings and resources needed to perform those operations at the lower levels and control of the system's overall efficiency;
- regional management is responsible for the tactical choices, with the task of updating the resources and controlling the activities of the agency level (coordination level);
- the agency level, corresponding to the administrative division of the provinces (operating at the territorial level), is primarily responsible for supplying the service and telecommunication needs expressed by the different usage steps, following and interpreting the market's needs. At this level, managers must also see to the management and maintenance of installations, as well as to the management of human resources.

According to the company's leaders, the organisational choices made were to guarantee the achievement of a greater decentralisation of functions and were not only concerned with increasing specialisation, but were also directed towards greater integration for the attainment of 'common objectives'. Decentralisation was seen chiefly as a 'management and delegation method'.

This involved an extension of the regional managements' and agencies' responsibilities. The regional managements became characterised by 'real autonomous entrepreneurship and profit centres', the agencies became, in effect, 'centres of sales and no longer only of technical and commercial service' and had to be concerned with the development of the market 'through a more precise satisfaction of the service needs expressed by the various users'.

In addition, the change plan did not overlook the micro-organisational aspects. Such objectives as the improvement of productivity and of service quality, the recovery of the system's global efficiency, could be reached only through a new work organisation and, therefore, through a different utilisation of the existing professional resources, in addition to the creation of new professional figures.

In fact the new technology contributed to making obsolete some traditional forms of professionalism. The new systems put at the operators' disposal a considerable volume of information hardly manageable through the existing professionalism: in short, the need was more and more evident for the company to change its policy, to abandon the pre-existing work organisation, rigid, fragmented and repetitive, in favour of solutions aiming at guaranteeing a greater autonomous responsibility for the operators through forms of job extension and enrichment.

This implied the introduction of profound changes in all the company's sectors, above all in the market areas (user services, commercial, subscriber installations and user systems) and the network areas (exchanges, transmissions and so on).

Policies of industrial relations and problems of change implementation

Industrial Relations at SIP up to the 1980s

In the corporate change programmes at both the macro- and micro-organisational level, significant importance was attached to the choice of industrial relations policy, in partciular to the type of relationship to be adopted towards the union when experimenting with and implementing the new structures.

Until then the history of industrial relations at SIP had been no different from that of the other state corporations, being bureaucratic and functionally centralised. The relative stability of the industrial relations system was the product of both the union being sufficiently representative, even if on a slightly declining basis (from the peak level of density, equal to 68.1 per cent in 1977, to 61.9 per cent in 1982) and the action of recognition and support performed by the company. Conflicts were mostly concentrated at the time of the renewals of the national agreement and towards the middle of the bargaining period and they too, in any case, were declining (in the last five renewals between 1972 and 1984 the number of strike hours per worker had been equal to 54, 24, 31, 20 and 14).

A further factor was the nature of the union representatives: most of them were of corporate extraction and possessed deep and specific knowledge of the company's problems. Negotiations were very meticulous, attentive even to the smallest aspects and peculiarities of the various sectors of the company. The negotiation processes were slow, tiring, but continuous and could be brought to a settlement/ mediation of the reciprocal interests. The agreements entered into at the central level generally did not leave much margin for negotiation by the periphery. Moreover, there was a considerable cultural and background gap between central and peripheral union leaders. In terms of content, before the 1980s most attention was paid to subjects of a normative nature or concerning union rights.

Industrial relations at SIP in the 1980s

During the 1980s, in parallel with the greater corporate commitment to technological and organisational change, there was a growing interest from the unions in the themes of labour organisation and professionalism.

A union representative made the following comments:

The union had realised the importance of the problems concerning the evolution of professionalism and the need for an overall negotiation of the changes induced by the introduction of new technologies.

The union's objective and challenge was that of contrasting the company's trend towards the unilateral introduction of technological and organisational changes which have repercussions on professional activities, with playing a more active role in the company's strategic decisions and developing the ability to analyse and solve problems on these themes.

To the union's wish to be involved and participate in the restructuring process, the company responded through cautious 'openings', establishing more direct and systematic information channels on actions to take at both the central and peripheral level and gave to FLT (*Federazione dei lavoratori delle comunicazioni*) the role of an authoritative source of suggestions about the process being experienced. The steps in the relationship with the union on the themes of organisation were expressed in the meetings of October 1981 and in the first half of 1982, as well as in the agreement of 1982 in which the two parties, on the renewal of the collective labour agreement, resolved to parcel out the organisational aspects with a view to defining them successively in a way consistent with the development process in operation. In this agreement, the national level was fixed on for managing the transition process from area managements to regional managements; there was a division of tasks, contents and contractual procedures between the national and the regional headquarters; there was the identification of some tools for solving problems of excess and/or shortage of personnel between the different areas (voluntary redundancies, early retirement, privileged treatment of transfers etc). There was a certain contractual autonomy in the management of the process and in the achievement of the pre-established objectives which were delegated to the regional level.

A tool particularly useful for managing organisational change processes was the creation of numerous company/union mixed committees (composed of an expert from the company's personnel function with an expert from the technical or line management concerned and one or more members designated by the unions) to examine a wide range of problems (for example, working time, non-returning workers, reduction of working areas, utilisation of company vehicles) or for checking in the field the progress of company projects (for example, the adequacy of training and development for the new technical and organisational needs).

In this way the company aimed at obtaining a greater involvement of the union and, therefore, the possibility of consensus among the workers on the change in progress. Simultaneously, the unions were trying to increase their level of knowledge of the company's strategy and their power and credibility in talks with the company.

The company emphasised that the need for a non-conflicting relationship between the parties was particularly strong, taking into account the context of deep technological and organisational change, which affected all aspects of the employment relationship.

With the relationship systems in operation, an advance was sought, through organisational innovations, towards a gradual move to a union culture of the 'propositional' type, open to the problems of company management.

On the opposite side, the union's wish to review its relationship with the company on the themes of reorganisation can be found in a note of July 1983 by FLT, which read as follows:

> In view of the policies and changes enhanced by the company, it is necessary to clearly define the sales strategies, the choice of the products, of the systems and of the techniques towards which to direct the sales and service activities since, in our opinion, an initiative directed to cover the whole range of products now present on the market would not be effective.

The dispute on the renewal of the labour agreement

The first meetings of the bilateral Intersind-SIP and FLT committee took place in February 1984. The committee was composed of technicians, labour organisation experts and labour policy experts of both parties and its purpose was to examine the problem of the company's reorganisation with reference to labour organisation, work positions, hierarchy and the related human resource training needs. The meetings were directed, in particular, to:

> the search for the formulation of new criteria of human resource utilisation that could take into account the predicted organisational innovations, a different organisation of the shift system and of the workers' availability, as well as an overall review of the human resource training and development system with a view to keeping it adequate to the changes in progress and to the dissemination of technological innovations.

In addition, the objective of the meetings was that of pre-arranging the elements necessary to define the 'bargaining configurations' to be developed during negotiations for the renewal of the collective labour agreement, which had expired on 31 December 1983.

The overlap of the two objectives mentioned and the approach of a complex stage of confrontation and negotiation saw the union engaged in a search to extend the opportunities for intervention in structuring processes at a peripheral level. The company was over-stretched in defending both the need to achieve organisational models and working conditions homogeneous throughout the whole national territory and the need to 'include every negotiation in the more general framework of competitiveness, the responsibility for which is placed at the central level'.

The confrontation between company and union became more tense after the presentation by the union of the bargaining package, in which FLT claimed 'the acquisition of adequate intervention tools and bargaining seats (at national and regional level) to obtain union control and the management of all the factors of the corporate reorganisation and productive qualification process'.

In particular, FLT declared its wish to qualify 'the right of intervention and of access to information, adjusting the bargaining places and tools with reference to the organisational changes'. In this context the national agreement had to 'foresee its organisation and dynamics, as well as the decentralisation of bargaining on specific subjects, defining their scopes, criteria and ways'.

In the initial stages negotiations proceeded very slowly. In fact, SIP wanted to wait for a more definitive completion of the new organisational structure on all territorial levels. In addition, the company could not leave 'the solution of the problems connected with the definition of an adequate framework of financial coverage and of economic compatibility'. The company was also waiting for the related government measures, with specific reference to the investment programme of 1984–85.

The members of the joint committee had to confront their respective positions on many occasions, without however arriving at significant convergences. In particular, FLT was definitely in disagreement with many of SIP's proposals, which it judged directed to 'fragment the salary and normative treatments, centralise the management of the agreement and of the human resources, identify salary treatments also through forms of unilateral disbursements, propose wage increases strongly punitive as regards quantity and considerably unbalanced as regards quality.'

The 'centrality' of these subjects of controversy and the lack of results reached by the committee led the company to further emphasise its position on the themes considered most important. In substance the company, through declaring itself ready to develop further confrontations with FLT on all the controversial subjects, confirmed that it would take a stand in order to achieve a cultural change in the organisation.

The direct consequence of taking this stand was the national strike of June 22, with the subsequent mobilisation and action of all the workers who, through the union, intended to respond to the unwillingness of SIP to deal.

The will of both parties to overcome these conflicts and the awareness of having been in the past – and of wishing to be in the future – 'a model company, in which to develop and experiment with industrial relations so that we can transfer the benefits to other companies of a crucial sector for the country's development' constituted the premises for defining a proposal of agreement.

The new collective labour agreement

The new collective labour agreement was signed on 1 November after a conflict whose duration and intensity was unusual for SIP. It followed a significant turning-point in bargaining strategy, presenting various 'chapters' which took a wide perspective on specific subjects. This provided real 'agreements within the agreement', which gave rise to a series of procedures on information, joint examination and verification destined to be extended over time, according to a model of continuing but regulated bargaining.

A union leader remarked, 'This time the opening of an agreement has meant more than ever the opening of a dynamic stage in the management of the agreements.' The most significant points of the agreement are discussed below.

Company–union relationships

One of the most significant parts of the agreement concerned the definition of an ordered system of industrial relations in tune with the need to cope with organisational technological change. With this perspective a considerable effort at social engineering was made to complete a gradual decentralisation of contractual activities, even if these were controlled from the centre.

The new structure foresaw a process of collective bargaining greatly extended and articulated into many stages. These included passing on information in advance and confirmation of information later, joint examination, real negotiation (formalised in an agreement), experimentation, verification, or possible reopening of the process.

The system of company–union relationships was articulated on a territorial basis in the following way:

- national level, at which to carry out a budgetary meeting, in the course of which the company's management set forth to the unions strategic policies with regard to investments, technological development, new models of labour organisation and so on;

- regional level, where two meetings were foreseen: the first with a budgetary nature on the programme to be carried out during the year, the second a review for verification of the results obtained on the particular territory;

- agency level, at which to hold a meeting which reviewed the results obtained in the territory.

Human Resource Development

Following the changed organisational, technological and procedural context and the consequently greater and different human resource training and professional needs, the training and development system was redefined with respect to both the different types of intervention and the methods of implementation.

In this way the company tried to realise specific development actions, according to the training content and methods agreed with the union, equal to a total of 1,100,000 hours per year for clerical workers, 200,000 hours per year for staff and 48,000 hours per year for executives and managers.

Economic aspects

As far as compensation was concerned (the aggregate of the increases was equal to lire 190,000 per worker) a greater acknowledgement of differences in terms of professional and work contributions was foreseen. That emerged from the review of the traditional pay systems (minimum pay and annual bonuses) and the introduction of two significant changes: the possibility of reviewing the annual bonus at the 'interim' agreement bargaining, on the basis of different contributions to the company's production by groups of workers and an incentive plan for salespersons' results.

The agreement on the methods of giving incentives to the sales functions was particularly interesting, as follows:

- The intended motivation of staff by incentives utilised a two-sided forecast with reference, on the one hand, to the activity of the salesperson directed at the major public and agency user systems sectors and, on the other hand, directed at the sector of regional management user systems. This was because of the different types of sale and of the consequently different criterion of attributing the users according to territorial area and portfolio.

• The determination, on three levels, of the economic measure for individual incentives for all salespeople as a function of the corresponding performance levels.

The payment by incentives plan was such as to make possible, in the framework of the system of company–union relationships, precise evaluation at regional and agency level of the overall pattern of sales activity; in particular, at budget level, examination of the annual acquisition programme and distribution of objectives among the salespeople constituted the main company–union relationship on this theme.

Working time

Significant innovations were also introduced as far as working time was concerned (it was reduced by 28 hours per annum for 1985 and by 36 hours per annum for 1986). It was made more responsive, both to the flexibility requirements of the production process and also to the workers' needs.

Labour organisation

Recognising the importance of identifying the organisational variants affecting the structure and the consequent implications for the utilisation of human resources and for workers' professionalism, company and union defined the basic criteria of classification and utilisation of human resources, with a view to making possible 'the best professional activity and the most efficient approach to the service'.

After the agreement

In an editorial, published in *Notiziario del lavoro* (edited by the research department of SIP's industrial relations division), the company's management expressed its satisfaction with the signed agreement and claimed that 'with respect to the extreme complexity of the external and internal reference scenarios which made difficult the search for a balanced connection between the conditions of corporate development and the employees' expectations, important objectives had been reached:

1. The definition of a new labour organisation consistent with the inspiring principles of the company's reorganisation.
2. The rationalisation of the ways of delivery of different types of performance, directed to fulfil specific programmes of quantitative and qualitative development of the company's activity.
3. The concrete acknowledgement, still in the respect of the substantial homogeneity of treatment for all the workers, with packages of norms, differentiated with reference to the various emerging professional and functional specialities.

Underlining, then, the innovative importance of the agreement, the following remark was made:

In order to supply a mixture of normative, compensation and relationship answers and to consistently combine all these aspects during the negotiations, it was necessary both to have a deep knowledge of the traditional institutions governing work processes, framing them in a different light according to the various positions which we were obliged to take and to create innovative tools in the new environment of industrial relations.

In fact, the implementation of the change processes assumed:

Firstly, the treatment and the solution, as far as possible preventive, of the problems with a view to creating real conditions for reducing conflicts. Secondly, a functional approach different from the traditional one taken concerning relationships as far as both bargaining level and employees are concerned.

Consistent with these evolutionary policies and in particular in the awareness that the management of technological innovations and operational decentralisation involves a parallel development of the bargaining dynamics, it should be seen that the new approach foreseen in the agreement represents a particular advance in the system of industrial relationships. This is to be able to identify, at the regional level, appropriate policies and also to experiment with different organisational models.

In fact, in this way there is a move from a relational model which delegated to the peripheral parties a substantially 'adaptive' function of what had been defined at central level, to a model in which, through 'experimenting', the bargaining adapts, while respecting the principle of the centrality of the relationships, to the new role or responsibility at the territorial level. However, the most important aspect of this functional change is the awareness that, at a similar stage of the corporate plan to that presented here in which all the perspectives of development are tied to a rigorous programming of the allocation of available resources, the role of industrial relations must be that of giving certainties to the development of the production process through common research, by all the actors, of strategies and the most suitable tools.

The unions expressed their satisfaction with the results obtained. One of their statements was that the renewal of the agreement strengthened the 'union's capability to define a strategy directed at integrating the traditional bargaining role with an actual management role in changing the organisation'. They cited, for this purpose, the following conditions for trade unions:

1. The maintenance of a unitary approach to organisation and to contract. This has required a collective reflection by the union on the concept of equality through an updating of the priorities and values on which the union's initiative will have to develop in future, since the union will wish to represent an increasing number of workers. Therefore the acceptance of differentiation of economic and normative treatment, depending on the workers' professional commitment, are included in this vision. This helps the union to realise a new ground of unity and solidarity between workers, salespeople, staff, technicians and managers.
2. The updating of the corporate functions, identifying in the commercialisation of management interests the prevalent task to which all the corporate factors will have to respond. In addition, an adjustment of the professional profiles, directed towards the workers' enhancement, according to the changes deriving from new technologies and the market.
3. The proposal for an active labour policy to be achieved through the flexibility of working time (part time, flexi-time, shifts).
4. A strengthening of the system of company–union relationships through the extension of the agreement articulated at the regional

level, aimed at the realisation of a structure of management which is in a position to respond to the workers' needs and methods.

Case analysis

The SIP case was the subject of attention and comment on the part of authoritative industrial relations researchers. Tiziano Treu, analysing the recent history of industrial relations within the company, remarked that:

> To the initial technological and market pressures recorded so far, the company has responded by adapting the contents of collective bargaining in an integrating or 'weakly' participative direction. Obviously the new contents are already innovative with respect to the average framework of industrial relations, in a context characterised by a public management of consultative orientation and by a type of union consolidated and oriented in the same direction through productivity, labour organisation and mobility and human resource development. Equally meaningful – and already fruitful – is the extended use of communication and consultative procedures. The point is that their use is still limited to the occupational effects of innovation and not extended so far to the strategic aspects of corporate decision making.

Treu also raised the question of the future of industrial relations at SIP:

> If this is an orientation identified by research in many contexts of industrial relations, the research itself suggests that, chiefly in corporate contexts characterised by a faster technological and organisational evolution, midway responses or intermediate models do not hold out long. The responses tend to polarise either towards trends of the new *laissez-faire* policy, of unilateral governance, of changes by the management, with marginalisation of the union and growing individualisation of the relationships between employers and employees, or towards more markedly participating trends, of involvement of the union in the various change processes. If this is true, the choices of industrial relations and of employment policy proposed to the company may

result in more drastic changes than the significant ones used in the past. . . .

There are a number of implications from this study. The first is the need for consistent implementation of decentralisation. A second need concerns the explicit and intentional design of the professional structures, roles and stratifications which need to be integrated with strategic and technological planning. Other issues are essential to every participative orientation of industrial relations. First of all there need to be participation procedures for the company representatives with respect to the strategic choices of innovation – not just communicating information after the event for bargaining about the effects.

This participation does not imply either a surreptitious invasion of management's decision-making prerogatives, or any confusion of roles, but produces a real exposure of managerial choices to influence from unions and hence helps the design through experimentation and joint control of the application stage. It is a challenge to the culture which, so far, has been met by both parties. This challenge has been considered indispensable in other environments in obtaining the necessary consent to the changes faced by the traditional forms of bargaining and participation.

8

Telespazio:
The Telecommunications Sector

Francesco Paoletti

For some years people working in the telecommunications sector have been going through considerable change. The creation of new products and services has stimulated an already substantial demand characterised by very high growth rates. The rate of change has broken the traditions of an industry which seemed unchangeable.

Even more significant consequences derive from the globalisation process taking place, with a gradual liberalisation of the markets through the abandonment of national regulations and the adoption of common standards; this way seems the only viable one in Europe to reach adequate dimensions of demand and allow the sector to make the necessary developments. However, for this individual companies this involves the loss of the safe protection of the national monopoly, an event which might represent a serious problem to companies which have been completely dependent on one market, such as the Italian firms Italtel and Telespazio and the British firms Plessey and GEC. However, this also provides an opportunity for those companies such as the French firm Alcatel and the Swedish firm Ericcson, which have diversified to a greater extent.

Telespazio is a non-quoted, publicly owned, joint-stock company; it is within the system of State shareholdings, IRI group. Since its establishment in 1960 it has been concerned, as the monopoly concessionaire, with the development and operation of satellite telecommunication systems (TLC).

In the early 1980s, seeing the first signs of greater competition inside the sector, companies decided to start a process of developing innovative products and markets. It was a complete strategic and cultural reorientation: From the space communications business to the selling of services and applications in the space field (eg environment surveys), this represented a change from a managerial role in an institutional service, to that of receiver and proposer of new application opportunities related to the use of space technology.

The technical competences seemed to be present. The company considered thorough knowledge of the technology tied to satellites as its real strength. However, greater weaknesses were apparent in managerial know-how, in particular owing to insufficient economic and financial sensitivity among the 'professionals'.

The strategic reorientation has been followed by the definition of five strategic business areas (ASAs) which represent the core business, in their turn responsible to as many SBUs (Strategic Business Units). Institutional telecommunications (via satellites and video telephone connections) have been complemented by such innovative services as those described below.

Firstly, there are closed user network systems, that is, private networks for the satellites broadcast of data in competition with traditional cable/land networks. The systems are distributed by SIP, which is the monopoly concessionaire for private users. However, the relationship with the final customer has to be very close. In fact the supply consists of a standardised technology (purchase of licences and appliances from American suppliers) which is adapted to the customer through Telespazio's systems expertise in network planning and software. The high-tech image and guarantee of high reliability and very rapid response for service make it possible to succeed economically, by obtaining prices on average 15–30 per cent higher than traditional networks.

Secondly, supporting spatial systems have been developed. They include the analysis of and research into space systems, mission control and the management of the structure in orbit. In this case Telespazio's strong point consists in the knowledge of the technology related to the satellite and in the quality of the control software; therefore, it is particularly important to succeed in transferring this knowledge so as to satisfy requirements in the best possible way.

There is also a service known as 'telebearing': this concerns using the satellite to collect environmental information. There are new markets to be developed and, partly, to be created such as agrometeriology, the exploitation of land resources, climatology and oceanography. Consequently success depends on the ability to identify possible applications and propose them to the customer.

Finally, the company undertakes studies and experiments: such studies take on a central role for the development of know-how with consequences for the other SBUs, who therefore seek, in their turn, to acquire research contracts (mainly thanks to their strong connections with national and international bodies).

To protect the related business areas, that is the activities most distant from the core business, a policy of agreements, shareholdings and cooperation with various companies and agencies has been adopted, through the creation of *ad hoc* external structures including joint ventures, consortia, commercial and R & D agreements. The objective, in this case, is to be present in markets which might represent important development opportunities, through the acquisition of technological knowledge without, however, creating an excessively complex structure which, even just to cope with the growth of the main business sectors, is confronted with development rates of 10–15 per cent per year.

The competitive approaches inside the various ASAs are highly differentiated and the current organisational structure is divisional in form. In particular, the new services require a market-oriented approach, rather different from the one typical of institutional telecommunications, since sales turnover is not secured by rates, but by the ability to negotiate the customer's requirements as far as possible. For example, user systems, though being distributed by SIP in a monopolistic system, have required the pre-arrangement of an after-sales system which was quite a new experience to a company used to offering service mainly to itself. It has been necessary to develop a 'logistic' culture which did not exist before. Nevertheless there are still difficulties in correlating costs and revenues of the individual parts of the contracts.

However, a greater sensitivity to the market seems to be necessary even for the professionals who operate in the sphere of institutional telecommunications, both because the environmental dynamics press in this direction and also because it is difficult for two different approaches to coexist in the same corporate environment.

There is, however, resistance to change because it is the 'technical' culture of the past that still today represents Telespazio's competitive, critical and distinctive factor. In this context the role of the function which governs human resources appears to be particularly critical. HRM constitutes the main asset of a knowledge-based company like Telespazio and presents significant management problems for professionally qualified employees, problems which are aggravated owing to the need to achieve in a short time the reorientation of the corporate culture through the introduction of new management systems.

Therefore the HR function must take on the role of 'facilitator' of the change process and this requires it to propose itself as an authoritative interface with the corporate units. It is necessary for those who operate inside the HR department to be fully aware of the direction in which the company is going and to be able to talk to the senior managers with the same views and language. It is therefore appropriate briefly to run through again the evolution of personnel management systems in the 1980s.

The personnel function: from the administration to the management of human resources

The personnel operating at Telespazio doubtless represent its most important resource and are highly professional. The work-force is composed of about 60 per cent of employees possessing a high school certificate, nearly always electronic or electrotechnical experts, and 24 per cent university graduates in various scientific subjects (mainly engineering, physics and mathematics). This percentage, however, is growing rapidly, since in recent years the intake of university graduates has been around 50 per cent of the total.

While the management of high school graduates does not usually cause excessive problems, that of university graduates – that is, the potential 'professionals' who represent the company's critical resource – produces a series of difficulties because they are in heavy demand in the market.

In the early 1980s, personnel management was limited to the activities of administration and the management of labour relations. It is in that period that the first units were created which were responsible for human resource training and development, organisational development and the definition of compensation policies. These changes continued into the mid 1980s adding, through the support of a firm of management consultants, some tools for evaluating jobs and performance and the first interviews for assessing human resource potential.

The subsequent developments (1986–87) were preceded by the adoption of the divisional structure, which should have brought clarity in the definition of responsibilities. However, the system of management by objectives which was introduced has proved unsatisfactory in practice and has not assisted in the orientation towards the market.

At present a profound revision of personnel management systems is in progress: consequently, it is perhaps appropriate to describe the changes taking place.

The 'management by objectives' (MBO) system has been extended to executives and managers and foresees responsibilities based on qualitative objectives (for example, the client's satisfaction) as well as on quantitative ones. However, a series of problems, which can be partly attributed to the limits of the theoretical model and partly to internal resistance, have made problematic the extension of the system and the definition of individual objectives consistent with the distribution of decision making. In particular, the distinction between routine and 'challenging' objectives has not been considered, thus *de facto* rewarding some 'mediocre' employees just because they performed their ordinary duties satisfactorily.

The company's results were good and were improving, but not to the substantial extent expected in connection with the MBO data; for this reason it was not possible to give the bonuses expected, thus leading to disappointment for employees and the conviction that the incentive mechanisms were not very clear and not easily related to individual performance.

The new policies currently in progress will result in a revised MBO programme at executive level and the use of performance and potential evaluation as far as managers and supervisors are concerned.

With regard to job evaluation, the previous experience has enabled the company to overcome some of the limitations of the Hay method, which tends to penalise those professional skills for which it is not possible to define individual positions accurately and to redistribute them logically 'by families'. The system has had to be manipulated through the invention of 'metapositions' (that is, of dummy boxes which do not exist in corporate reality) and carefully reconsidering the weighting of the three key criteria of experience, decision-making autonomy and sales turnover, so as to define values more in line with the actual strategic importance of the different roles to the company.

Quasi-quantitative parameters, directly negotiated with the section manager, are utilised for the evaluation of performance; the manager is also called on to offer some indications on the behavioural characteristics of his subordinates, on the basis of grids of elements judged to be essential for the success in the professional family to which reference is made. The grids have been created through interviews which have involved all managers.

The evaluation of potential is extended also to young university graduates for whom, in addition, it is particularly critical for identifying the most capable, on whom to concentrate professional investment.

The connection with the incentive system is not necessarily direct, in fact performance and potential evaluation can be used as a basis for internal mobility and the connection with remuneration is based on career advancement.

It is clear that the success of a system of this importance must depend on the contributions of the managers, who are the only people possessing the information needed to evaluate their subordinates. Unfortunately, in this respect the managers showed a number of deficiencies which led them to propose, almost indiscriminately, actions in favour of all subordinates, leaving to the personnel function the task of deciding what steps to adopt. To encourage managers to take responsibility for directly managing their staff, merit rating scales were required which could be subsequently utilised as the basis for assigning rewards. The next step consisted in creating the evaluation system, so as to support the manager in the 'subjective' part of the process, enabling him to distribute the rewards within the forms and limits defined by corporate policies. This resulted in a new challenge to the personnel function, which had to reduce its direct decision-making activity and transform itself more and more into the role of an internal consultancy.

On the other hand, with the new tools it is also necessary to supply a new 'culture'. Some episodes which occurred in the past are indicative of the risks that may result from excessive delegation in personnel management where the ground is not sufficiently prepared.

So, for example, in a given year a budget of resources available for the distribution of rewards has been allocated for each manager; the budget has been designed to grant deserving young engineers, hired in the last 18 months, additional salary increases between lire 150,000 and 300,000 assuming an average value of around lire 200,000. Actually the average value of the rewards attributed was lire 160,000 because the managers, with a view to rewarding all workers, ended by levelling the individual awards downwards to fit within budgetary limits.

Another example of the 'distorted' use of the system has been identified in the growing trend of granting additional bonuses at the end of the year (so as to make them appear in the reward budget for one month only and to grant a greater number of them).

The result of these actions can be inferred, on a global level, from the data concerning use of the different incentive mechanisms: during 1989 23 per cent of workers were promoted to a higher category, additional increases were awarded to 16 per cent, and a one-off payment to another 18 per cent; consequently, 57 per cent of employees got some form of additional reward and this percentage rises to 75 per cent in the most recent interim statements concerning 1990 (which was, however, an 'exceptional' year, coinciding with the world football championship and the move to the new headquarters).

In any case it is evident that, in a company like Telespazio characterised by a steadily growing work-force, the career system constitutes the hinge of the reward system. In the past there was no career planning; development was based on what had been foreseen by the contractual agreements, while access to the highest levels (management) took place through 'cooption' from the top. In the course of time, some non-formalised career paths dependent on seniority or permanence in the position were added.

The large increase in the size of the work-force (from 581 employees in 1983 to the current total of 960) has made necessary the formalisation of paths based on systems of professional promotion to appropriate job families.

At present, nine contractual categories are foreseen besides, of course, those of executives and managers. Today, however, some of these categories are empty or are disappearing while others, the highest of the staff level which correspond, among other things, to the access level for new graduates, now represent a very substantial share of the work-force and produce an upward pressure which no longer finds an outlet in further promotion opportunities. In fact the access to management proves difficult because of the limited number of vacancies available.

In order to enable some vertical mobility, personnel planning techniques have been introduced through the working out of specific replacement tables. In addition, a new superior professional profile has been introduced in the category of managers, to which the company intends gradually to attribute a status close to that of the executives.

Nevertheless, there are insufficient opportunities for promotion. There are also signs of an increase in labour turnover and exit interviews proved that this problem could, at least partly, be solved by starting horizontal mobility processes which, among other things, are also included in the company's objectives. This is appreciated by the young and dynamic workers, who would like to widen the sphere of their experience but are hindered by managers who have generally grown up within only one function, who do not consider their employees' potential and, above all, who do not want to deprive themselves of the best resources. At present horizontal mobility is utilised chiefly as a way to solve interpersonal conflicts between managers and subordinates and, therefore, has a 'pathological' connotation which the company would like to reverse and render positive.

To this end a careful analysis of successful professional and behavioural characteristics for different roles has been made and its compatibility at corporate (not sectoral) level has been verified; so some cross-career paths, which are going to be formalised, have been defined. Personnel training and development activities are extremely significant in the support of those processes; it is a matter of intervening in such a way as to fill the gaps (professional and behavioural, never technical) which emerge at the various stages.

Equally critical is the role of selection: the true problem, however, is not so much in recruitment, because the good image Telespazio enjoys and its strong connections with the university world in any case enable the company to attract a good number of suitable candidates. The differences arise more when the problem is that of checking the candidate's personnel characteristics, in particular the homogeneity of values, needs and attitudes to the social context he or she is going to enter. This is an activity which cannot be standardised, because of the limited number of employees hired for each individual profile. This requires the close involvement of the personnel function, through their deep knowledge of the different internal sub-environments.

The last aspect which should be considered is connected with the evolution of industrial relations which are presently conducted in a good climate, but are also affected by rapid change. The union is losing power and tends to represent the most vocal groups which, however, are also the least important to the company. In fact, 'new' and graduate workers tend not to join the union, preferring individual to collective relationships. This produces an increase of 'microconflicts' and a heavier burden for the personnel department, which has to solve a series of individual controversies previously covered by company agreements.

Case analysis: The new critical areas for the personnel function – towards the management and development of human resources

The development of operating systems and the gradual decentralisation of the management of human resources to the individual SBUs represent the necessary conditions for a further evolution of the personnel function towards a strategic approach.

The importance of this process is evident if one considers that it is exactly the technical and managerial knowledge held by employees that represents the 'invisible assets' on which competitive advantage is built and that the employees represent the main lever of organisational change.

Therefore, it will be the duty of the personnel department to understand the need for change and to anticipate it through development policies; this also requires the achievement of greater integration between the various sub-functions and operating systems.

For example, if the system of performance evaluation identifies any professional gaps, these must be transmitted to the training and development section, in order to define action programmes; this information, if concerning recently hired employees, could represent important feedback for the manager in charge of selection.

So, one perceives the need for a wider dialogue between the various sub-functions, which could also be carried out through organising an effective personnel information system. This, at present, is limited to salary analyses utilised for the budgeting process or in labour relations (for the evaluation of the 'cost of the contract') and is totally insufficient from the management viewpoint. It is necessary to add qualitative information resulting from the evaluation of potential and extend the availability of quantitative data to managers responsible for the various SBUs who need such information for economic evaluation of the various job requirements. Labour costs amount to over 50 per cent of operating costs and although in the past one could be content with using approximate estimates – by increasing them through the addition of wide margins – today it is important to have at one's disposal more analytical data for the definition of pricing policies.

This change to an information system is necessary in the long term and is especially important as a means of increasing the familiarity of managers of the various SBUs with the economic and financial aspects of the utilisation of human resources.

In order to satisfy the anticipated need, the company expects to introduce a system of strategic personnel planning. The labour relations department will be asked to take on the role of 'researchers' on external labour market changes and culture.

Obviously, as the development of these projects takes place the systems of Telespazio's personnel department may become more important. The trends which have led to the greater valuing of and attention to the personnel department can be summarised as follows:

- a very high education rate with a strong growth of the incidence of university graduates;
- a rejuvenation of the professional population, chiefly in the areas which show a high technical specialisation and are particularly critical for the company;
- a steady and marked growth in the size of the work-force;
- a significant restructuring of the work-force, with a relative decrease in the professional areas of general services and direct labour, against an increase in the sales and marketing professional areas as well as in the more technical areas of research and development.

In order to face these challenges the personnel, organisation, labour relations and information systems have been engaged for some time on an agenda which presents the following critical aspects:

- to cause top and line managers to make explicit a more visible framework of prioritising organisational requirements, so that the organisational development function may be less and less compelled to undertake 'on call' interventions and therefore be the 'lightning conductor' of organisational conflicts. Instead the organisation development function should express wider and more flexible organisational policies;
- to enable the system of labour relations to reduce the lack of flexibility in the present system of workers' classification and contractual hierarchies;
- to enable the company's training and development system to

prioritise some critical objectives of internal communication and of dissemination of a new corporate culture, especially through more specific and better targeted inputs and development needs;

- to orient the systems of personnel evaluation and remuneration towards greater attention to the critical nature of some corporate objectives, by using variable payment systems;
- to favour, over a period of time, a clearer and more explicit assertion of systems for distinct and differentiated 'professional families', so that personnel policies are devised which are capable of understanding with greater sensitivity and precision the different expectations and requirements of management and professional development.

9

Valma Industries

Carlo Turati

'Americans do not greet anyone when entering the office in the morning, Europeans do. OK, after a month you learn that, and that's all.' Mr Pilati, an engineer, has been abroad since 1983; since 1985 he has been responsible for a complex Anglo–Italian international project, included in a joint venture agreement between his company, Alza Italiana and Vertigo, one of the leading European manufacturers of high speed elevators. Since 1 January 1990 he has been the chief executive of Valma USA, a three-party joint venture between the partners of the preceding venture and a North American giant.

'I have entered this adventure since its start. At that time there was a gag among our workers: 'This company is like its product: it stands still in mid-air, it goes neither up nor down'. When the alliance started we were convinced that our ideas would never coincide with theirs. We looked with mistrust not only at the alliance with our English partners, but also at the very hypothesis that the company might survive the general crisis of the sector. Now the company is asking me whether I am willing to manage a new alliance in Canada. In principle I would like to answer affirmatively. From my European experience I have learned a lot. I just wonder whether our executives too have learnt anything: from strategists to human resource specialists.'

The Valma alliance: background and introduction

Alza Italiana is an Italian public company, established in the early

1980s. Like Vertigo, it employs about 3000 workers. Like Vertigo it has a primary interest in the high-speed lift technology sector and a declared will to stand out as the sector's leader. In this decade both companies have a strong propensity for cooperation. Indeed this is almost a compulsory choice; the two companies are too small to compete singly in national markets or to exploit sector niches. A necessarily international scenario, the pressure of new entrants to the market, the introduction of new technology and a sharp rise in R & D expenditure are all factors which have made recourse to cooperation inevitable.

A brief description of Valma's story follows, and the organisation structure is shown in Figure 9.1. In 1982 a prestigious customer of Vertigo's communicated his intention to renew his lift systems in the near future. As this was a very interesting job, Vertigo started a

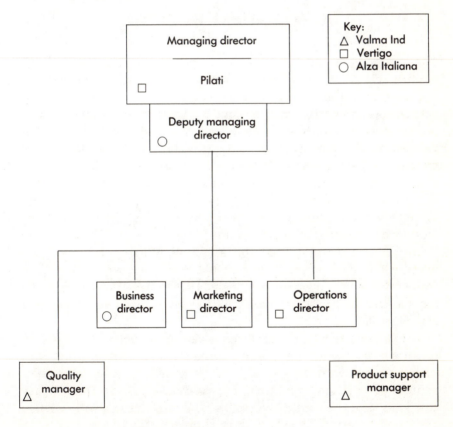

Figure 9.1 *Valma Industries Organisation*

preliminary survey directed to give the technical specifications the customer required. At that time, in the same circumstances, a firm closely connected with Vertigo presented itself to Alza Italiana. The tie between the two potential customers, the synergy between the two projects and the technological and competitive difficulties already pointed out constituted an incentive for Vertigo and Alza Italiana to decide to evaluate a cooperative strategy for the development of the new project. The cooperation structure evaluated foresaw the launching of a joint project for the design of a product, system A, and its variants A1 and A2, one designed for Alza's primary customer and its counterpart for Vertigo. Once the stage of negotiation between the two companies and between them and their respective customers had been completed, Valma was launched on 1 January 1985.

The Valma alliance: the structure

The common objectives assigned by the parent companies to the joint venture relate to the design, development, production, sale and after-sale support of the new product. The capital structure foresees joint participation by Vertigo and Alza and is characterised by an organisational structure which is complete even if not all the detail has been worked out. The partners have also jointly contributed the human and technical resources necessary for the operation of the joint venture.

Six people – three from each company – were involved in the definition of the operation of the alliance, with the objective of building the technical content of cooperation. They worked out such areas as workloads, the sharing of semi-manufactured products between the parent companies and used the assumption that, once the joint venture had been started, they would keep their role in both the technical and management responsibility. On behalf of Vertigo, the members of the project group were three engineers: Pilati, Pennarola and Ticinelli.

The organisation of the alliance consists of a double structure, on the first level of which there is an international group interacting with customers and with the second level of the alliance, the Valma joint venture. The latter, in its turn, has relationships with the primary customers and the parent companies. The relationships with Vertigo and Alza are very close on both the technological and decision-making levels. In fact, on one side of the two parent companies are directly responsible for the production of parts which are destined to be important elements of the final assembled product. In this way the parent companies are in a position to influence Valma's technical choices. In addition, each strategic, legal, financial and organisational decision is jointly taken by Vertigo and Alza, thus depriving Valma of any decision-making power and making it more of a 'hinge' between the two parties.

The subdivision of operations between the partners created problems not only during the assembly stage, but also with the parent companies' cost accounting. The philosophy of total cooperation between the two parties required also a fair subdivision of manufacturing costs. Since Vertigo and Alza utilised two different systems of cost accounting, it was particularly difficult to define universal criteria. Through rejecting the idea of cost apportionment based on monetary value, complicated by exchange rate problems connected with the partners' different currencies, a more suitable system was identified, based on subdividing the contributions as a function of the amount of labour used.

A site near Vertigo was chosen as the registered and operational headquarters. The official language adopted, the one which was to be used for all meetings and the various mass of technical and procedural documents necessary for the working of the alliance and the relationships between the partners, was English. On these conditions the joint venture between Vertigo and Alza was begun on 1 January 1985.

People and personnel

'The technological, industrial and financial aspects are doubtless important to define and start an agreement, but it is human resources, with their own initiative, the ability effectively to communicate to the others in multicultural contexts, to value and take on risks in the decisive moments and to utilise the right level of autonomy, jointly with the ability to cooperate with various functions within the team and complex functional relationships, which determine the alliance's results in each criteria stage. This is more or less what Salvemini, our company's managing director, told us when we inaugurated the joint venture – it sounded like this, remembers Pilati, 'I felt unsuited to the role.' In that speech there was something that reminded us of the manual of the perfect manager, something also that evoked the ghost of Superman. I had attended no master course and there was no phone box in which I could transform myself into a superhero.'

The engagement of human resources agreed with Vertigo foresaw an allocation of 120 people to the joint venture, 15 per cent of them to cover key management and design positions and the remaining 85 per cent technical staff. In view of the localisation of Valma's plants and the need not to deplete the company's technical lines, Alza judged it convenient to limit the direct transfer of staff to the main key positions, filling the lower-grade jobs with staff recruited externally on the market.

'As far as transfer to the joint venture was concerned, the choice was limited to the executive level,' remembers Dr De Monte of Alza's personnel department. 'The potential available personnel was about 150. Our task was to choose from them an initial pool of three people to start the project. We began their selection in September 1982.'

'By the end of 1982 Dr De Monte, of the personnel department, called me to her office,' said Pilati, 'and in a short time she summarised to me some events that I already knew concerning the alliance just initialled with Vertigo.'

'The most delicate starting stage of an international joint venture is the selection of the people to be included in the project group,' said Dr De Monte. 'The initial stage of the screening took place in an indirect way, by sifting the information in our files on the elements which seemed more suitable from the viewpoint of technical competences and the personal profile. It was immediately clear that, with respect to the 150 potential candidates, the number of valid ones was drastically limited. The discriminating factor – and this makes one smile in a company of international vocation like ours – was represented by the scarce knowledge of English. On a second level of exploration we contacted the most interesting candidates for a preliminary interview.'

Dr De Monte explained to the candidates: 'Our company intends to make a success of this alliance, in which connection I have called you here. The person we want to hire should go abroad for an initial period of two years.' Pilati remembered 'she adopted a participative approach, she asked me whether I was still interested in an international experience, what my availability was and, more generally, how I saw the project of alliance.'

Decastri, the engineer in charge of the design office and Pilati's direct superior, said: 'When the round of the interviews began, I did not like the process very much. The fact that mainly my cleverest collaborators were contacted irritated me. Pilati, for example, was engaged with an extremely important project on the point of becoming operational. He was very well acquainted with the work performed so far and his good relationships with the production people had helped us to manage the usual frictions which accompany the passage from the research to the mass production stage. I disliked the idea that he – or others like him – might be moved to that joint venture. I will tell you something more: not one of the top management had had the idea to explain to me how I would meet the delivery time I had promised, with fewer men and, moreover, without the cleverest ones.'

'After talking with the people directly concerned,' continued Dr De Monte, 'it was decided to interview their direct superiors. Our objective was that of supplying the line with a further deep examination of the project in process of being defined. At the same time we tried to sensitise the other staff to the strategic character of human resources, chiefly with a view to continuing the internal programmes in the parent company and to implement a non-traumatic replacement plan.'

'When a work programme is started, you understand me,' added Decastri, 'all those who work there become a large family. Interpersonal relationships are basic: replacing a person is much more than exchanging picture cards. It is necessary to maintain the equilibria which have been created. In my case there were clever and less clever people and, no wonder, the clever ones are those who can hardly be replaced.'

'After the first talk with the staff of the personnel department, my boss, Decastri, called me to his office and asked me what I was thinking of doing,' said Pilati. 'I answered that I was hesitating, but it seemed to me a good opportunity for my future. He told me that these opportunities were opening also inside our group and proposed I continue these for the near future. I answered that I was going to think about that. The feeling was that he was not going to accept my indication of availability for the new operation. You can call them weak signals, however they are quite clear: some social isolation in the meetings, a request for greater formalisation of my work, more support for a younger colleague and so on.'

'The personnel people came to me and told me that Pilati was candidate number one for the position of operations manager at

Valma,' responded Decastri. 'They assured me that this was not going to impoverish the structure. But to me, personally, it was not important to have ten Brambillas (ie ten colourless candidates) in exchange: Pilati was clever and knew everything about the project he was on. When I asked whether they realised the cost of training a person and of the risks of delays in the project Pilati was engaged in, they told me that it was an aspect which they had evaluated and which, definitely, had been considered also by the top management. I just knew that nobody has ever come, either then or later, to tell me that the delivery timing had been changed, or that it was possible to give the customer something of a lower quality.'

'Considering also the work climate as it was changing, at last I resolved to accept the proposal,' said Pilati. 'Leaving aside the initial stage, the idea of taking a position of management responsibility was exciting to me. It was a way to increase my internal visibility and to perform a role I had never played seriously: that of the manager!'

'At the end they succeeded in convincing him that it was worthwhile,' commented Decastri, 'and I have lost one of my most valuable collaborators. If they had sent one of my Brambillas would it not have been better for everybody?'

The management of expatriates

'The first two years do not count,' stressed Pilati. 'From 1983 to 1985 we tried to get to know each other by working partly here in Italy, partly in England. It was hard work, more than full time, through the need to keep good contracts with production (on flexibility analysis, future work sharing, costs and specifications) which made me spend a lot of hours at our plants. Many more than before: it was as if I was responsible at the same time for research, development and first attempts at passing to mass production. However, it was still under old Decastri.'

'Here is the point: I had a collaborator who cost me – even if only partly – but who was fully engaged in an external project,' added Decastri. 'He was calling on us in order to get opinions, to evaluate with his colleagues possible proposals to be made to the British. More time was lost for the most urgent activities!' After evaluating our staff as well as the British staff and after deciding to confirm on the joint venture two out of three of our engineers (the British did not like

Ticinelli), from 1 January we started the stage of the operation proper.'

De Monte remembered: 'The transfer of the expatriates – six altogether, three of them directly from the preliminary project group – occurred through a system of temporary transfer. The salaries continued to be paid by their present company. Compensation policies were oriented to preserving compensation before the transfer through adding an extra contribution to make up for the inconvenience. Depending on the circumstances and on the performance achieved, further increases could be granted. In addition, it should be pointed out that, at the moment of his return, the expatriate would retain the salary level reached abroad. Besides, Alza agreed to bear all the expenses concerning housing and children's education. All this in order to facilitate a radical change of life of the executive and his family.'

Perrone, an engineer in Alza's design office, had been one of the candidates for the position of Valma's technical manager. He was not a member of the trio engaged in the design team and, consequently, he would have reached the position starting from 1 January 1985. But he had already been alerted by the personnel department in July 1984. 'It was an important step in my career. When I was informed about that, I was going to leave for my holidays. I can assure you that August of that year was a hellish month: interminable discussions. My wife did not want to have anything to do with England: first of all she did not know English, nor did she wish to learn it; secondly, some problems connected with her parents made it not very easy to leave Italy. We arrived at the point of considering the idea of a separation. When I was back at the company, Dr De Monte called me and told me that the management had decided not to send me to England. In my case I took some months to restitch the relationship with my wife.'

In connection with Perrone, De Monte said: 'That of Perrone is the classic case where it is your partner that selects the job as well as yourself. They told us they preferred other candidates, so we informed him that the matter had come to nothing.'

'Perrone was really furious,' remembered Pilati, 'and I myself was a little dubious about the future; I thought that the company was not behaving well towards us. Another signal is Bodega's case. Bodega is another engineer in our design office. At first he had not been involved in the project because he was engaged in activities which were highly strategic for the company. When, for reasons which still escape me, it was decided that Ticinelli would come back to the company, someone planned to involve Bodega in his place. Now may I say that Bodega is an excellent, professionally very valuable man, and we agreed on the choice. However, on one side he was extremely skilful in negotiating his conditions for the transfer, on the other side the company was perhaps in dire straits: the fact is that he obtained a compensation package far superior to ours, a company car and other fringe benefits. Pennarola and I did not like this very much and so we did not hesitate to express our dissatisfaction. You know, money is not everything but, in business language, it is an important signal: have you ever seen a chief executive earning less than a function executive? Besides, Decastri was furious as he had been obliged to give away Bodega in exchange for Ticinelli, who had always created some relationship problems.

'We have tried to be always very flexible in the management of an expatriate,' continued De Monte. 'On the other hand they are men so different from each other and with such different motivations. Bodega obtained something more, but Pilati and Pennarola, on their coming back, were going to benefit with higher positions. The problem of personalising the decision about the management is present, for example, in the evaluation of the return and of the extension of the presence in the joint venture. Some people, after two years, wanted to come back by any means, others, having decided to settle abroad, resigned from Alza and were directly hired by Valma.

'Anyway, no preferential return paths for the expatriates are foreseen. However we try to do some internal marketing with the line. We launch messages such as 'Mr I intends to come back to headquarters starting from next year . . . he has done a good job, professionally he has widened his knowledge, and so on.'

'Even if, formally, I was still on Alza's payroll, my tie with Decastri was broken. In my transfer to Valma I had lost the previous hierarchical position. This involved two problems: formally I found myself to be the chief executive of the new company and, therefore, in the condition of requiring from Decastri what was useful to me, being able to utilise the direct institutional phone line with Alza's top management. On the other side, substantially, I was (or I was perceived to be, and there is not the least difference) a subordinate of his. In both cases I had problems in asking him for support from Valma.'

Pennarola said: 'I have found myself in an ambiguous position. I was not yet Valma, but I was not even any longer Alza. After the first two-year period abroad when we were, *de facto*, coopted for two further years, a couple of problems arose: we had lost a lot of contacts with the line at Alza, either the people had moved to other companies, or we had . . . Our main link was the personnel department; with the line there was some friction.'

'Very often the former manager of an expatriate is unable to respond to the new problems of the person,' added De Monte. 'The personnel function must operate as an interface, maintaining a constant contact with the expatriate. It is as if we said to our manager "We are here, in any case!".'

'The problems with the production department were the same I had to face when I was in the neighbouring office,' said Pilati, 'with the addition that they were able to tell me stories more freely. The biggest problem was with the design department. Leaving aside the fact that British people measure in inches and yards, and this is no negligible fact when we talk about tolerances in hundredths of a millimetre, the perception was that nothing of what Valma's technical office produced complied with Alza's quality standards.'

'At the end of the fourth year in Valma, my job of project engineer could be considered as concluded; we had definitely passed to mass production. All of us, Bodega, Pennarola and myself, asked to rejoin the company and at this point a rather funny thing happened: faced by our requests for a rehiring that might take into consideration our international experience and not penalise us too much, the personnel department asked us to be patient for a while. In fact what had happened was that our absence had determined the advancement of other colleagues and, in the company's personnel policy, we had slightly slipped into a second echelon. Not out of a lack of esteem obviously, but merely owing to the fact that we were not present at the headquarters. Then we asked to talk with Salvemini about our position. He was very kind and asked us to dinner. At a certain moment, while we were pressing him about the problem, he said to us: "How many managing directors and chief officers do you know in this company? There are only two! Apart from you, of course, we are really too few to have had your type of experience. Would you like to repeat it? The opportunity of an alliance in the U.S. is at hand. . . . Understand?"!'

Care analysis

The problem is the management of human resources in inter-firm alliances.

The topics covered by the case are:

1. The problems typical of human resource management in joint ventures and, in particular:
   - the selection, allocation and induction of people;
   - the management of relationships with the parent company;
   - the re-entry of expatriates to their home organisation.
2. The need to analyse the individual's 'identity requirements':
   - who do I belong to?
   - who am I to be faithful to?
   - what are the interests at stake?
3. The need to analyse the individual's 'stability requirements':
   - what will happen about my career?
   - who do I report about my actions to?
   - what will happen when I come back or when the joint venture ends?
4. The need to analyse the individual's 'development requirements':
   - what can I learn from the experience?

In addition, the analysis of the case proposes a series of classic themes of managing a joint venture:

- compatibility between the partners (problems of language, differences of know-how and of technical knowledge, 'not invented here' syndrome);
- the structural and organisational inadequacy of the parent company (absence of roles and organisational positions devoted to the joint venture at the parent company, lack of systematic and well understood human resource strategies and so on);
- the negative counter-effects of the joint venture (interpersonal conflicts, demonstrations, uncertainties and inconveniences in critical roles).

Commentary on the Italian case studies

The analysis of the cases related to the Italian context has enabled us to point out, with reference to a more specific thorough examination, some of the general themes discussed in the introductory chapter on Italy.

In particular, the SIP case has enabled us to:

- demonstrate the main phenomena of the strategic and competitive business context which determine new organisational requirements in corporate systems, such as the requirements of anticipation, flexibility, productivity and participation and involvement of the workers;
- point out the theme of the critical protection role of the human resource department in the processes of organisational change, with particular attention to the focus on corporate strategy.

The Telespazio case has enabled us to:

- investigate thoroughly the critical area for the human resource function related to segmentation criteria for internal clients of the function itself;
- investigate the theme of the performance of the human resource department;
- explore the theme of human resource management as a service.

Finally, the Valma Industries case has enabled us to:

- reveal new models of economic and corporate development which have a particular impact on the needs for change internal to the human resource function;
- connect these models with the emergence of a new profile of professional skills and values for the specialist human resource staff.

Part 4
Spain

10

Human Resource Management in Spain: Strategic Issues, the Economic and Social Framework

Ceferi Soler I Vicente

This chapter will describe the strategic issues which impinge not only on Spanish human resource management, but which are also key concerns throughout Europe. These are the changing nature of trade unions, the move to 'brain workers' and the consequent awareness that people are a significant source of competitive advantage, the need for quality and a customer focus, and the resulting issues of corporate culture, communication and management in a multicultural context.

The second part of the chapter provides a detailed analysis of economic social and demographic data on human resource policies in Spanish companies.

Contingencies and uncertainties

Living the life of a business is synonymous with living a social, economic and political life – and one of its attractions consists in managing the unexpected. Generally speaking, people are fragile and ephemeral and so are organisations when they are affected by individuals. Organisations plan, design scenarios and as a rule their leaders apply vision, a sense of mission and strategies to achieve their objectives.

But no matter how objective their strategies may be, the inevitable subjectivity of the individual means that contingencies and uncertainties are bound to occur either before or after decisions are made. This subjectivity is what enables us to live the life of a business and shape a corporate culture day by day.

Corporate culture, as a process of identifying individual and group values and the values of our environment, generates a feeling of belonging and helps reduce the uncertainty and complexity that arise when organisations emphasise flexibility and the management of interpersonal differences.

Trade unions: from initial agreement to final confrontation

In the future we will look back on 1990 as the year when confrontation was greatest between Spain's leading trade unions, the Communist-oriented CCOO and its Socialist counterpart, UGT. Paradoxically enough, the year began with the two unions signing social pacts. Unfortunately, electoral interests proved stronger than the strategy of cooperation which brought the unions their greatest success: a nation-wide general strike on 14 December 1988. After two years in which dialogue between the social actors of the country proved impossible, it is a pity that no one can now reach an agreement to make Spanish business more competitive.

The trade unions which emerged from the Franco years are unions focused on in-company action. Once freedom to unionise was established by Spanish law and works councils and union sections legally recognised, Spanish trade unions began striving to increase their political influence rather than concentrating on developing strategies and tactics for negotiating with employers.

This led to a double union structure: one which is limited to in-company action and the other which is a nation-wide political structure. This has caused a general feeling of disenchantment and brought union membership to its current low (see Table 10.1) Business has started to take matters into its own hands by setting up corporate and/or organisational development projects by means of which employee commitment is encouraged and stimulated by each employee's immediate superior. This has resulted in a reduction in the number of days not worked in the period 1988–90 (see Table 10.2).

In order to guarantee acceptance of its pact for social progress, the government is engaging in bilateral negotiations with political parties and with business and labour. The pact for social progress may well provide the opportunity for a thorough discussion of the current union crisis.

The unattainable pact on competetiveness

Although no agreement on competitiveness has been reached, labour did manage to get Government to approve a controversial measure: union control over all labour contracts for jobs ranking below the senior management level. The Spanish employers' association, CEOE, immediately lodged a formal protest and is now waiting the opinion of the European Community and the verdict of Spain's constitutional court.

So far it appears that the Spanish Government succumbed to labour pressure without asking anything in exchange. CEOE's annual study reveals that in 1990 the cost of wages increased on an average of 9 per cent in Spain as opposed to 4.2 per cent in other industrialised countries. In other words, the private sector preferred to pay salaries in excess of the consumer price index rather than risking strikes. This tactic has turned into a nightmare for the monetary authorities and

Table 10.1 *Trade union delegates and membership trends*

| Election | Total of all delegates | Trade union delegates | | |
		CCOO	UGT	USO
1978	193,112	66,540 (34.40%)	41,897 (21.70%)	7,474 (3.90%)
1980	162,959	50,1116 (30.80%)	47,741 (29.30%)	14,811 (9.10%)
1982	140,770	47,016 (33.40%)	51,672 (36.70%)	8,327 (4.64%)
1986	162,298	56,065 (34.50%)	66,411 (40.90%)	6,200 (3.80%)
1990*	165,127	59,334 (35.91%)	69,792 (42.24%)	4,908 (2.97%)

* Preliminary results (70.67% of votes cast)
Source: Ministerio de Trabajo

Table 10.2 *Strikes developed – main features*

| Period | Absolute figures | |
	No of strikes	Days not worked
1988[1]	1,193	11,641.1
1989[12]	1,047	3,685.4
1989[1]:		
August	36	21.7
September	44	34.8
October	74	50.5
November	68	46.4
December	78	35.8
1990[1]*:		
January	68	67.6
February	107	47.7
March	175	520.8
April	165	357.2
May	174	464.2
June	137	217.3
July	72	57.1
August	39	12.1

Notes:
[1] No data from Basque country.
[2] Variation calculated without taking into account the strike on 14 December 1988.
* Provisional data.

Source: Ministerio de Trabajo (1990) *Revista de Economía y Sociología del Trabajo*, Diciembre.

has justified charging high interest rates in an attempt to keep inflation from spiralling once again.

The pact on competitiveness continues to be delayed and the European single market is just around the corner. Just as CCOO and UGT were collecting the highest dividends on their unity of action, the fight for supremacy in the union elections neutralised their most recent successes. After a 15 year period of democracy Spain's labour unions are going through an adolescent crisis: the unions have good ideas but have been unrealistic. They are not prepared to look to a future beyond their day-to-day struggle. Curiously enough, they share this shortcoming with a number of Spanish firms which do not invest in research or training. There will soon be a rude awakening: Spain urgently needs business–labour cooperation in order to improve competitiveness, but the Government's only response to this need has been delay.

Flexibility

As of 1990, 23 per cent of all job contracts in Spain were part-time, temporary contracts. Young people looking for their first jobs are the hardest hit by this situation (see Figure 10.1).

Another peculiarity in Spain is that non-executive personnel have little or no geographic mobility. The labour unions are fiercely opposed to an open labour market which would facilitate people moving from one part of the country to another. Nor do they accept the idea of temporary part-time contracts unless they evolve into permanent ones.

Rigid hiring regulations and the difficulty involved in dismissing personnel do nothing to facilitate the entry of foreign companies into Spain. Companies who are thinking about investing in Spain will discover that if they want to get rid of an employee they will have to

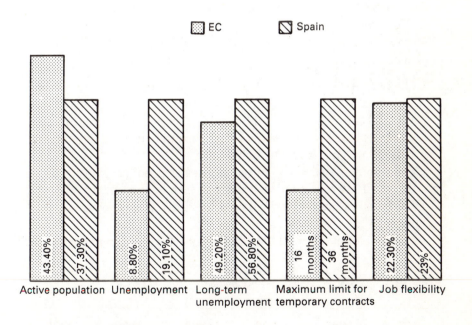

Figure 10.1 *The EC labour scene*

pay him/her the equivalent of 42 months' salary – one of the highest indemnity rates in all of Europe.

Returning to the earlier comment about the adolescence of Spanish labour unions, this is revealed in their petty struggle to be the leading union with the most members.

The economic environment

The slow but steady recovery of the Spanish economy is all the more valuable, if we keep in mind that Spain had to undergo two acid tests simultaneously: the political and the economic. While drastic political changes were taking place inside the country, the whole world was in an economic quagmire. The oil crisis had played havoc with the world's economy. Inflation rates had sky-rocketed everywhere and unemployment was rampant. Spain was, therefore, made doubly vulnerable. No wonder, then, that inflation and unemployment figures went at one point in time well beyond the 20 per cent mark. Something drastic had to be done and quickly. This was the core issue in 1977 of the so-called Moncloa Treaty.

A few current economic indicators will substantiate this steady improvement.

1. The per capita income is US$ 9,791.42, placing Spain 18th among Organisation for Economic Cooperation and Development (OECD) countries. *El Pais*, 11 July 1991, cites the Banco de Bilbao-Vizcaya's latest report, stating that per capita income has gone up to 1,330,000 pts = 11,670 US$.
2. The average real GDP (gross domestic product) growth from 1983 to 1989 has been 3.94 per cent (5th in the OECD ranking). The latest estimates by the Banco de Bilbao-Vizcaya place it at 3.18 per cent for 1991.
3. The development of GDP in billions of US$ (at current prices and

Table 10.3 *The growth of GDP in US$ (billions), 1980–90*

GDP	1980	1985	1988	1989	1990
	214.49	295.10	344.49	380.01	491.10

Table 10.4 *The growth of GDP by sector, 1980–89*

	1980	1983	1986	1989
Food products	7.1	6.5	6.0	6.1
Industrial	38.6	37.8	37.6	28.3
Services	56.0	57.6	58.3	57.9

exchange rate) for the last ten years shows a steady increase (see Table 10.3).

4. The GDP growth rate from 1980 to 1989 by sector suggests a gradual decrease in the relative contributions from the food sector (agriculture, fishing, hunting etc) and industrial sectors, and an increase in the service sectors (see Table 10.4).

5. The rate of inflation and the relationship between earnings and prices are significant because they directly affect the ordinary citizen. At 1985 prices, representing a base of 100, an index of prices is as follows:

Table 10.5 *The relationship between earnings, prices and inflation*

	1987	1988	1989	1990
Hourly earnings	119.3	127.0	138.8	na
Consumer prices	114.5	120.0	128.2	136.8
Inflation	4.6	5.8	6.9	6.5

6. This brief note on the Spanish economy must include a reference to tourism. The sun is to Spain what oil is to the Middle East. Without the income from tourism Spain could not have survived its endemic commercial trade deficits. The flow of tourists into Spain has been steady and at times spectacular (see Table 10.6).

Table 10.6 *The influx of tourists into Spain, 1980–90 (millions)*

	1980	1985	1988	1989	1990
Tourists	38.027	42.785	54.173	54.021	56.524

It is always difficult to translate these figures into dollars and cents, but it is estimated that tourism makes a contribution to the Spanish exchequer of between 15,000 and 20,000 million US dollars a year.

7. Finally, a look at a few indicators of the standard of living can throw some light on the economists' impression that Spain is slowly staggering to its feet and joining the group of developed nations. The figures in Table 10.7 (in thousands) may prove the point.

Table 10.7 *Indications of an increase in the standard of living* (millions)

Telephone lines	10.972 (281 per 1000 inhabitants)
Radio receivers	11.473 (295 per 1000 inhabitants)
TV receivers	14.314 (368 per 1000 inhabitants)
Passenger cars	15.681 (403 per 1000 inhabitants)

The two pivots on which the Spanish economy hinges even today are the 1959 stabilisation plan, and the 1977 Moncloa Treaty. The 1959 stabilisation plan was prepared at Franco's request by professional economists, hailing from Spanish universities. They were not politicians. The gist of the plan was to promote development in real terms by seeking a greater integration with world trends and policies.

The second decisive factor in reviving the economy was the Moncloa Treaty of 1977. It was a sort of tripartite gentlemen's agreement among unions, managers and government meant to ensure a steady economic growth for the country. It was a two-pronged attack by making a sort of 'economic spring cleaning', and by introducing a drastic budget and fiscal reform.

It all went well during the first few years, until government–union relations soured soon after Felipe Gonzalez's re-election in 1986. It all came to a head in the general strike of 14 December 1988, already referred to. Even to this day, the relations between the PSOE and the UGT unions (both of socialist inspiration) are not yet what they used to be. There are some feeble signs (as of July 1991) that another Moncloa Agreement is in the offing, being proposed by Carlos Sochaga, the minister of economy, finance and trade, as a competitiveness and progress treaty.

Table 10.8 *Employment by sector (millions)*

Working Pop	Employed	Agriculture	Industry	Services	Unemployed
15.005	12.621	1.400	4.180	7.041	2.384
100%	84%	9%	27%	47%	16%

* Percentages by sector are of total active population

Source: Boletin Economico: (1991) Banco de España, Mayo

Labour markets

Against this political and economic background, information about the labour market may be clearer.

Working population

Spain's working population is estimated at 15 million men and women. The total number of employed and unemployed and the employment by sectors is given in Table 10.8.

The proportion of men to women is approximately 2 to 1, ie women represent one third of the working population. Another interesting feature is that in the working population there are 2.1 million working in the public and 7.034 million in the private sector. To complete the picture, the number of self-employed people amounts to 3.348 million.

Unemployment

One of the as yet unsolved problems of the Spanish economy is unemployment. Inflation is being tackled with some measure of

Table 10.9 *The rate of unemployment, 1987–90 (%)*

	1987	1988	1989	1990
Unemployed	20.0	18.4	16.6	15.9
Men	10.6	9.3	8.3	7.5
Women	9.4	9.2	8.6	8.4

Table 10.10 *The rate of unemployment in the 16–24 age group, 1987–90 (%)*

	1987	1988	1989	1990
Age group: 16–24	47.1	43.3	38.4	33.9

success; but unemployment still remains a major problem. The data in Table 10.9 speak for themselves:

These figures are all the more tragic when attention is directed to the 16 to 24 age group who have not yet had any work experience (Table 10.10):

There is a clear downward trend in the level of unemployment. Actually, the latest provisional estimates according to a study by the Banco Bilbao-Vizcaya of June 1991 (*El Pais*, 12 July 1991) indicate that the total number of unemployed is 2,227,748 (ie 14.8 per cent of the working population). It is needless to emphasise that in spite of the observed trend, the numbers are far too high for the government to remain unconcerned. Its intention is to keep fighting. Much of the urgency in arriving at an agreement between Government, employers and unions comes from the recalcitrant behaviour of the employment market.

The recent OECD study on the evolution of unemployment rates for this year and next set off alarm signals in the EC and all its member states. The EC unemployment rate is expected to increase from the 8.4 per cent (registered) in 1990 to 8.7 per cent in 1991 and 9.3 per cent in 1992. (See Table 10.11)

This predicted development marks the end of the steady improvement which was registered throughout the 1980s and reached its peak in 1990.

Although the OECD report includes Spain among the countries whose unemployment rates will remain steady (15.6 per cent) government, business and labour are all pessimistic following the breakdown of negotiations on the Pact on Competitiveness, also known as the Pact for Progress, and fear that unemployment will rise as a result of failure to reach an agreement.

Spanish expectations

These predictions could not have come at a worse time for EC member

Table 10.11 *Unemployment (% of active population)*

	1989	1990	1991	1992 (estimated)
United States	5.3	5.5	6.7	6.3
Japan	2.3	2.1	2.2	2.3
Germany	5.6	5.1	5	5.1
France	9.4	9	9.4	9.7
UK	6.2	5.5	8.2	9.6
Italy	12.1	11	11.3	11.2
Canada	7.5	8.1	10.1	10.1
Spain	17.3	16.2	15.9	15.6
OECD Europe	8.5	8	8.7	9
Total OECD	6.4	6.2	7.1	7.1

states, most of which view the Community's economic future with caution.

Long-term measures

Inasmuch as neither governments, business nor labour have shown any foresight in their planning, human resources experts are demanding that they avoid short-term, vote-getting solutions now that unemployment is on the rise. Effective solutions to unemployment, just like effective management techniques, must be focused on the long term. We must re-educate our society to realise that nothing can be achieved without hard work and that this is the basis for social acceptance and equitable distribution.

It is essential that Spanish educational systems be improved, particularly occupational training, and that university studies which lead only to unemployment be refocused. It is also very important to keep inflation down and to make laws on hiring as flexible as possible while simultaneously fostering high productivity rates and good quality.

Catalonia

In an attempt to discover how Catalan businesses view the prospect of the single European market, CIDEM (*Centre d'investigació i desenvolu-*

pameni empresarial) sent out an extensive questionnaire, to which 573 companies replied. The results give a reasonable idea of how local business people rate the impact of the EC.

The questionnaire was divided into five parts:

- strategic needs;
- impact on costs;
- impact on sales;
- opportunities and risks derived from the single market.

The opinions expressed are shown in Table 10.12.

The opinions expressed by this sizeable sample of the business community reflect the belief that Catalan firms will be able successfully to meet the challenge of 1993. Another sign of this confidence is the fact that 2000 new businesses have opened in Catalonia since 1989.

A large number of Japanese, European and US companies also expressed their opinion that Catalonia's chances for the future are good. These companies have invested and are continuing to invest in setting up offices and plants or enlarging their factories in order to gain an ever stronger position in Spain and in Europe and in doing so will also strengthen Catalonia's position and productivity.

Table 10.12 *Needs, costs, sales, opportunities and risks in the Catalan market*

Strategic needs	
Increase productivity	51%
Expand and/or increase specialisation in product range	41%
Research and development	38%
Impact on costs	
Costs will increase	46%
Costs will decrease	27%
Costs will not be affected	18%
Don't know/did not reply	9%
Impact on sales	
Sales will increase	63%
Sales will decrease	7%
Sales will not be affected	30%
Opportunities and risks	
Opportunities will be greater than risks	56%
There will be roughly the same number of opportunities as risks	37%
Risks will be greater than opportunities	7%

These are a few of the reasons why we can be optimistic about the 20th century's greatest challenge to the Catalan business community, competing without protectionist measures in a market of 340 million people.

Mergers: 1988–1990 (financial sector)

Mergers are part of the fight for a larger share of the market and for greater power. Power is defined in A's ability to influence B's behaviour so that B makes decisions which would not otherwise have been made.

Despite the theoretical advantages of being bigger in order to better meet the challenge of the single market, mergers between Spanish financial institutions are not proving an easy matter. Furthermore, size can not always be said to be synonymous with competitiveness and competence. On the contrary, it can be argued that greater size means greater problems, which executives are not always prepared to confront and analyse, failing therefore to propose various alternatives, to discuss them and reach a consensus so that an appropriate decision can be made when required.

Moreover, it is surprising how docile Spanish boards of directors are proving to be when it comes to approving mergers. And yet, the merger process suffers from a basic defect: it gives the impression of being a Socialist Government manoeuvre to gain more effective control of the financial sector.

It is not good for the ethics of the financial profession when the Banco Bilbao-Vizcaya and the Caixa de Pensions de Barcelona are viewed as strange bedfellows of the current government. But one cannot help but wonder about several operations that are vitally important to the country's energy plan: it seems somehow odd that both BBV and the Caixa are shareholders in Repsol and the new gas company.

As agencies dealing with economic resources and promoters of saving and investment, banks should have freedom of thought and action in order to design their strategies for the single market. While the time is not yet ripe for analysing what is happening in these two financial institutions, visible signs, both external (1990 performance) and internal (working atmosphere), indicate that short-term success is going to be hard to achieve despite bigger volume and a larger share of the market.

Executive development

In the 1990s human resource management has become a strategic priority for innovation and success in Spanish business firms. The economic and social climate is changing rapidly, but the art of managing individuals and groups of personnel is still very slow to evolve. Managerial attitudes and values should play a key role in accelerating this change.

Strategic management of human resources is not a technical job involving complicated formulas. Instead it is a matter of channelling personal energy in order to generate confidence and the feeling that a brighter future lies ahead.

Executives who deal exclusively with complex techniques spend most of their time and energy keeping an eye on things and doing other people's work. They do not delegate functions because they have no confidence in others. Learning that the manager has an important role to play in getting the right people for the right jobs is a lesson that often proves difficult and costly for companies and they usually only learn it when they encounter problems in implementing even the best conceived strategies.

People who are well suited to their jobs enjoy what they do. Furthermore, it is important that people feel proud of what they are doing, proud of the company they work for and proud of their company's aims.

Experience has revealed that as competition becomes greater and the life cycle of products becomes shorter, true managerial guidance is much more important than control simply for the sake of control. If we are to prepare young leaders for global management, their training should always involve lateral and inter-functional mobility. Executive training should involve moving management trainees from one job to another, always providing them with the assistance of experts who will teach them the pragmatic aspects of problem solving which are overlooked in the classroom. Executive development must be a strategic priority in Spain if the country's businesses are to become more competitive. Executives must learn something that is at once new and old: how to manage the real dissatisfacions of their personnel and create a good working atmosphere. By managing to do this they will avoid strikes which can destabilise a company. (For examples see the Bimbo and Edicli SA cases that follow this chapter).

If young management trainees are rotated through various jobs they will acquire a broad knowledge that will enable them to reduce corporate bureaucracy to a minimum by opening better channels of communication between different units and divisions and creating small inter-divisional working groups.

Executive development is the most powerful tool for creating companies that are oriented towards the future and have specific corporate projects that respond to the needs of their customers, both internal (employees) and external.

People: a vital resource for our society

Studies of major economic cycles unanimously reach the conclusion that the new technological model, which is going to be the basis of a coming economic boom, involves a combination of microelectronics, computers, telecommunications and information systems technology. This new model is the information revolution, which will bring an end to Taylorism and its pseudo-scientific, mechanical approach which overlooked the skills that differentiate one person from another, making them individuals. In the future, productive labour will depend on the creative talents that differentiate one individual from another.

Production in the information society (Punset *et al*, 1987) will be characterised by the following:

- industrial robots and computers;
- economies of scale will be replaced by flexible, robotic-run production systems able to manufacture differentiated products;
- quality-based competition will become as important as price-based competition;
- the quality touch will be that element of creativity and craftsmanship obtained through skilful management of interpersonal differences.

If managers are to be able to accept and respond to this new information-based society whose needs will differ greatly from what we are accustomed to, they will have to analyse these needs in order to be able to integrate young people from this new society into the business world.

Integrating brainworkers

Brainworkers (von Gizycki, 1989) are the new generation of employees who will control the 'intelligence' of the information society's production systems and innovate new ones. They will know how to solve complex problems; they will be good at Edward De Bono's lateral thinking and they will be able to transfer experiences from one field of operations to another. They will be virtually essential to promoting and maintaining our capacity for innovation and to assure that interpersonal differences are managed as objectively as possible in order to solve anticipated problems.

Brainworkers usually have extensive personal networks through which confidential information circulates. They are hungry for new knowledge, generally tend to be workaholics and nonconformists. They are opposed to established hierarchies, bureaucracy and money-based values. This means that the employer who needs them will have to give them special treatment. Brainworkers are the business world's most fragile resource. They are motivated by recognition, meaningful interpersonal relationships and career plans which offer them creative opportunities. These employees are difficult to keep unless they can be offered work on an attractive, long-term business project. They are capable of resigning simply because they do not agree with their employer's financial policy or because they feel that the marketing campaign is deceptive or because the senior management team lacks a sense of ethics. Fully integrating these employees into the company is a challenge for any good personnel manager.

Employers: Their image and how they are viewed by brainworkers

Employers are a complement to the brainworkers described above. Employers are people capable of mobilising goods and services for business projects that encourage responsibility and initiative. Companies, departments or divisions involved in this kind of business project must be flexible: hierarchy may be on the basis of products, geographic areas of functions and sustained by task forces working on specific projects within a well defined time frame and with clear objectives so that they can be creatively and flexibly managed.

Innovative companies provide their brilliant employees with their own projects to be independently developed. They encourage the development of small innovative companies outside the parent company and do their best to encourage inter- and intra-company teams. This is the corporate project for companies that want to channel the independent energies of brainworkers who are continually striving for a way to do things better every day.

Employers who can retain these high-energy employees will have to be role models for these people, inspiring them to blaze career paths that will culminate in setting up their own businesses: small, medium or large.

Training and quality

In the new technological order of things, all knowledge is subject to change and updating. The fixed working hours, set vacation periods, rigid retirement rules that were part of the industrial society are giving way to flexible hours, part-time employment, leaves of absences for studying or undertaking new projects.

If they are properly prepared the new employees can become good in-company trainers, transmitting their experience and spirit of enterprise to the employees coming up behind them.

In order to satisfy their thirst for the latest knowledge, managers must take the opportunity to reflect on their company's successes and failures and invite their brainworkers to participate in designing the next steps in their corporate project. Team work, experimental study plans that are adaptable to any job situation and devised by bosses and employees alike will be the ingredients of quality employee training.

Attitudes and values that encourage satisfaction and independent thought, belief in research: these are the same characteristics that enable people actively to resist the pressure to conform or accept rigid, outmoded ways of thinking.

And where do the differences lie? In the way the differences are managed; in whether training is considered an expense or an investment; in the way individuals are controlled; in whether we worry about employees whose minds wander from their jobs or if we only worry about those who are physically absent.

Investment in training

Society, technology and production systems are all undergoing a process of change. Business firms, universities and management schools must all prepare the coming generations so that they will be equipped to work in an environment in which productive employment will depend on the creative talents of each person and his or her ability to obtain satisfaction from the job, rather than the current labour market where jobs offer little in the way of attraction and value added and people looking for work sell their professional and personal talents in exchange for a salary. This is the challenge of a future that has already begun.

The issue of quality

Quality is a competitive factor in the information society. The 'no mistakes' concept is not enough in information technology or the single market.

A strategy that aims at maximum quality implies:

- a participative structure;
- group tasks and rewards;
- communication groups;
- a social balance sheet that reports successes and failures;
- a corporate project that includes the stated mission, communicating it in such a way as to encourage employee participation and integration.

Quality strategies mean that personnel managers must be creative in order to combine different systems of remuneration with maximum flexibility in terms of individual career plans, providing quality training in order that the pursuit of excellence will cause employees to identify with, and feel a part of, the global corporate project and the transmission of the key values and attitudes inherent to the corporate culture.

In the old European industrial society competition was the result of using a company's economic and human capital. The object was to earn maximum profits through maximum productivity and the individual was a resource to be exploited. In the new European business society innovation is looked on as a continuous, dynamic process that has no fixed limit. This society needs employees who will be committed to their projects, their companies, their community, to quality and to excellence in their work.

Within the next few years, ie when we have felt the impact of the single market, the human resources strategy for managing this new group of brainworkers will inevitably contain certain denominators for excellence:

- customised leadership;
- leadership in the market;
- solid corporate culture;
- a shared corporate project;
- a market oriented towards free competition;
- outside customers shared with other companies.

These concepts are described in more detail below.

Customised leadership

- Ability to select the best collaborators.
- Motivate them by showing confidence.
- Evaluate their performance.
- Prepare career plans.
- The right person for the right job at the right time.
- Consistent but flexible values and attitudes.
- Accept paradoxes and unintended errors.
- Promote the corporate project in order to channel energies and capacities for commitment.

Leadership in the market

- Innovation in marketing.
- Research and develop new products.
- Permanent contact with customers.
- Differentiate product/service through value for money and brand image.
- Concentrate on products/services that you really know and do well in order to become a leader.
- Focus on short- and long-term profits.
- Policy of honesty in customer relationships.
- Reinvest part of profits in order to build up capital.

Corporate culture

Values and attitudes to take into account:

- Integrity: seriousness, honesty and sincerity in the corporate project.
- Commitment and trust in each person, accepting the paradox of managing the differences between individuals and working teams through a customised style of leadership that is skilful enough to integrate the values and attitudes of the individuals into the corporate project.

The corporate project

- Assures that inter-divisional strategies are coherent.
- Serves as a tool for coordination and motivation.
- Is a means of in-company communication.
- Is a statement of aims/values.
- Is linked to the key values of its leaders and their environment.
- Generates a sense of identity and belonging.
- Must mobilise the logic of professional success.
- Is rooted in the company's history.
- Focuses on the immediate future.

The project must provide for employees' professional development through:

- ambitious medium/long term objectives;
- a chain of command designed to promote efficiency;
- fluid communication;
- constant training;
- autonomy in decision making;
- an attitude of listening, analysing, settling real complaints;
- participation and commitment.

Communication and the corporate project

There is evidence from the Price Waterhouse–Cranfield–ESADE research (Price Waterhouse/Cranfield, 1991) that managers should place ever greater emphasis on direct relationships with their employees through personalised communication.

Communication is part of management style. Listening to people should be regarded as a medium-term investment of time which will pay off in innovation. Mobilising energy and enthusiasm by talking openly to people will lead to concerted agreement and encourage responsibility.

The mistakes you will read about in the first part of the Bimbo case and in the case about Edicli might have been avoided had senior management had a corporate project that was shared with employees and had communication not been limited to contacts with the labour unions. This style of management was a waste of the social and economic resources that all of Spain has paid for.

The management challenge: managing differences

The first key action for the immediate future is to promote the management of differences. It is obvious that managers must be prepared to manage differences if they want to get the best performance out of their employees and their working team. This means accepting the difference between individuals and finding the right person for the right job at the right time in order to optimise management results.

This can best be stated as follows: we should accept general or sectorial labour agreements but each one of us should study how we can apply them in our organisations in order to meet our company's needs in terms of:

- professional categories;
- performance of each work centre;
- individual performance in achieving objectives;
- geographic territory.

Managing differences means taking a pragmatic, operational approach to the flexibility that most of our organisations require.

Considering each individual as a valuable asset will enable us to mobilise our employees' energies, guiding them and integrating them into the goals that were set by mutual agreement with these same individuals and the attainment of which will formalise and update the essence of our corporate culture.

Every company should be aware that individual differences do exist and that they have both positive and negative effects on the potential of its human resources. Attempts have been made to apply a variety of theories about equality in some educational systems and idealistic companies, but all these theories overlook the basic principle of individual differences.

A corporate culture that is accepted and updated by means of a corporate project, the key features of which are participation and commitment, helps reduce the uncertainty and complexity which is an inherent and logical part of the operations of our companies which are faced with the challenge of the single market, constant technological developments and the difficult task of integrating brainworkers who demand quality in their relationships and in products and services. Moreover, the need for flexible approaches to managing, guiding and integrating differences will enable us to become better acquainted with the professional talents of our employees and assign them to the jobs for which they are best suited.

If we refuse to recognise this situation we are closing our eyes to the complexity of the challenge that all of us have helped to shape.

Recruitment

Responses to labour market shortages

One ray of hope in the economic gloom is that companies are realising that the executive managerial skills that served us well during the 1980s will not necessarily do so in the 1990s. Judging by the recruitment briefs of leading headhunters, executive managers now have to demonstrate a track record of innovation, a firm grasp of marketing, be as financially numerate as the financial manager and have a wide appreciation of the European market.

European fever has reached Spain in the last five years. In recruitment terms this means demonstrating an international awareness and ability to do business at a pan-European level, even for companies that operate mostly in Spain.

These changing requirements will have important implications for an individual's career development, for mid-career managers and for organisations. Aspiring executives will have to find jobs that give them such a range of experiences. Relying on the company's management development system will not be enough.

Since a few young managers have started to change jobs on average

Table 10.13 *Main groups specially targeted in recruitment*

Long-term employed	15%
Women	47%
School leavers	74%

every three or four years, most are used to job mobility. This is the new fashion from the USA and Europe that Spanish students from business schools and universities now imitate. But in future they will have to assess how a move will benefit their long-term career goals and not just look for greater job satisfaction and a larger salary.

Up to now the great risk for many mid-career managers has been whether or not they would survive company restructuring. Examining some of the reasons why individuals are made redundant provides some clues (see Table 10.13).

Spain does not yet have firms experienced in outplacement. The working society does not accept unemployed people, managers or otherwise. When they need communication and relationships to help open new doors, companies prefer people who are actively employed.

Methods of recruitment

In Spain the personal job interview is used by more than 80 per cent of companies. When unemployed people have to answer a standard questionnaire that will open the door to a personal interview, they all too frequently find the door closing and someone perhaps giving them a nice smile and explaining that there are too many applicants.

The chief criticisms are:

- interviews are not reliable predictors of subsequent job performance;
- interviewers typically make up their minds about a candidate in the first ten minutes and are rarely swayed by subsequent developments. Be careful about first impressions!
- candidate's non-verbal behaviour in the interview can sometimes be more important than what he or she actually says, but few interviewers really have such a thorough knowledge of the different connotations of non-verbal behaviour.

In an attempt to make the selection system more objective a large number of Spanish companies have begun using personality tests. The companies that are using them explain that 'we can see precious little evidence even when the best personality tests are used that job performance can be predicted'.

A few companies are making use of assessment centres. These tend to be rated favourably by candidates and employers alike, but the problem is the higher costs.

One selection system attracting a growing number of fans and few critics is the structured interview in which the candidate is asked a series of predetermined questions. The interviewer has the advantage of knowing the best answers, having systematically studied successful performers in that same job. The most significant replies could be stored on a personal computer disk and average replies for every job level or category could be seen on your computer screen.

Structured interviews give impressive results in predicting subsequent job performance. A number of studies show that candidates recruited using this method make a significantly greater contribution to bottom-line profit, change jobs less frequently and are rated higher in terms of customer satisfaction.

There are no quick fixes: in the final analysis it will be those companies that are able to select and motivate talent that will gain a sustainable competitive advantage over their rivals.

Employment law

The economic challenges and, above all, the political changes that had to be faced in the democratisation of Spain entailed a serious revision of the country's legal fabric. Spain rose to the occasion. Three years after Franco's death, the Spanish constitution was approved by a universal referendum (December 1978). This was the beginning of a radical change, which obviously had an impact on employment practices. Of course, there are many issues still pending. In general, however, the progress made should be duly acknowledged. Five years after Spain's entry to the EC, its employment legislation has been adapted to the EC social charter.

Sources of the law

The constitution, the civil code and the workers' statutes are the main reference points. In addition, legislation applies to Spain as a member country and due attention is paid to ILO (International Labour Office) rules and regulations. The constitution (title I, chapters II and III) states the fundamental rights as well as duties of every citizen. Applied to work, the fundamental rights are freedom to form unions and the right to strike, consonant with the basic principles of a democratic society. These principles assume a number of duties on the part of citizens.

The workers' statutes bring together ways in which the constitutional rights and duties are to be understood and applied. They were the result of a long negotiation process between the CEOE (the employers' association) and the UGT (the socialist union), which were finally subscribed to on 10 March 1980.

Labour courts and industrial tribunals

The 'tribunal constitutional' was set up to watch over the faithful understanding and application of the constitution in all spheres of Spanish life. After 12 years, observance of the constituion has been satisfactory, with some question marks which call for minor revisions. Between this tribunal and the ordinary employer and employee there are a number of subsidiary bodies that help decide in doubtful cases and correct malpractices. In case of conflict between employer and employee, the appeal must follow this hierarchical order from the lowest to the highest court of justice.

- The CMAC (*Centro de Mediación, Arbitraje y Conciliación*) which studies the case and decides according to existing laws, rules and regulations;
- *Juzgado de lo Social* (court for social issues), which is the next step if the CMAC decision is not accepted;
- *Tribunal Superior de Justicia* (high court of justice), which is the highest court at the level of autonomous government. Failing this, appeal must be made to the centre.
- *Tribunal Supremo de Madrid* (Madrid's supreme court). It is possible that high courts in various autonomous regions may have different criteria to decide on labour problems. The contending parties may appeal to the supreme court in Madrid.
- *el Tribunal Constitutional* (supreme court for Constitutional matters), whose prerogative is to study cases which may be unconstitutional. It is the highest organ of justice in Spain.

The Government is subject to *el Tribunal de Cuentas* which is the supreme fiscal organ to inspect the Government's accounts and economic policies. It enjoys a long tradition, dating back to the 13th century, later confirmed by the first constitution of 1869 and corroborated by the constitution of 1978.

Most industrial disputes are decided at the CMAC level of each autonomous government, without appeal to higher courts of justice. Monthly information is made available about the number of cases decided for or against the worker or employer.

Major Acts

In addition to the constitution, the Spanish civil code and the workers' statutes, there are many acts that regulate the application of the basic principles and laws to day-to-day situations. There are five of these Acts that stand out quite conspicuously:

1. *Ley General de Seguridad Social* (Social Security Act) which regulates all aspects of social security from the time of workers' registration to their death. It was issued on 30 May 1974.
2. *Ley de Contrato de Trabajo* (law regulating work contracts) issued on 26 January 1944.
3. *Ley Organica de Libertad Sindical* (law regulating the free exercise of the right to unionise and to strike) issued on 2 August 1985.
4. *Ordenanza General de Seguridad e Higiene en el Trabajo* (ordinance regulating health and safety requirements at work) issued on 9 March 1971.
5. *Ley Bàsica de Empleo* (regulating the various requirements connected with the beginning and termination of service) issued on 8 October 1980.

Contracts of employment

With the intention of satisfying the employer's and employee's various needs, the legislation recognises a number of standard contracts. They start from the ordinary formal work contract, which assumes work to be full time for an indefinite period until retirement. Different standard contracts cover the following cases which show how the employer and employee may find the right relationship:

- physically handicapped people;

- workers who are 45 years old or older;
- vacancies created by anticipated retirement;
- jobs created for very specific temporary tasks;
- special production requirements;
- temporary assignments;
- launching of a new project to last no more than three years;
- creation of new jobs to reduce unemployment;
- new needs resulting from partial retirement or from converting full-time jobs into part-time jobs;
- jobs implying work-training and apprenticeship;
- part-time jobs or cyclic job requirements;
- work at home;
- group contracts, including sub-contracting.

Termination of employment

The reverse side of the coin is how services should be terminated. This is a cause of constant irritation. On the one hand, unions try to make it almost impossible to dismiss any one; and the employers, on the other, leave no stone unturned to get rid of workers if they are not as efficient as the employer would like them to be.

Apart from 'leave of absence' and temporary suspension of the work contract, the termination of services implies the breaking of the employer–employee relationship. This can occur by mutual consent or by the decision of one of the parties. If the worker asks for termination of the contract because the employer has not fulfilled it, compensation must be paid. In the case of voluntary resignation, the accepted traditions of the organisation should be followed.

On the other hand, if the employer decides to terminate services individually or collectively, several situations can arise. The different solutions proposed boil down to notice periods (from one to three months depending on the worker's seniority) and compensation to be paid as specified by the law.

In the case of substantial change in the firm's statutes (either by change of ownership, bankruptcy or the employer's retirement or death), the relevant authorities have to be duly informed in writing and the workers will have to be compensated according to the circumstances of the case.

It must be noted that in all cases, except when the worker voluntarily resigns he/she will be protected by unemployment benefit (ie two years' salary paid by social security up to a maximum of 2,400,000 pts, ie 21,000 US$). For an up-to-date account of current employment laws see Barrenechea and Ferrer, 1991.

Pay and benefits

Spanish employers have moved away from rigid pay structures and have increased their use of variable payment schemes. A recent survey, conducted by Price Waterhouse and Cranfield (1991), showed that more than 50 per cent of the respondents in the 1990 research and 60 per cent in the 1991 research have introduced more flexibility in pay systems during the past three years.

This means that over three-quarters of Spanish firms, particularly in the retail and distribution sector, have made variable pay an increasingly important part of their reward packages.

Incentive payment schemes: significant provision

By far the most noticeable development in flexible payment has been the introduction of incentive pay schemes. Unlike remuneration systems aimed solely at recruiting and retaining, incentive pay is designed to link the individual's reward package more closely to the organisation's objectives.

All types of employees can benefit from immediate incentives. Although managers are given incentives more often than other staff categories, bonuses and various other forms of merit or performance pay are available at all levels in many organisations.

Performance related pay is the most widely used type of short-term incentive. 33 per cent of the respondents to the 1990/1991 survey said that managers are much more likely than other employee categories to receive performance related pay. Moreover, 58 per cent said that technical and professional employees received performance related pay. Payment of group bonuses is considerably less popular in Spain.

Non-financial benefits

Non-financial or fringe benefits have been a popular means of providing pay flexibility and have been used imaginatively to support recruitment and retention policies. Spanish employers use creative non-taxable benefits as an important feature of competitive reward packages at a time when they need to offer further incentives to attract key managers and technical staff.

The influence of tax regulations and culture on the willingness of organisations to adopt non-financial benefits is illustrated in new Spanish legislation coming into effect in 1992, when the majority of non-financial benefits such as company cars, vacations, school fees, private homes will have to be declared as personal income.

Setting pay rates for individual employees only becomes a significant practice at senior staff level. However, the 1990/1991 research findings indicated that 37 per cent of respondents felt that non-financial benefits are becoming increasingly important in Spain.

One of the main challenges for the 1990s may well be learning how to manage tax regulations as well as the cultural and historical needs and preferences of every company in order to get satisfaction from their recruitment and retention policies.

Corporate culture as a strategy for social competitiveness

Business has survived under governments of different ideologies and has caused Socialist governments radically to change their opinion of business.

Corporate ideology is beginning to be studied by professionals in the fields of communication, sociology, psychology and economics, all of whom are involved in analysing the behaviour of organisations led by individuals applying particular strategies. The past decade has seen the appearance of corporate charters, corporate projects, corporate images, all promoted by trail-blazing professionals who are working in and for the business world.

Corporate culture is a specific application of the culture that exists in the working world. Culture in corporations plays the same role as culture in society. It is a system of integration, differentiation and, above all, a system that provides points of references for organising the corporation and imbues the actions of its members with a certain significance.

If Spanish businesses do not have written strategic human resource plans which will give their employees incentives, stimulate them and get them moving, then unfortunately they do not have the spirit necessary to manage differences and face up to a situation as complex as the current one. There must be a revision of the old cliché that maintains that it is more important for managers to do their jobs than think about them and the company's working atmosphere.

Conclusion: an end to acting like amateurs

There are two conditions which must be observed throughout all stages of a plan for competitiveness:

- the appropriate group of people must **participate**: every action is an occasion for learning how to reach constructive agreements;
- **organisation and study**: there must be precise projects on facts and measures of proven validity. Social innovation, like technical innovation, requires study and research.

It takes more than amateurs to get real results in terms of social change. Future-oriented specialists and managers are what is needed, not people who only look back in order to see what can no longer be done. Commitment generates trust and participation and these are key values in the process of change.

Sociologically speaking, the 1990s can be predicted to bring some changes in the converging lines of power and influence in our organisations. In the 1980s these lines ran from the pinnacle down to the base of the organisational pyramid. In the 1990s the path of influence is reversed and is now a bottom-up affair.

This change has put the emphasis on human resources which have justifiably became the major asset in any business. This has been endlessly repeated in boardrooms, but was never actually reflected in the policies and practices of the 1980s.

This new state of affairs is the result of social, technical and economic circumstances. It involves a radical cultural change which will reach into every corner of western industrial societies. This change has been triggered by the notable population decline in industrialised countries, amazing technological developments, the gradual specialisation of individuals, the new strength of the labour force (fewer people who do more work) and in the pressing need to place our businesses in an advantageous position *vis-à-vis* the competition.

Being competitive in the 1990s means attaining levels of productivity, quality and flexibility that were unimaginable in the 1980s. This cannot be done simply by effectively cutting costs and investing in product development and technological improvements. Companies must also have full confidence in the value of investing in human resources and using an innovation strategy to manage them.

There are reservations about traditional systems of personnel management which may not be flexible enough to be able to adapt to this new situation where creativity and innovation are essential ingredients of corporate approaches to strategy, tactics and operations. It is logical that this should happen and it is fitting to state here at ESADE, one of Spain's leading management schools, that there is a tremendous body of scientific knowledge about human behaviour in the organisation, but this knowledge is not synonymous with the *ability to solve the operational problems derived from this behaviour.*

The challenge facing business schools and professionals working in the field of human resources is to translate theoretical knowledge and the progress that has been made in psychosociological research into daily practice in the management of human resources in our changing society.

References

Barrenechea, J and Ferrer, A (1991) *Guia Laboral*, Ediciones Deusto, Bilbao.

Price Waterhouse/Cranfield (1991) The Price Waterhouse/Cranfield Project on International Strategic Human Resource Management, report, Price Waterhouse/Cranfield.

Punset, E, Rodriguez, A and Fernandez, J (1987) *La Sociedad de la Informacion*, Ciencias de la Direccion, Madrid.
von Gizycki, R (1989) *The Brainworkers*, Oldenbourg Verlag, Munich.

THE CHOICE OF CASE STUDIES

The cases contained in the following section have been selected because they reveal certain significant features of human resource management in Spain's most recent past (from 1976 until the present day).

Although the leading labour unions, CCOO and UGT, have become an increasingly important force in Spain's business organisations, small in-company unions are still able to exist. They have a great deal of strength, as illustrated by the second case about Edicli, SA, a publishing and printing company.

The third case examines the decentralisation of the multinational Bimbo, SA, which was founded in Mexico with Catalan capital and ideas. This is another common feature of the Spanish business world: the steady increase in the number of local companies purchased by foreign investors. Spain is completely open to foreign capital investment. This is part of democracy and the way things ought to be. Spain is currently doing its best to attract foreign currency and is open to new ideas and new projects that are part of the information society. A brief example of this can be seen in the first case, Sociedad de Servicios, SA, which deals specifically with brainworkers.

Spanish employers are spending large amount of money on information systems and technology in an attempt to make up for the years lost up to 1975 and the death of the dictator who believed he was saving the country. During the 15 years since then, Spain has been buffeted by the gales of fast development, ranging from democratic labour unions, through new information technologies to a dizzying array of new products, services and capital from abroad.

Labour unions, new capital brought in by multinational companies and the explosive growth of information technology are all part of the development of the Spanish market and its brainworkers. Universities, management schools and businesses will all play a decisive role in developing a new style of human resources management based on customised leadership and managing differences.

11

Sociedad de Servicios, SA

*Samuel Husenman**

Sociedad de Servicios, SA sells computer hardware and software to large companies. It offers a wide range of products and services and has an excellent reputation. The company is particularly well known for its empathy with its customers: its technicians and sales personnel never give up on customer problems.

The computer service industry is a difficult one. Unforeseeable problems are forever cropping up, often in the middle of a job. Quality of service depends on a number of things, but one of the most essential is how customers are treated. In Sociedad de Servicios, as in all companies of this type, personnel motivation is a strategic issue.

Sociedad de Servicios was founded in Barcelona 15 years ago by a group of companies who had nothing to do with the computer business but were enthusiastic about its future. Some of the founders also viewed the company as a way to satisfy their own needs for computerisation.

---

* This case is based on real events. The names and circumstances have been changed at the company's request. This case aims only to provide a tool for discussion and learning, not to judge whether the executive behaviour or management decisions described are correct or incorrect. Only God can know that. If the reader is an atheist, he can refer to Socrates and the idea that 'the only thing I know is how much I do not know', or Timon, a sceptic who said 'Everything that I believe to be absolutely certain today, may be only likely tomorrow'. In other words, this case aims only to stimulate thought, not to provide certain knowledge.

Juan Ramirez, a promising young executive, was appointed managing director. From then on, the founders more or less forgot about Servicios. Apart from keeping an eye on the company's finances, the board of directors left the running of the company entirely to Ramirez.

Ramirez believed that his business was not just any business but a source of qualified employment that made an essential contribution to the country's economic development. Under his leadership Servicios grew rapidly and became a leader in the Catalan market where it had a reputation for utter reliability.

Ramirez was absolutely convinced that company growth could only be sustained by opening offices in Spain's major cities. So about six years ago he opened offices in Madrid and Bilbao, as well as a small research operation in Valencia. The Madrid and Bilbao offices also serviced outlets located in a number of medium-sized cities. At the same time he increased the company's range of products and services, with varying degrees of economic success.

Company structure and management

Since it was founded Servicios has undergone numerous changes in its organisational structure. This is consistent with the growth and expansion of operations, but can also be explained by a tendency to adjust its structure to the individuals working for the company.

Generally speaking, the company's definition of jobs and responsibilities is rather vague while its concern for the individual is great. Although Servicios is not an individual or family business it shares many of the same characteristics, with Ramirez occupying the role of the respected company leader.

Ramirez believes that employees should participate in company management and tends to delegate responsibilities (too much so, in the author's opinion). Furthermore, most of the senior executives and technical personnel started out with Ramirez and many of them have held different jobs depending on the company's needs.

All this means that the working atmosphere is extremely warm and that people have a great deal of freedom in their jobs. It also means that there is a fair amount of confusion.

Appendix 1 (page 255) shows the organisational structure of Servicios. At the time the events described here took place, this structure had been only recently introduced. Previously the company was organised by functional areas whereas now it is organised by divisions.

This radical change in organisation is part of the company's efforts to clarify its situation and respond to the financial difficulties it has suffered in the past several years. Recently the company has had an increasingly hard time meeting its financial goals and the end of every year is like a war. Some of the staff, including Ramirez himself, feel that they are permanently called on to perform heroic feats.

Most of the problems can be traced to the Madrid and Bilbao offices. These offices tend to go pretty much their own way. They criticise the head office in Barcelona. They feel that their demands are ignored and they regard all involvement and assistance from Barcelona as 'an invasion'. The arrival of executives from Barcelona is heralded with comments such as 'The *barretinas* are coming', and anyone who agrees too readily with the head office is criticised for 'wearing a *barretina*.*

The feeling in the branch offices is that people from headquarters don't know much, that they are unfamiliar with the local market and that there is 'more than one Athens'. A report from an independent management consultant did, in fact, point out the company's traditional problems in 'transmitting its culture' to the branch offices. Headquarters finds this hard to understand, but they have not managed to settle their differences with Madrid and Bilbao.

A point worth mentioning here is that the Barcelona office, which is in close touch with headquarters, is prospering and dominates the local market, whereas Madrid and Bilbao have traditionally been poor performers. Bilbao manages to more or less break even, but the Madrid operations have never really developed.

Servicios' entire management team knows that the company needs to grow in Madrid, where there is a large market. They have practically reached the limit of their possibilities in Barcelona and Bilbao is too small a market to provide any real growth with the kind of products and services the company offers.

The Madrid office

Despite Madrid's tremendous potential market, Servicios' office there has never turned in a satisfactory performance. Resentment of 'the

---

* These expressions refer to the traditional headgear of Catalan peasants.

barretinas' is particularly marked. On more than one occasion Madrid has requested that the head office be moved to the capital so that the company would cease to be 'provincial'. Although the request is reasonable enough, such a move would be exceedingly difficult.

Madrid has had two different general managers in the past four years. The first, a native of the capital, was a brilliant intellectual who relied so heavily on his sales manager that he eventually lost control of company operations. Devoting himself to little more than public relations, he was eventually fired. The sales manager was so openly anti-Servicios that he was completely unmanageable. He ran the Madrid office with an iron fist which made decision making there particularly difficult.

Headquarters decided to transfer one of their top sales executives to Madrid along with a new technical manager, Juana Prats. Until then, the technical staff in Madrid had been more or less completely ignored and employee turnover was 20 per cent higher than average for the computer service industry.

The change was not a success. The new manager soon found himself in a situation similar to that of his predecessor and three months after taking over was unable to deal with the sales manager. The Madrid office was now split in two and the two sides barely spoke. On the one side was the managing director with Juana Prats, his technical manager (both of whom were from Barcelona) and on the other, the sales manager and the entire sales team.

The link between the two factions in the Madrid office was nothing more than a formality. There were frequent clashes, but they were not talked about for fear of causing an open break. This precarious situation lasted for a year, at which time the sales manager quit to take a job with another company.

Around the same time the managing director clashed with Juana Prats, his technical director. Finding himself completely alone, he asked for a transfer back to Barcelona.

What had really happened was that Juana Prats, a truly talented technical manager, had managed to stabilise her team. They were now getting at least minimal results and the thorny problem of sales management had been solved. The Barcelona management team had now survived the problems of Madrid for slightly over a year.

However, it was no longer possible to ignore Madrid's troubles and more definite solutions were called for. At this point, the company began searching for a new managing director. This coincided with

Servicios' reorganisation into a division-based structure (see Appendix 1). In other words, the situation was, or could be, entirely new.

The new Madrid office

Angélica Font, the manager of Division II, was determined to make a success of the Madrid office. She had accepted the high economic targets set for Madrid, even though the situation was as described in the previous pages.

Sergio Guerra was chosen to manage Madrid operations, now to be known as the Madrid business unit (see Appendix 2 on p. 256). He had previously been employed by a leading firm of international computer consultants where he had been a successful account executive with several major customers. Becoming Madrid manager of Servicios was an important step up in terms of both money and prestige. Had he remained with his former employer it would have taken him years to reach such a responsible position.

All the reports about Sergio Guerra indicated that he was a gifted salesman with little technical background but a lot of experience in managing customers and business operations.

Angélica Font was worried by these reports. Management was not her division's strong point. All the business unit managers were highly skilled and extremely intelligent technicians. Guerra's background in consultancy bore little relation to the way Servicios worked.

Before long it became evident that Angélica Font had grounds for her concern. Guerra was hired in January 1990, just a few months after the new divisional structure went into operation. In February all the business unit managers met in Barcelona. Naturally, Guerra was introduced to them there. His ideas and opinions about the business differed considerably from what the company had done, and done well, in the past.

Because Guerra had no technical background the other business unit managers did not accept him as an equal. Refusing to be ignored by them, Guerra did a great deal of talking in an attempt to show off his knowledge, but it was not easy to impress the other members of the group.

Angélica Font realised that the other unit managers had observed a polite silence in regard to Guerra. Still, it was Guerra's unit that needed to grow and she decided to let Sergio Guerra make his own decisions.

In mid-February Guerra hired Marcos Buonorotti, an Italian who had been technical manager with Guerra's former employer. This made Juana Prats exceedingly nervous, but Guerra insisted that Buonorotti was a top quality professional and essential to the Madrid operation.

At the beginning of March, Angélica Font got a telephone call from Juana Prats, saying it was impossible to work in Madrid. According to Juana, Guerra dealt exclusively with Buonorotti, shunting her aside and giving her no information. 'They've isolated me,' she complained. She was obviously upset. Angélica Font calmed her down, asking her not to do anything rash and to give Guerra 'a vote of confidence'.

Angélica decided not to mention the telephone call to Guerra, sensing that it might cause a blow-up. Instead she decided to ask Sergio Guerra for a report on his plans for organising the Madrid unit. Enough time had now elapsed that he should have a clear idea of what he proposed to do and, judging from Juana's telephone call, the prospect was not too good. A week later Guerra sent her a one-page fax, proposing that the Madrid unit be jointly managed by Buonorotti, Juana Prats and himself.

Angélica started wondering if Guerra had really been the best choice for the job and began to feel trapped by her decision. She met with Guerra in Madrid, rejected his proposal and said that she regarded him as the manager of the Madrid business unit and Juana as technical director. Sergio Guerra made a vague attempt to defend his proposal and the matter was left at that.

At the end of March the Madrid office's performance was normal, but it was a continuation of work begun the previous year. Guerra had told Angélica that he and Buonorotti were looking for new customers and workers, but that was all she knew.

Buonorotti began working as project manager. In theory he answered to Juana Prats, but in practice he was completely independent. He had two project chiefs, Agustín Pedralbes and Martín Domingo, working under him. Juana supposedly monitored Buonorotti's activities but they didn't get along and she limited herself to controlling the costs of the projects in which Buonorotti was involved.

Buonorotti soon proved to be a difficult person. He was technically outstanding, but had serious problems with interpersonal relationships because he was convinced that he knew more than anyone else. His customers trusted him completely and he had a well earned reputation throughout Madrid. According to him, his project chiefs were no good: Agustín Pedralbes knew a lot but worked little and Martín Domingo – well, he was incompetent and didn't know much.

In may, Angélica Font got a second telephone call from Juana Prats, who reported Buonorotti's problems with his project chiefs. Juana was even more upset than before and asked for assurances about her future with the company. She said it was impossible to deal with Buonorotti and complained that he beat down his subordinates, especially Martín Domingo, telling them they were incompetent. Once again, Angélica managed to calm her down. She asked Juana to give her time to make a decision and assured her that there would always be a place for her in Servicios. When she hung up Angélica recalled that Juana herself had frequently complained that Martín Domingo was not very knowledgeable and on occasion had asked that he be replaced. What is more, Angélica was acquainted with Agustín Pedralbes and knew that he was rather vague. But from there to 'beating them down' . . .

The next day Angélica got a call from Sergio Guerra. He said he was having serious problems with Juana who was 'in cahoots with the project chiefs'. Although she was against him, he acknowledged the quality of her work and professional skill. He defined his problems with Juana as 'jealousy between her and Buonorotti'. He also reported that Buonorotti was doing a magnificent job and that negotiations with new and very important customers were in progress.

Angélica Font felt that the situation was a bad one and thought perhaps she ought to get rid of Guerra before it was too late. She wondered how there could possibly be so many personal problems. Before making her final decision she decided to get in touch with an outside consultant who knew Servicios very well and had frequently worked with Ramirez on general management problems.

After reporting the situation to the consultant, their meeting developed as follows:

Angélica: Do you think I should fire Guerra?

Consultant: Is he meeting the Madrid business unit's goals?

Angélica: As far as numbers go, things seem to be proceeding normally, but we aren't getting those new customers that would permit us to grow in Madrid.

Consultant: That's not something that can be done overnight.

Angélica: I know that. In fact, it's impossible to get results so fast. But what should I do about Juana?

Consultant: Juana Prats had problems with the former Madrid manager and now she's having problems with Guerra.

Angélica: That's true but ... (*pause*) what about the problems with Buonorotti and the project chiefs?

Consultant: Is Buonorotti wrong in his impression of the project chiefs?

Angélica: No, he's more or less right, but he shouldn't treat people the way he does. In a business like this you've got to have a good working atmosphere. We're not manufacturing just any old thing. Besides, Martín Domingo is directing a single project worth over 200 million pesetas and he's a personal friend of the information services manager. If we lose Domingo we're liable to lose the customer too and we're not in a financial position to withstand a blow like that. If we lose that account we won't meet our goals and we can't allow that.

Consultant: All right! As you say, you're not manufacturing just any old thing, but what you've been doing in this matter is 'just any old thing'. Don't you trust Sergio Guerra?

Angélica: ... (*pause*). No, not much. He's new to the company and, as you know, we're sort of special here. His background is in consulting.

Consultant: In other words, you don't have too much confidence in him but you say that the business end of things is normal? And he's just told you he's got some good prospects. That's what you want, isn't it?

Angélica: You can never be sure until you actually get the customers. Guerra tells me he's got good prospects, but he seems to be working only with Buonorotti.

Consultant: (*interrupting her*) ... who is technically very good and highly respected by the customers.

Angélica: Yes, but the two of them work together independently of Juana. Guerra hired Buonorotti because he himself doesn't have a technical background.

Sociedad de Servicios

Consultant: It could be that he doesn't get along very well with Juana, who also had problems with the former managing director, and so he hired somebody he knew and could trust. You know what the Madrid office was like before Guerra came in, don't you? Let's find out what kind of a job Guerra's doing in the market. Can you tell me that right now?

Angélica: No, I can't tell you right now if he's really working the market or not. My impression is that he's not headed in the right direction. The customers he's brought in so far are small businesses and they don't fit in with our line of strategy. They're the kind of customers who would be better off with a consulting company and that's what Guerra knows. Our business is something else entirely. He's adapting our business to his background. The person who's really running our kind of business is Juana.

Consultant: Our kind of business . . .

Angélica: That's right. You know, the kind of projects we've always been involved with. What Guerra is doing is filling little gaps with things that will bring us short-term profits. He's selling something that isn't our basic business.

Consultant: Guerra is part of our business too . . .

Angélica: Stop playing psychologist for a minute and give me some practical advice. Naturally Sergio Guerra is part of our business. Do you think we've done a bad job of integrating him into the company?

Consultant: That's up to you to decide. As division manager you know how much time you've devoted to him.

Angélica: I frequently have meetings with him in Madrid and we talk on the phone a lot. I've tried to leave him alone and give him time to get better acquainted with the business, but look at the mess we've gotten into (*she laughs*) in such a short period of time. So, I want your advice.

Consultant: Why don't we find out for ourselves how we're doing in the Madrid market?

253

Angélica: I could send the marketing manager down to take a look at the projects and find out about these prospects of Guerra's. That way I'd know exactly what's going on, but Guerra would take it badly.

Consultant: Your marketing manager is pretty tactful and besides, control is a management tool. You want information; you're not trying to interfere in Guerra's market decisions.

Angélica: OK. I'll keep you posted . . .

Two weeks later Angélica received a written report from the marketing manager indicating that Madrid's sales prospects looked very good and that one of the deals was about to be concluded involving a major customer which Servicios had repeatedly and vainly tried to win away from one of their competitors. The marketing manager had visited several prospective customers with Guerra and reported that Guerra was an experienced salesman. There were some new customers that were small and not exactly the type of customer with which Servicios usually worked, but Guerra maintained that they brought in short-term earnings which were necessary in order to be able to work in peace. Although the marketing manager felt that this point could be argued, he agreed that it did make some sense.

Angélica Font breathed a sigh of relief. Guerra had protested loudly about the marketing manager's interference. Angélica had insisted that it was simply a market control, but they both knew that was not true.

In May Guerra sent Angélica a memo reporting that three new project chiefs had been hired and would all be working under Buonorotti. No mention was made of Juana Prats.

At the end of May, a major contract was signed with one of Guerra's prospective customers and Madrid's performance far exceeded the goals set in the budget. Angélica Font was now truly relieved. It looked like the Madrid office was at last beginning to go according to plan.

On 1 June Angélica got a phone call from Martín Domingo, one of the Madrid project chiefs. He reported indignantly that Buonorotti had 'humiliated' him. It seemed that in a meeting with a customer, Buonorotti had dismissed one of Domingo's applications, saying it was 'a botch-up'. Domingo told Angélica that Buonorotti was impossible to deal with, that he (Domingo) was in charge of the project and that they were now liable to lose the customer. He also told her that Buonorotti had told the customer that he would personally 'patch up the mess' and that this had ruined Domingo's reputation with the customer. 'I'll never be able to face him again . . .'

While Angélica was talking to Domingo, her secretary entered and left some papers on her desk. Domingo kept repeating his complaint over and over. Angélica glanced at the papers, automatically reading the top one which was a short handwritten note from Ramirez. His large letters read: 'Juana Prats has asked for a meeting with me. Can you give me some background on this?' . . .

Appendix 1: General organisation

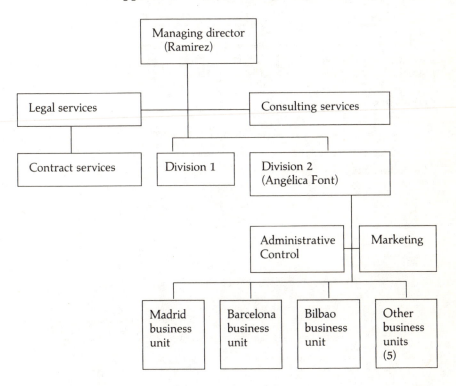

Appendix 2: Madrid business unit organisation chart (theoretical)

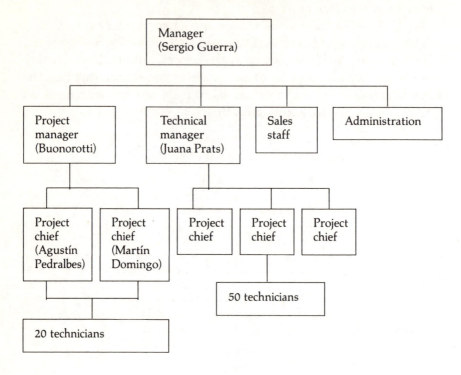

Questions

1. Why is motivating personnel a strategic issue in this service company?

2. Analyse the situation in order to determine whether the divisional structure is appropriate in Sociedad de Servicios, SA's current phase of growth.

3. What are the basic and operational difficulties involved in transmitting the company's culture from its Barcelona head-quarters to its other branches?

4. Analyse Angélica Font's professional role and behaviour as manager of division II and in relation to the Madrid branch.

5. Analyse Angélica Font's meeting with the consultant from Ms Font's point of view as division manager.

6. Did the consultant help the division manager?

7. If you had been the consultant, what advice would you have given Angélica Font?

8. What information should division manager Angélica Font give the managing director so that he can prepare for his meeting with Juana Prats in Madrid?

12

Edicli, SA

Joan Cornudella

A brief history

Ediciones de Comics y Libros, SA was founded in Barcelona on 1 January 1950 as the continuation of a publishing operation that had been started by a single individual half a century before.

Over the years the company expanded its distribution network throughout Spain and Latin America and began printing and distributing publications for other publishers in addition to producing its own material. The high point of its expansion was the plant constructed on the outskirts of Barcelona in 1973. In 1980 Edicli invested heavily in new machinery.

The company mainly published magazines and other type of periodicals, most of which were distributed and sold to Distribuciones Editoriales, SA, the exclusive distributor for Edicli publications in Spain. Another division of the company, Distribue, SA, distributed other non-Edicli publications for the national market through its extensive sales network. Foreign distribution was taken care of by Edicli itself, through its subsidiaries abroad.

Because it had its own printing plant, Edicli also produced magazines for other publishers.

Edicli

Events leading up to the crisis

In the early 1980s the company was hit by an economic crisis, the causes of which will be examined somewhat further on. The financial situation was shaky and the very survival of the business was in danger. In June 1982, both Edicli and Distribue (the two divisions that comprised the company as such) were authorised to declare a moratorium on payments. At this time, the company was deeply in debt.

Among the reasons for this situation were:

- the crisis of the Spanish economy, which had been further aggravated by a world crisis;
- lack of government aid to rationalise the publishing and printing industry;
- lack of equity and the non-availability of credit with good enough terms to permit the company to reorganise and adapt to new conditions;
- it was impossible to obtain funding by floating a stock issue;
- in February 1982 a major publishing group rescinded its contract with Edicli's printing division and the company's turnover dropped 1,200 million pesetas per year;
- the constant social, political and economic upheaval and the drastic currency devaluations in Latin America caused one of the company's most important markets to deteriorate;
- the situation was particularly bad in Mexico and Argentina, which accounted for 70 per cent of Edicli's export market;
- the company was set up in such a way that it was virtually impossible to adapt to changing market situations: among its fixed costs were salaries for 1,411 employees;
- intra-company management was weak (there was no coordination between the publishing, printing and distribution divisions);
- the operating margin was gradually decreasing while the company's financial costs were steadily rising.

Economic and financial analysis

Obviously, drastic changes were called for, particularly in three essential areas:

1. The financial situation forced the company to apply for a moratorium on payments and come to terms with its creditors in order to settle its debts.
2. The company had been registering heavy losses since 1961 and would definitely go under unless it took steps to economise.
3. The number of permanent employees had to be reduced so that it would be commensurate with the real market demand.

The proposal for overcoming the crisis

The company's problems were due more to its structure than to any particular trend in the economic cycle. A detailed feasibility study was called for, but meanwhile steps had to be taken in order to avoid a short-term loss of confidence and the reduction in the value of its capital assets.

To this end, the company established a schedule of aims and actions to be taken in the different functional areas. This case will deal only with the measures involving personnel.

The objectives in terms of personnel were the following:

1. **Short-term objectives**

    - Encourage voluntary resignations by negotiating agreements with individual employees and with the consent of the works council.
    - Encourage early retirements as permitted by Spanish law, negotiating individual agreements as in the foregoing point.
    - Farm out certain in-house services (transport, mechanical typesetting etc) to employees who would be paid incentives to set up as self-employed suppliers.
    - Cut costs by temporary lay-offs and/or reduced working hours.

2. **Medium- and long-term objectives**

    - Carefully analyse the company's viability, with representatives of management, labour and outside experts participating in the process.
    - Study the possibility of applying for help from public sources, specifically the Catalan regional government's department of labour.

- Make joint decisions in the light of:
  a) the way business developed over the ensuing 6 or 12 months;
- b) the feasibility study.

The company proposed the following methodology for all the aforementioned measures:

- Information should be open, above board and regularly provided.
- Economic and financial studies should be made jointly by management and labour.
- Specialists in organisation should be commissioned to carry out studies of the company's structure, functions and working methods.
- Outside specialists and representatives of management and labour should all work together and provide each other with regular information.
- Briefing sessions should be held regularly and in accordance with a pre-established timetable.

The company did not have sufficient funds to make the first, second or third quarter bonus payments to its employees and wanted to postpone them for two years. In return for agreeing to this, the works council would be entitled to monitor the company's operations and balance sheets, particularly its cash and bank balances.

After presenting this plan to the works council, the chief executive officer wrote a personal letter to every one of the employees, just as he had done to announce the moratorium on payments. After commenting on the problems the moratorium was causing as regards the company's customers, suppliers and banks, he turned to the matter of personnel:

> To conclude, I would like to discuss the subject which is causing the most concern among our employees: survival of their jobs. I will try to be as clear on this point as I have been in my other attempts to explain the situation: management will thoroughly study the structure of the company and then begin negotiating with the employee representatives. Our study will be totally objective and will be made with the assistance of independent and accredited specialists. As regards negotiations: if necessary we will request that the regional government, the *Generalitat*, and the Department of Labour act as our advisers and arbiters. Mean-

while and during a period of six months, which will most likely be extended a further six months, all jobs will be maintained. The future depends largely on our ability to react and on the appropriateness of the decisions we make.

If, during the aforementioned period, high costs force us to eliminate any currently existing jobs, the employees affected will be reassigned to other departments on terms which will be duly negotiated with the works council. The council will also be informed of any voluntary resignations which may take place as well as the terms of any early retirements, disability or other pensions that may be agreed with individual employees.

Management and the works council met a number of times in July in order to set up a schedule for paying the personnel up until 10 September, another schedule for payment of back wages and for salaries payable from September on and a final schedule for submitting the plan for reduced working hours and/or temporary lay-offs.

On 30 July the works council published a bulletin that summarised the situation as follows:

Works Council Bulletin (30 July 1982)

In the Works Council's meetings with management a schedule was agreed on for payments up until 10 September. Management has repeatedly announced that there will be a *reduction in working hours*. The company had promised to submit its plan for reduced hours to the council by 19 July and had even announced this in the press. However, this promise has not been kept and the plan was not submitted until 29 July.

It is now the last week of July and management and the works council have agreed to postpone negotiations on reduced working hours until the end of August when the summer vacation period is over and the employees will be able to take a collective stance.

When we return from our holidays, we will have to study management's proposal to reduce working hours. This will not be the only issue on which we will have to take a stand. We will also have to consider *all aspects of the situation* caused by the moratorium on payments.

It is true that part of the plan for reduced working hours was not submitted to the works council until the beginning of August. According to management, the delay was caused by changes in the estimated work-load. The plan can be summarised as follows:

1. The proposal to reduce working hours basically stemmed from the pressing need to cut production in accordance with the actual possibilities of the market. The company had for the moment decided against lay-offs, preferring to wait and see how the market would develop over the next few months and carry out the feasibility study.

   Management argued that if production was not reduced, the company would have to continue borrowing in order to get temporary relief from the effects of its accumulated losses. This would result in a persistent and extremely high deficit that would quickly drive the company into bankruptcy.

2. Given the situation of the company and its market, the company could no longer support the burden of salaries for so many employees. Salaries were already being paid late and the company was having an increasingly hard time meeting these payments.

   The proposed reduction in working hours responded to the functional needs outlined in the existing working plan. This was illustrated by the lists which accompanied the plan. These involved a breakdown by tasks and an explanation of why it was necessary to reduce working hours. This meant cutting personnel by about 32 per cent.

Trade unions: their position in the company

Before describing the negotiations that took place prior to Edicli applying for authorisation to reduce working hours, the situation of trade unions in the company and how the negotiating procedure had worked in the past must first be explained.

The company's outstanding economic performance in the 1960s and the first half of the 1970s had made it easy to negotiate labour pacts proposed by management itself.

The *Jurados de Empresa** who negotiated on behalf of the employees were practically all independent *enlaces*** who were fairly well content with the company's paternalistic policy. In addition, there were a few former union leaders who had gone over to the 'official' labour

---

* *Jurados de Empresa* represented company employees during the Franco years and were roughly equivalent to works councils.

** Representatives elected by the *Jurados de Empresa*.

organisation of the Franco years and did a great deal to foster this paternalistic approach from their positions both inside the company and in the vertical trade unions.* Later on, when the political/labour system began revealing its first signs of obsolescence, a split occurred within the ranks of the *Jurados*: many of the younger members became restless and began demanding higher wages and improved social benefits, most of which the company was willing and able to provide. But the political transition in Spain brought a substantial change to labour relations. Employees began organising in an assembly movement led by young university graduates who had joined Edicli's publishing division within the two previous years. Some of them came from splinter groups of CCOO** and others from organisations with anarchist leanings. After forming their own union within the company, these leaders proceeded to win a landslide victory in the company elections, virtually eradicating the other candidates who had originally been part of the assembly in the hopes of dominating it after the election.

The company was pleased with the results of the elections: management felt it could meet the increasing demands of the new labour leaders and, moreover, the victory of an in-house union meant that the company could continue its tradition of solving its problems behind closed doors. Management was convinced that any industrial relations problems were likely to be on a sectoral level and was at first willing to raise salaries and increase benefits if that was the price that had to be paid to keep the company out of potential conflicts. This tactic worked until the market recession made it impossible to continue and it became abundantly clear that the company desperately needed restructuring, which would involve drastic cuts in permanent personnel.

The negotiating process

On 26 August the employee representatives informed management that they could not respond to the plan for reducing working hours until after the summer vacation, when a general assembly of employees could be held.

---

* The Franco regime's version of labour organisations.
** The communist-inspired trade union.

On 1 September 1982 management sent a memo to all employees, stressing the need to reduce working hours because the wage and salary costs were too great a burden for company finances to bear. Once again, management reiterated its willingness to negotiate the terms of such a reduction as well as a schedule of payments for amounts outstanding and a new system for making future bonus payments.

> While the company is on short hours, salaries for hours actually worked will be fully paid by the company and the hours not worked will be covered by unemployment insurance. Nevertheless, total salaries will be lower than normal. I would like to clearly state here that the company is willing to study proposals for reasonable and equitable solutions to this problem. I believe that it is essential for the company and its employees to reach an agreement which will enable us to continue our normal operations and permit our customers, bankers and suppliers to maintain their confidence in us.

On 5 September the works council submitted to management a document which had been discussed and approved by the general assembly of employees. Among the paragraphs appearing in the document were the following:

> **The feasibility plan:** Cutting production to a minimum and putting employees on short hours will leave management free to devise a definite plan for salvaging the business, ie a feasibility plan. Management intends to do this a few months from now, around December, when we employees are expected to be accustomed to ridiculously low production, shorter working hours and lower salaries paid irregularly. This much touted feasibility plan will then be no more than a way of formalising the current situation. The plan will attempt to demonstrate that production must be kept low and that, as a result, one-third of the personnel is redundant. The cut in working hours is simply a trial run for what is to follow. If the company can keep going for six months with one-third less than its usual staff, what will happen to this one-third once we go off shorter hours?

> We employees must reject this situation and be ready to fight hard to keep from being gradually steamrollered by this plan.

> Wouldn't it be much more appropriate for management to

abandon its chronic short-sightedness and search for medium- and long-term solutions that would allow the company to grow or at least maintain its current size? It strikes us as being suicidal to permit net sales to drop from 7,000 million pesetas in 1981 to 4,300 million in the period from 16 September 1982 to 15 September 1983.

There is a good deal that can be done before starting to talk about cutting down working hours. Management must come up with a reply to the plan presented by the assembly; they must provide a feasibility plan that guarantees our jobs. The company must pay its outstanding debts to the employees and we must be paid our salaries regularly. Once these problems have been solved, and only then, can we discuss whether or not working hours need to be reduced. If we permit working hours to be reduced before these other issues are settled, we will be heading straight to the slaughter.

Management and labour obviously held radically different opinions about the right strategy to apply. Still, on 14 September, they managed to come up with a series of 'agreements', which included a possible reduction in working hours and temporary lay-offs, both of which measures would be subject to ratification by the employees' assembly.

In the end, the assembly unanimously rejected management's plan and equally unanimously voted to present the following report:

Steps to be taken: The employees' assembly has voted to take the following steps:

1. The employees shall present a report to management and shall further present a financial report drafted by their advisers.

2. If management does not announce the commencement of the period established by law during which employees will be consulted on the proposed reduction of working hours, said employees shall assume that management intends to study the employees' report and use it as a basis for drafting a feasibility plan. Such intention shall be announced within one week (no later than 20 September). In the event management demonstrates its willingness to negotiate (by not commencing the aforementioned period of consultation), the works council shall assist in drafting the feasibility plan and in all

necessary negotiations with the competent agencies. So long as the intention is to maintain all existing jobs, the employees recognise that a temporary reduction in working hours may be necessary.

3. Should management commence the aforementioned period of consultation, the employees shall assume that management is not willing to negotiate and intends to forcefully impose the reduction in working hours. In this case, the employees shall resort to pressure in the form of:

a) a press campaign denouncing management's unwillingness to negotiate with the employees;

b) contacts with the creditors meeting in order to explain the company's true situation and prospects;

c) contacts with official agencies to report management's unwillingness to design a feasibility plan;

d) a legal strike, subject to ratification by the general assembly of employees.

After receiving this document, management sent the following reply to the coordinating committee of the works councils for Edicli, SA and Distribute, SA:

Gentlemen:

The assembly has made certain observations on the agreement which was reached on 14 September and which imply substantial changes in the said agreement. You are now proposing something entirely different from what we had jointly agreed upon. Under no circumstances can we accept your statement that you have ratified this agreement when you have arbitrarily changed its content. This is a lamentable occurrence, giving rise to a great deal of confusion, and we regret to inform you that your action forces us to conclude that you have violated the agreement. This conclusion is borne out by the fact that it was the coordinating committee itself that proposed that the assembly change the very agreements said committee had originally signed.

Obviously, we fail to understand why you have violated an agreement which was so difficult to reach but which, in our opinion, was an important step towards assuring the survival of the company and the jobs of all its employees.

Throughout the bargaining process we repeatedly emphasised

several points. However, given the current situation, we feel we should once again remind you that:

a) The company's current billings are insufficient to maintain the entire staff of employees.

b) Under these circumstances, we have no choice but to reduce working hours in order to avoid having to fire any of our employees.

c) Reducing working hours is an emergency measure. Unless we adopt this measure, every job in the company will soon be in jeopardy.

d) Reducing working hours will give the company a breathing space, financially speaking. Without this breathing space it will be impossible to pay the back wages owed to our employees.

e) Unless the company continues to operate normally and present a good image to the rest of the world, our customers, suppliers and bankers will withdraw their support, without which the company cannot survive.

The aforementioned points are vitally important and the current situation is so serious that we cannot accept any further delay or neglect our responsibilities. We therefore declare that the compulsory period for consultations on the reduction in working hours shall begin on today's date and we take this opportunity to inform you that we are willing to negotiate the terms of the said reduction within the period of time established by law.

Application for reduced working hours and temporary lay-offs

On 14 October the Company finally applied for authorisation to cut back the working hours of between 33.33 per cent and 37.5 per cent of its 333 permanently contracted employees and temporarily lay off 105 others on certain days for a period of six months. The works council submitted its report opposing the application and on 18 October the employees went out on a one-day strike, staging protest demonstrations in the streets.

In its report the works council requested that the company's application be refused, arguing that the company had 'limitless possibilities for growth' and needed to take 'maximum advantage of its personnel', ie to adopt a policy similar to that proposed by the former managing director, who had been so severely criticised by the works council itself.

The works council made generalisations about the existence of 'much more attractive and profitable alternatives' without ever specifying what they were and continued to insist on full employment totally ignoring the true market situation. Because the application was contested, the final decision in the case would be made by the Government.

On 27 October 1982 the provincial branch of the labour authority issued a resolution, authorising Edicli to reduce working hours and temporarily lay off employees until 31 January 1983 (half the period applied for), 'by which date the feasibility plan must be completed so that in the light of the said plan, a clear and coherent decision can be made on the measures to be adopted as regards company personnel'.

Conclusions and effects of the disagreement

- The employees' attitude was that the company should continue producing at full capacity even though it was in a state of crisis.
- The high rate of union membership and the variety of unions made it difficult to reach any sort of agreement and simply complicated, delayed and made matters more expensive.
- The high rate of unionisation and the fear of trouble led management to be very tentative in its attempts to overcome the crisis and in the long run this proved ineffective.
- In this particular case, the legal machinery did not slow the process down. However, the need to obtain government authorisation to reduce working hours and temporarily lay off employees usually involves additional attempts to reach some sort of agreement. This makes the negotiating process longer (and generally more costly) than usual and causes the situation in the company to deteriorate still further. In many cases, the very survival of a company depends on how rapidly decisions are made.
- Edicli is a good example of this. Reduced working hours went into effect in November when the decision could actually have been made in August, had it been legally possible to do so. Once management/labour negotiations reached a stalemate, a good deal of time and trouble could have been saved had the company been

entitled to make at least a preliminary decision to cut back working hours for a certain amount of time, without having first to apply for government authorisation.

The board of labour report which served as the basis for the decision read as follows:

On the grounds of the background material to this case and the statements made in meetings held with one or both parties on 18, 19 and 21 October 1982, the board of labour hereby states that: there are two different, though closely related, facets of the situation: a) the financial problems of the companies involved which led directly to the application for a moratorium on payments motivated by the impossibility of going further into debt or drawing on the company's apparently exhausted equity, and the lack of attention paid to the financial obligations incurred in order to continue operating despite the losses registered in the past several years; b) the gap between production capacity and current market demand, which demand has dropped due to a number of different circumstances which may or may not be cyclical in nature. This gap is due to a number of reasons ranging from an internal situation which led to the application of some unfortunate sales and management policies, to loss of customers (essentially involving publications for outside customers) and including the failure of the company's distributors (South American subsidiaries) to meet their financial obligations. The combination of all these circumstances caused stock to increase more than advisable or endurable for the company, particularly during the period from August 1968 to February 1982. The board of labour considers that the company is in a genuine state of crisis, although the said crisis can be quantified or evaluated differently by each of the parties. As regards the measures for which application has been made, the board of labour considers that the different measures designed to cut down working time as permitted by current legislation are aimed at regulating a temporary, cyclical situation and normalising the company's operations. However, due to the complexity and importance of the company's economic–financial problems, the said normalisation requires an in-depth study of the said problems and the possible solutions thereto, which should be set out in a feasibility plan which we understand to have been duly requested of the pertinent organisations, who were to submit said plan before 31 January 1982.

Case for analysis

In 1982 Spain registered its highest unemployment rate in decades. Curiously enough, most of this unemployment was caused by eliminating jobs. New jobs were not being created and in addition the energy crisis had proved devastating to an industrial system based on the obsolete economic model inherited from the Franco years and already plagued by serious structural defects. Moreover, the economic crisis coincided with the political transition, the need to consolidate democracy and employees' recovery of their right to organise.

This was the background to the crisis described in this case. Granted, the union situation in Edicli was by no means typical: the country's two leading labour organisations – the communist-inspired CCOO and the socialist UGT – were outnumbered in Edicli by an anarchist union which radicalised the situation and made it difficult to negotiate an agreement that could have put an end to the crisis.

This case describes the first round in a lengthy process of crisis and negotiations which ended in 1986 with the demise of the company. The first attempt at management/employee negotiations ended in failure, forcing management to file for Government permission temporarily to reduce working hours and lay off personnel – measures it believed to be essential. It must be noted here that in Spain such measures require Government authorisation regardless of whether or not the employees have previously agreed to them. The difference is that when both sides are in agreement the Government automatically grants its approval, providing no pacts have been made that violate the law. When no prior agreement has been reached the Government must analyse the particular case and make the final decision.

Winning the right of decision in cases like this is one of the longstanding aims of Spanish employers.

Questions

1. Under the terms of Spanish legislation, any employer wishing to reduce his staff must first obtain the labour authority's authorisation to do so. How do you feel about this regulation and what influence do you think it had on the negotiating process in Edicli, S.A.?

2. What is your opinion of the board of labour report which served as the basis for the final decision in the case? How do you feel about this decision?

3. To what extent can the failure of negotiations be blamed on the composition of the works committee and the fact that in Spain employees' representatives are sometimes influenced to take certain actions by the tendency to decide through general meetings of employees?

4. Given the pre-crisis situation in the company, do you feel that the works committee could really have had a clear idea of how much the company had deteriorated?

5. Do you agree with the measures proposed by the new management team and the way they handled the issues of information and negotiation? Give reasons for your answer.

6. If your reply to the above question was negative, what alternatives would you suggest?

7. Why do you think the management team proposed a gradual solution for overcoming the crisis?

13

Bimbo SA:
Corporate Culture and Strategy
for Change

Manuel Marcet

Introduction: December 1977, a time of uncertainty

Two years after the death of Franco (who had gripped Spain in an iron-fisted dictatorship for 38 years) and once democracy and the right to union action had been formally reinstated, a violent 36-day strike broke out in Bimbo, SA. The strike itself was not unexpected, but its length and violence came as a surprise. It was triggered by Spain's soaring inflation, which that year reached 27 per cent.

In an attempt to keep inflation from rising even higher, the entire spectrum of political parties met in the presidential palace, *La Moncloa*, and set a tough ceiling on wage increases, with an absolute top of 18 per cent.

The trade unions, who had not been party to the pact, reacted violently to this certain loss in purchasing power and took to the streets to protest about what they considered a grave injustice.

Bimbo was the scene of the first strike. When the company began negotiating its annual labour agreements, following the Moncloa pacts to the letter, the unions rebelled and the company's employees marched through the streets of Madrid, Barcelona, Malaga and other cities brandishing signs that read 'They're stealing 180 million from us'. The company was paralysed for 36 days: production and deliveries stopped and orders went unfilled.

The shelves in all the large grocery chains were empty of Bimbo products and the company's competitors took advantage of the opportunity to move in. The end appeared to have come for a company that had once been prosperous, well known and appreciated by consumers.

A brief history

Bimbo, SA started in Mexico. The Spanish Bimbo company was actually a replica of the original Bimbo which was founded in Mexico City in December 1945, just a few months after the end of World War II.

The company was founded by a group of Mexican businessmen who were descendents of Spaniards from Catalonia. They felt that 'sliced bread' would be an ideal response to the needs of a nascent middle class whose life-style and consumer habits were rapidly changing.

Bimbo's founders intuitively built their business on two basic principles. The first involved the kind of product and the second the kind of customer sevice they would give.

They aimed to produce high quality sliced bread, made with the best ingredients and under perfect conditions of hygiene. The bread would be delivered in a protective wrapper. It would be not just an alternative to regular bread, but could also be the basis for more informal kinds of meals. Customer service would involve delivering the product fresh and regularly.

These two features were the key to Bimbo's growth and success. It was not long before the Bimbo logo and mascot were serving as a guarantee for a broad range of bakery products.

Twenty years later one of the company's founders decided to build on this success by setting up the same company in Spain, using the same corporate symbols and philosophy. Since then the paths of the two companies have been parallel, but independent.

Bimbo, SA was founded in Barcelona on 4 March 1964 'with the corporate aim of producing and selling bakery products'. Operations began on 25 February 1965 when the Granollers factory turned out its first loaf of sliced bread.

Although by 1977 the company had spread throughout the entire country, it still did not have a proper core structure which would have permitted it to unify all company policies and establish common operating standards for the entire organisation. Bimbo's success in terms of demand, production and sales led the management team to opt for short-term, money-making operations. Meanwhile, employee grievances were building into a hotbed of resentment, which exploded in 1977–78 in a strike that shook the company to its foundation.

1978: The moment of change

The big strike left the company in a shambles. Relations between management and employees were tense. The Bimbo image had been seriously damaged. The company's competitors seized the opportunity to move in on all sides. The Mexican partners were utterly discouraged. Company executives were demoralised and had lost their confidence in the company. It was extremely difficult to make a comeback on the market. The losses were enormous.

Faced with a situation like this – further complicated by the fact that after 38 years of dictatorship Spain was taking its first tottering steps towards democracy – there were only two alternatives: either radically change the company's focus and management or close and sell out, sentencing the company to death.

The Mexicans decided to sell. The Americans were willing to buy. And so Bimbo became fully owned by Campbell Taggart Inc at the end of 1979.

A new board of directors was appointed and they named as managing director a man who was a lawyer, economist, faculty member of the ESADE management school and who had solid experience in the business world. Later he was also appointed as chairman of the board. This man led the entire turn-round process. He had the full suppport of Bimbo's shareholders and power enough to do what had to be done, undo whatever had been done wrong and make any changes that were necessary. The first thing the new chairman did was confirm the appointment of the new personnel manager, a fellow ESADE faculty member, so that the company could work with its executives and employees alike to design a new policy that would allow for the normal management of Bimbo.

By strengthening operations management and giving a more professional shape to management/employee relations, Bimbo embarked on a new path aimed at changing its future prospects completely.

Corporate strategy

In 1978 the CEO set two goals: survival of the company and regaining the shareholders' confidence. He began by floating a sizeable stock issue. This gave Bimbo a solid image in the eyes of banks and suppliers. He then proceeded to develop a methodical and global corporate strategy which is described below.

Remodelling the company's structure and organisation

The company was structured in the standard functional areas with a specialised service staff to provide support. Because there were so many branches in so many different places, management had necessarily to be decentralised. This was compensated for by centralising policies and systems designed to guarantee the various functional operations.

General management first separated and made a clear distinction between manufacturing and sales operations. Although the two areas would be independent and autonomous, they would be coordinated by the senior management team.

A factories manager was appointed to head up industrial operations, which consisted of six factories strategically located throughout Spain. Each factory had its own plant manager, who managed seven departments: production, maintenance, distribution (including warehousing of finished products and shipping to the various sales offices using its own fleet of vehicles and drivers), quality assurance (including quality control, manufacturing hygiene and industrial safety), administration, industrial relations and vehicle repairs and service. In addition, each plant manager had his specialised support staff.

Sales operations were headed by a commercial manager who coordinated marketing and sales. Spain was divided into eight different territories and a sales manager appointed for each of them. Each sales manager was responsible for sales offices, which varied in number according to the particular territory involved. Each sales office had its own team of salesmen, its own delivery trucks, its own office personnel etc. A number of marketing and sales specialists completed the staff of the commercial department.

The departments of factories and sales management were located in the Barcelona headquarters along with the personnel, administration and public relations departments, engineering, research and development, purchasing, data processing etc. The mission of these centralised departments and services and their technical and clerical staffs was to unify the policies to be applied in each area and ensure that all decision making was as professional as possible. With this system, the new senior management team assured the coherence of the operation and the decentralised operatives encouraged a high degree of initiative in the rest of the staff.

Back to basics: quality and service

The CEO was not out to invent anything new. He simply wanted to regain what had been lost, what had instinctively been the essence of the business: delivering fresh bread every day. Bimbo were bakers and proud of it. All the CEO's policy decisions were guided by pride in the profession.

The company instituted a control process that gave customers a total guarantee of the product's quality. The process began with careful selection of the raw materials and ingredients to be used. These were laboratory tested in each factory to assure that they met the specifications. A state-of-the-art product research and technological development centre was opened in Granollers and the best flours were subjected to tests there. Employees were given basic and specialised training to develop their skills and become increasingly professional. New technologies were constantly introduced into manufacturing processes in order to improve the final product. Once the product was finished and placed on supermarket shelves, a specialised agency used statistical sampling techniques to check the quality of the product when it finally reached the customer.

Once quality was assured, the company set up a marketing and sales service that made Bimbo a household word. The advertising campaign *'Los frescos del barrio'* (which roughly translates as 'The freshest guys in town') was tremendously successful in selling the image of Bimbo salespeople as service-minded, early risers who were always on the spot.

Soon Bimbo salespeople and their delivery vans became a familiar sight in all the towns and cities in Spain, as did the huge semi-trailers that plied the nation's highways carrying the product from the factories to the sales offices. And no wonder. Every day 1300 vans visit thousands of customers as the company aims to deliver its product daily to some three million consumers.

The reason behind all this is simply service. Bimbo produces a perishable product and it must reach the consumer as quickly as possible. That is why the factories work round the clock every single day of the year, including Sundays and holidays. Huge trucks deliver the freshly baked goods to offices throughout the country so they can be sold the following day. The slogans 'we're bakers' and 'the freshest guys in town' have become the company's operating philosophy.

Towards a more professional management style

The CEO established a five year plan which is updated every year. The most important thing is that employees know 'where we are headed' and that there is a definite path to follow.

Every year a budget listing sales, costs, expenses and earnings is drawn up. This is faithfully adhered to. Once set and approved, the budget serves as a tool for management and control. Periodic budget reviews serve to indicate what remains to be done and what results must be obtained.

Another of the CEO's early aims was gradually to recoup the company's losses and put it back in the black, with the invested capital making good profits. In order to make the company increasingly solid, he applied a policy involving amortisations, self-financing and investments which gradually led to Bimbo's current image as a leader in its field. During his first years at the helm annual investments amounted to approximately 1 billion pesetas: machinery was replaced, two new factories were built, new offices opened, the company's trucks were renewed and the entire accounting process computerised.

This display of daring, coherent management, open and above board gradually restored the confidence of executives and employees alike. Little by little, confrontation between bosses and workers gradually gave way to mutual respect and shared interests.

Obviously all these improvements led to better market penetration. The company's market share increased and Bimbo's visibility was higher in all communications media.

Training the management team

One of the CEO's first priorities after taking the reins at Bimbo was to shape a management team that would regain confidence in its own abilities and in the future of the company. In order to do this he took a series of steps which can be summarised as follows:

1. He applied a totally open and above-board policy, providing constant information about 'where we're coming from, where we are and where we're going'.
2. He adhered strictly to the five year plan, which was constantly updated and which provided an assurance that the company was following a definite path.
3. He scheduled one meeting a year in a quiet place away from the office at which the annual budget was prepared and operational alternatives discussed.
4. He scheduled one meeting a month at which the performance of the previous period was analysed, compared with the updated budget and any deviations corrected.
5. A meeting for all plant and sales managers was held quarterly in order to analyse the performance of the previous period, compare it with the budget and with performance in the same period a year earlier and define the actions to be taken in order to assure closer adherence to the budget.
6. A day-long course was held once a year for senior and middle managers and supervisory personnel in order to explain the company's situation, the results of the previous year as well as plans for the coming year and how they fitted into the five year plan.

All these actions gradually led to unified objectives, established the accessibility of the CEO and created a feeling of limitless confidence in the man who is the indisputable leader of the process of change.

Personnel strategy

At the same time as the CEO was gradually shaping a 'new' company with a new management style, the personnel manager was having to put another process into motion. It was his job to try to heal the deep scars left by the long and violent strike, put an end to the resentment and conflicts between bosses and workers and regain their lost confidence in the system.

It was not an easy job that the CEO gave the personnel manager, but he managed it successfully. Not only did he gradually develop an extremely well defined personnel strategy, but this strategy earned the CEO's full support and was fully consistent with the overall corporate strategy.

The following is a brief description of some of the personnel policies that the company began applying as of 1978.

Clarifying the rules of the game

This was as simple a matter as declaring that everyone should observe the labour laws in effect at any given moment. The strike had caused all sorts of clashes between bosses and workers, between supervisors and senior managers and between employees themselves. It had been a violent time. In 1978 one of the foremen said to the CEO, 'working for Bimbo is hell. Nobody pays any attention to you. The employees have no respect for you.'

The first rule now is one of mutual respect. This means that everyone is considered as an individual. Any violation of the individual's rights is strictly against the law and disciplinary measures are rigorously enforced – for everyone.

The first firing took place in 1978. A group of supervisors entered the room where an assembly was being held and an employee (who was, incidentally, a union delegate) said, 'What are they doing here? They're nothing but a bunch of parasites and leeches who do nothing to earn their salaries.' The employee was dismissed immediately. He refused to retract his words. The court judged in favour of the company stating that the dismissal was a justified response to 'a serious lack of discipline and respect'. But it cost Bimbo a second (and final) 15-day strike to maintain its stand that every member of the company is equally deserving of respect.

Several incompetent supervisors were also fired at that time, but after several years the rules of conduct began to be more closely observed. Individuals are now respected, supervisors and workers manage to coexist and differences are settled through dialogue and moderation. It is extremely important here that the principle of 'equal justice for everyone' is scrupulously observed.

Discipline is no longer an issue at Bimbo. Instead, there is respect for the individual, respect for legislation, respect for regulations and respect for legal proceedings in the event that any employee feels that his or her interests have been violated. This has led to a situation where even supervisors have earned the employees' respect and appreciation for doing their jobs and honestly evaluating the workers' efforts.

Respecting union action

Because the company had so many work-places, a great number of union delegates had to be chosen. The company provided complete facilities for union elections to be held. 154 union representatives were elected and CCOO (Communist-affiliated) and UGT (Socialist-affiliated) emerged as the two unions with the most votes, just as they were throughout the entire country.

In order to facilitate matters, a 27-member central committee was elected from among the 154 delegates. This committee was empowered to receive corporate information, settle global conflicts and negotiate the company's collective agreements.

In 1977 Bimbo negotiated seven different agreements, according to the zones where the company operated. In 1978 the first nationwide agreement, valid for all Bimbo workplaces, was negotiated.

Management's attitude towards organised labour changed from opposition and rejection to respect and even acceptance. The change was gradual and largely thanks to the way one of the unions, UGT, developed in terms of willingness to negotiate and reach compromises.

The works committees and personnel delegates in each work-place now negotiate all issues relating to job organisation and working conditions. It has become a matter of company pride to begin and end annual negotiations for the nationwide agreement during the month of December.

By 1988, trade unions had a firm foothold in Bimbo. There is now a growing spirit of compromise and the unions have become increasingly influential representatives of the employees, who are currently organising in union sections. Bimbo's union delegates have been totally freed from other tasks in order to attend to their union commitments and each union section has its secretary general who represents the union in the company.

The personnel department's policy towards the trade unions has been one of *rapprochement* and support of the way the unions are structured within the company. This has made it a great deal easier to unify objectives and policies and has facilitated communication and the possibility of negotiating and reaching compromises.

Organising the personnel department

Since 1978 priority has been given to unifying personnel policies and objectives. The new personnel manager applied the CEO's operational criteria to his own department, decentralising operations and centralising policies.

At the same time five central departments were gradually set up in order to assist the personnel manager in defining general policies for the entire company. The first to be organised was the human resources department, under the direction of a psychologist who defined policies for recruiting, selecting, evaluating and promoting personnel so that the entire flow of employees eventually became a planned process. A legal department was then organised with a labour lawyer in charge of defining labour policies in accordance with the legislation in force at any given moment.

Shortly afterward the departments of personnel administration, organisation and compensation, and training were set up and gradually developed policies dealing with administrative control, wages and salaries, job organisation and training programmes.

The personnel department's entire philosophy is based on defining and applying policies. Relations with management and personnel delegates are given top priority and direct dealings with the employees are improving, as is the habit of providing all personnel with immediate information on the company's situation. The CEO gives his full support to the personnel department and explicitly approves all its policies, guaranteeing that they are totally coherent with the corporate strategy he has designed.

At the beginning of January every year, the personnel department meets to programme their tasks for the year and analyse the current situation. The four-day meeting is held outside the company and traditionally concludes with an address by the CEO. At one such meeting in Palma, Majorca, he said to all members of the department, 'I charge you with a mission: it is up to you to make employee motivation compatible with the company's objectives so that we form a compact, united social entity.'

This then is the goal of the personnel department and, paradoxical as it may seem, the majority of the employees are beginning to share this goal. One day the secretary of one of the union sections said to the personnel manager, 'You've managed to integrate us into the dynamics of the company and now we feel we're stakeholders and responsible for the company's performance.' This is perhaps the greatest achievement of a department of mediators that provides continuous, specialised service to management, delegates and employees in general.

Informing and communicating as a 'system'

In December 1977 in the midst of the big strike, when losses were tremendous and employees were demonstrasting in the streets with placards reading 'they're stealing 180 million from us', management called a meeting of 150 senior executives to analyse the situation. At one point in the meeting the personnel manager spoke up, saying, 'Gentlemen, there is a lack of information in the company. The employees don't know what is going on. What this company needs is a newsletter.'

His audience didn't burst out laughing simply because at this point the company's situation was not a laughing matter, but most of them felt that his suggestion was downright ridiculous. Nevertheless, as of 1978 the personnel department has been committed to keeping all employees informed about the company's plans and progress.

Once again, the CEO gave his full support to the idea and began writing a quarterly letter about the company's financial situation. The letter is published in the bulletin, which first appeared in 1979 on a bi-monthly basis. It proved an ideal way to keep employees throughout Spain informed about events in a company as geographically wides-pread as Bimbo.

Conclusion: December 1988, a bright future

Ten years after the serious crisis that unleashed the strike and triggered the change in orientation, we can safely say that Bimbo has become a major and very solid company.

Shareholders have regained their confidence and continue investing in the company. Everyone recognises the CEO as a gifted leader. The unified strategy of general and personnel management is highly visible and tangible. The company has adopted state-of-the-art technology.

Working conditions have improved considerably and salaries have gained in purchasing power.

Profits and capital earnings have also increased year after year. The management team is now highly experienced and acts in concert under the leadership of the CEO. The employees recognise all these improvements and feel involved in the process. Even the unions feel as though they are participating and share the responsibility for the company's success. Union policy is now definitely focused on negotiation and compromise. The employees know their company and what to expect from it; no surprises, no uncertain futures.

To sum up, Bimbo's current strong points are:

- its solid economic and financial situation;
- the strength, size and enthusiasm of the sales force;
- the general working atmosphere;
- the motivation and corporate culture which is shared by all employees. Employees are proud to work for Bimbo and have gradually come to feel that they are genuine stakeholders in the company.

Still, it would be wrong to overlook a few weak points that do exist and might threaten the achievements that have been made. These weak points currently include:

- pronounced growth in the competition with a highly aggressive pricing policy;
- excessive satisfaction with the company's achievements and lack of creative measures designed to assure an even brighter future;
- middle managers who are governed by a single agreement negotiated by unions which do not really represent them;
- the fact that there is no pension fund designed to improve the living conditions of retiring employees.

Bimbo has come a long way. 1990 marked the company's 25th anniversary. This silver jubilee is a good occasion to move onward and upward to new heights, confronting the challenge of the 1990s and entry into the new Europe, the 'common house' of a new era.

Questions

1. Define the most important elements of the company's:

   - Change: the five year plan;
     the CEO's leadership talents.
   - Culture: information;
     the strategic union of general management and personnel management.

2. How can Bimbo's 'culture' be defined?

   - by being bakers;
   - by quality and freshness: 'the freshest guys in town';
   - by pride: identification with the profession and the company.

3. Analyse:
   - the information system;
   - the way factories and sales are separately organised;
   - the way work is organised as the baker's 'profession';
   - union action in the company: how powerful are the unions?
   - employee integration: how is it achieved?

4. How does the political situation affect personnel management?

5. What are the conditions that provoke change?

6. What are the advantages and disadvantages of a centralised/decentralised organisation?

7. What are the features of 'professional' management?

8. What are the results of Bimbo's information and communication policy?

9. Is Bimbo's policy one of an iron fist or a velvet glove? Why?

10. Has Bimbo managed to integrate union action into the company? What is meant by 'integrate'?

11. What is the best way to develop human resources? Analyse Bimbo's system and suggest changes and improvements.

12. Are salaries the prime integrating force in Bimbo?

13. How did Bimbo manage to organise work performed under difficult conditions?

14. Describe the advantages and disadvantages of job descriptions and evaluations and of a single negotiated labour agreement.

15. Analyse the way the personnel department is organised and relate the way it is structured to the changes in Bimbo and the corporate culture that has been shaped.

Commentary on the Spanish cases

A final brief note on the Spanish case studies may be helpful, as a final comment on the argument presented earlier.

The Sociedad de Servicios case brings us into the realms of managing knowledge workers and the interpersonal skills necessary for the integration of talented people into teams. There are no easy, factual solutions to these problems. The question of what the facts are is not readily answered – in human resource management, feelings are facts. Opinions on which people act must be taken into account. The case may therefore be helpful in showing how management in a fast-growing industry brings to the fore the difficulties of managing the new knowledge workers.

Edicli/SA, a printing and publishing company illustrates the legal and institutional framework of a more traditional industry. The problems and issues of managing industrial relations in this sort of climate finds a resonance with the Merlin Gerin case, the SIP case and the Coats Viyella case. Organisations throughout Europe are changing from traditional relationships and cultures. The Edicli case is therefore a good opportunity to see the connections between HR policy areas such as working hours and the industrial relations traditions of a country.

The case of Bimbo SA helps to show how the growth and development of a business affects the climate of employee relations. The position after the strike, when a unified strategy of general personnel management was developed, including recruitment and communication strategies, reinforces the points made in the introductory chapter on Spain. It is in the 'corporate project', the creation of a corporate culture with the help of human resource management, that we can see businesses changing and adapting to the new Europe.

Part 5
United Kingdom

14

Human Resource Management in the United Kingdom

Shaun Tyson

Introduction

The economy of the United Kingdom has passed through a cyclical series of booms and slumps since the Second World War ended in 1945. The 'slumps' or recessions have been of varying degrees of severity, causing unemployment and the closure of many businesses. The 'booms' or periods of rapid economic growth have typically been accompanied by rising inflation, higher wages and raised expectations. The purchasing power of £10,000 in 1970 had fallen to £2878 by 1980 and to £1375 by 1991 (source: Central Statistical Office).

By the time the Labour Government left office in 1979, the general public had become disillusioned by the pressures from trade unions on the Labour Party, the constitution of which accorded them a special status and influence. These pressures had manifested themselves in an outbreak of public sector disputes resulting in the 'winter of discontent', when public services broke down as the Labour Government tried to resist wage claims in an attempt to stem the tide of inflation. The new Conservative government under Mrs Thatcher came to power with a mandate to introduce widespread economic and social change.

The new Conservatives put forward an ideologically coherent argument. There was to be a change in society towards individual responsibility. 'Sound money' (low inflation and low government borrowings), a greater emphasis on property ownership as an essential condition for democracy to work and rewards based on merit were the keystones. Small businesses and entrepreneurship were to be encouraged, with incentives to create wealth.

The mechanisms for achieving this change in society were as follows:

- The sale of public assets such as the utilities (gas, electricity, water and publicly owned organisations such as British Steel, British Airways and British Telecom) was pushed forward rapidly in order to increase the ownership of shares, to reduce losses to taxpayers and to provide a lump sum of money which reduced Government borrowings.

- The sale of council houses to sitting tenants was undertaken in order to give working people a stake in society and a foot on the first rung of the ladder of property ownership. This was interpreted by socialists as a turning away from any commitment to housing as a social necessity.

- Reductions in public sector borrowing through reduced subsidies and rigid control over money supply, which were believed to be the central mechanisms for reducing inflation, were achieved.

- The reform of institutions such as trade unions and the 'freeing up' of the labour market were combined with tax cuts as incentives, in an attempt to encourage individualism.

- A minimalist approach to Government intervention in all forms of economic relationships was encouraged.

- Dependence on the welfare state was to be reduced by creating looser structures in the organisation of health and education services, so that private services became more accessible.

These characteristics of the ideology which came to be described as 'Thatcherism' were present for most of the period from 1979 to 1990, even with three general elections to Parliament during that period. It was a time when financiers came into the ascendancy. Money markets and trading, service industries rather than manufacturing became dominant. The 'young, upwardly mobile professionals' known as 'Yuppies' were role models for this society. There were, however, contradictions. The power of central government was increased at the expense of local government mostly because of a failure to find a sound basis for financing local government expenditure.

This debate in local government has now evolved into a broader question about more local decision making through federal structures in the UK, devolving power to the regions of Scotland and Wales. The issues of what constitutional changes and regional development should happen in the UK as a result of EC integration and the social purposes behind the single market are questions made all the more important to both main political parties by the return to high levels of unemployment in the deep recession of 1992.

However, even after Mrs Thatcher's departure from office, the ideological ground on which economic and social issues are debated has irrevocably shifted to the right. The Labour Party has largely abandoned its original socialist philosophy which leaves its relation-ships with the trade unions in doubt, in favour of beliefs which are more in tune with those of the social and Christian democrats in other countries. They have strongly supported the 'social charter', a minimum wage and employee involvement. The Conservatives, re-elected again with a five-year mandate, have softened their monetarist views and have pragmatically shifted towards a large budget deficit in the face of a recession. They remain committed to a free labour market and opposed to centralist restriction from the EC.

Labour markets

In keeping with many other developed economies, there have been significant changes in the occupational structure in the United Kingdom. There has been a move towards a knowledge-based economy, away from primary industries and manufacturing. This is sometimes represented as a move from blue collar to white collar. In the last decade mechanisation has accelerated, with new technology influencing all types of jobs, a move perhaps to 'steel collar'.

Robots and automatic processes have been developed which allow a linkage to be made between computer-aided design and computer-aided manufacturing, offering flexible manufacturing options with highly customised products. Similarly, most white collar jobs have been revolutionised by new technology – whether it is automated banking or word processing and the enormous range of software packages available for clerical and administrative occupations.

The main expansions in employment have been in the service sector which now accounts for 37½ per cent of national output: employment in retail, banking, leisure, professional services and all other services now exceeds employment in manufacture.

Changes have also occurred in the development of the secondary labour market. This was due to a desire to cut labour costs and the need for a more flexible approach to employment on the part of employers and a desire for less commitment to one employer by employees. The secondary labour market consists of part-time, temporary, casual and sub-contract workers whose employment can be flexed in accordance with market demands. There is therefore a core of permanent employees for whom all the normal conditions of service apply and a periphery of employees whose services can be used as and when the business requires (see Figure 14.1).

In addition to this form of contractual flexibility, there is flexibility of time and of task. 'Flexibility of time' is where contracts are negotiated which allow either the employer or the employee to vary the start and finish times. For example, flexible working hours (under the control of the employee) or annualised hours (under the control of

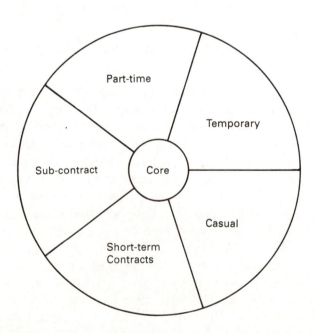

Figure 14.1 *The core and periphery labour markets*

management), flexible shift patterns (providing for people to change their shift) have all been developed by employers.

Task flexibility was encouraged by the breakdown of rigid trade union rules regarding the type of work members could perform, often negotiated as a part of a wider deal on pay and productivity. The intention was to avoid demarcation disputes between unions and to improve utilisation of craftspeople in such fields as maintenance.

Rising aspirations among women coincided with a demand for labour which could not be met by the male population alone. The changing demographic trends are common throughout Europe. In the UK in the period 1984–2000 there is a reduction by 23 per cent in 16–19 year olds and even among this smaller number of school leavers, there are more youngsters staying in further education thus reducing even further those available for employment. There is a corresponding increase in the number of people aged over 35. For employers to be able to recruit women who are at a crucial stage in the creation of their families, equal opportunity policies are needed. These are therefore driven as much by economic necessity as by values. In fact, the UK record on managerial or senior appointments for women is not impressive by European or North American standards. The majority of the five million new part-time jobs which were created were taken by women and, in spite of legislation, the positive action programmes and the appointment of equal opportunity managers in companies such as the National Westminster and Midland Banks, there still seems to be a shortfall between aspirations and reality for women in Britain.

The Conservatives have inherited a framework of employment laws including Equal Pay (1970) covering contractual terms and Equal Opportunities (1974) covering the non-contractual areas of discrimination in recruitment, training and development. However, legal intervention in labour markets was counter to their free market philosophy. One of the achievements the Conservatives claimed was that their employment legislation had freed labour markets, especially from any trade union control.

Institutional changes

Trade unions in the UK are mostly based on the occupation rather than the industry. Trade unions might therefore be found in any industry. There are exceptions: the National Union of Mineworkers, for example, is the main union in the mining industry. The old differences between 'craft' and 'unskilled' unions have now become less important as there are sometimes unskilled sections in skilled unions and white collar sections may also be found in what are often regarded as manual unions.

The power of trade unions was significantly reduced by legislation over the past ten years. The British system of industrial relations has frequently been described as a voluntary system, that is the relationship between trade unions and employers is governed by collective bargaining and the agreements between the two are, at the time of writing, not legally binding on each party. The Conservatives have stated their intention to introduce legislation to make such agreements legally binding.

The relationship between trade unions and the government has been distant over the past ten years. Collective bargaining has also moved away from the industry level to the local level, this being at the plant or firm level. This facilitates local agreements on pay and productivity and was a feature of the period from 1980 to 1990, when employers sought to increase productivity by changing working practices and bargaining arrangements.

It is through legal changes that the Government has sought to reform trade unions. In the UK there are two types of law: statute law which is created by Acts of Parliament, and common law which is based on precedent and which covers contracts of employment as one of many forms of contract. Common law is made by judges, whose decisions are recorded on each case as a guide to future action.

The legal framework under which trade unions operate is as follows:

- Trade unions do not have a positive right to strike or to take other action affecting employers, but are immune from common law prosecution for damages for breach of contract provided they fulfil certain obligations. These include the requirement for a secret ballot before action is taken. The trade union officials must themselves have been elected in a secret ballot.
- Any action by trade unions must be directed at the employer with whom they are in dispute. 'Secondary action' which attempts to put pressure on employers by indirect means is forbidden, as are political strikes.

- Employers do not have to recognise trade unions for collective bargaining purposes, but if they do, the trade unions have certain rights to consultation and information. Trade unions are not allowed to force employees to join.
- Trade unions have the right to be consulted on health and safety matters and to be given information where there is redundancy.
- Trade union officials such as safety representatives and employee representatives, known as 'shop stewards', have the right to time off to take part in union activities.

The statute law relating to employment also covers individual contracts of employment and is designed to prevent unfair dismissal and ensure that contracts are clearly specified. It also covers redundancy, equal opportunities and equal pay.

Complaints under the law relating to employment are heard at industrial tribunals, where three members (one employer nominated, one trade union nominated and one independent) decide the case. Employers can be ordered to make various kinds of financial restitution, but cannot be forced to reinstate employees. Appeals against industrial tribunal decisions are possible on points of law (not fact) to an employment appeal tribunal. Increasingly directives from the EC have an impact on employment law, as in the European court's equal value amendment to the equal pay laws, which instituted the principle of equal pay for men and women who do work of equal value, although the jobs themselves may be different.

Trade unions

Trade union membership has been falling steadily in the last decade. There are approximately 3 million fewer trade union members in 1991 than there were in 1979. In 1988 there were 326 trade unions with a total of 10.38 million members. By 1990 there were 305 trade unions with a total of 9.8 million members (Report of the Certification Officer, 1992).

The reasons for falling membership are not only because the Government has introduced strong legislation to crush union power, but more significantly because unemployment has occurred in those older traditional industries which either disappeared or were restructured during 1980–1981, where trade unions had a power base.

In addition, the exploitation of the secondary labour market and the increasing proportion of part-time contracts has made it difficult for unions to organise. There is also some evidence that women may be more reluctant to join trade unions than men and this has an effect as women now form around 50 per cent of the working population. New technology has moreover led to the restructuring of jobs and to consequential changes in membership. One response to these pressures by trade unions has been an increase in the number of amalgamations between unions who have to face severe financial problems.

In the fight for membership, divisions between unions have also become apparent. The Electricians' Union (the EETPU) left the collective association of unions – the Trades Union Congress (TUC) and together with the engineers (the AEU) they have typically sought to change the image of trade unions and have been more willing to cooperate in the restructuring of negotiations with employers. The recent merger between these two major unions reinforces their distinctive approach.

However, unions at 10 million members represent a substantial proportion of the working population of around 26 million people. They also exercise influence beyond their numbers, since the pay rises negotiated in key industries and companies, such as Ford and General

Table 14.1 *The disputes record in the UK*

Year	No. of days lost (thousands)	No. of stoppages
1980	11964	1348
1981	4266	1344
1982	5313	1538
1983	3754	1364
1984	27135	1221 (miners' strike)
1985	6402	903
1986	1920	1074
1987	3546	1016
1988	3702	781
1989	4128	701
1990	1903	630
1991	759	630

Source: Employment Gazette

Motors in car manufacture, produce knock-on effects on the rest of the economy as people try not to be left behind in the wage race.

There is also now substantial membership in the public sector, such as the civil service, local government, health service and in education. Many major disputes have taken place in the public sector – including those involving teachers and ambulance staff.

The number of days lost due to strikes has diminished although major disputes have had an impact (see Table 14.1).

When assessing the effect of government policies on union militancy, the impact of the labour market – of large scale unemployment – must not be forgotten.

Human resource management

The term 'human resource management' has entered the management vocabulary and signifies a new, more strategic approach to the management of people at work than is implied by the phrase 'personnel administration'. The most important changes are in the employee relations policies of organisations. The 1980/81 recession forced employers to rethink their employee relations policies.

The move to plant-level bargaining has generally been accompanied by the development of a strategic approach to industrial relations: that is, attempts to support the business strategy of change to improve competitiveness, greater efficiency and reorganisation. Policies in support of these objectives include new bargaining structures with reduced numbers of trade unions, formal communication policies, the introduction of flexible contracts and flexible working practices. These policies often constitute a coherent strategy aimed at reducing costs, increasing responsiveness to markets and improving quality and productivity.

The need to be competitive has forced companies to review their training activities and to strengthen the role of first line supervisors by giving them direct responsibility for discipline, training and reward. More recently the impact of quality initiatives has pushed the issue of total quality into all managerial practices.

The unifying theme in human resource management is the recognition of the need to utilise and develop people in support of business objectives. Thus non-employment options such as franchise operations are as much a valued technique for delivering quality to customers as human resource development policies.

While it is not possible to give a complete picture, the main current trends in human resource management can be described, under the various activities performed by human resource specialists.

Planning

There is still little evidence to suggest that HR directors play a major role in business planning; increasingly HR issues are dealt with at board level when, for example, mergers or acquisitions are planned, or when reorganisation and change are required and when pay rates are settled. The advent of software which models manpower has enabled scenario planning to be developed by HR specialists to inform management's choice of policy options. Boards do take a detailed interest in management development and succession planning and in any cost implications from union negotiation, or arising from salary restructuring.

Recruitment

Just prior to the 1990/91 recession, employers were searching for new recruitment strategies to overcome the shortfalls caused by demographic changes and skill shortages. With increased unemployment (heading up again towards 3 million) there seems little need to worry about finding enough people, although skill shortages do still exist. There has been an increasing tendency to recruit for jobs rather than careers, a trend encouraged now by the recession. This is complemented by an increasing emphasis on the competencies required for effective performance and consequentially by a search for techniques to measure competencies, such as tests and assessment centres.

Rewards

Productivity deals as part of a new approach to employee relations have encouraged reforms to reward structures. Performance related pay has grown in popularity, as have longer-term pay deals and a move towards single status, perhaps from the influence of Japanese companies in the UK. There is still much talk of cafeteria-style flexible benefits packages, but these more typically apply to the most senior levels. Pay in the UK tends to be industry specific, with little regional variation except in and around London. Managerial salaries vary by function and are also a function of the sales turnover of the business: higher salaries go with larger sales turnover in revenue terms.

Development

That skill shortages can coexist with high levels of unemployment has been seen as a commentary on Britain's education and training system. In the earlier recession, there were cut-backs in apprentice training schemes and the weaknesses of the technical and general education system have become obvious, even to governments. New initiatives, such as regional Training and Enterprise Councils, have been established in order to encourage and oversee training. There has been a marked increase in management development following a number of reports and government interest in the quality of management. The concern was with weaknesses in the volume of development compared with the UK's main competitors. A government and private sector sponsored initiative, known as the Management Charter Initiative, has helped to concentrate attention on defining managerial competencies and the different ways to attain them. Growing numbers of MBA programmes have been accepted as one response to the need for better trained managers. Perhaps most significantly, management development has been used as an important ingredient in change programmes, such as those at British Airways in the mid 1980s and at BP in the early 1990s. These programmes seek to 'empower' employees, to give them responsibility and the opportunity to perform a high quality job.

Summary

This chapter has described some of the main changes which are taking place in human resource management in the UK. The shift in emphasis to a strategically driven, business objectives-based version of personnel management is what prompts this to be described as human resource management, a shift in the models of personnel management which are found in the UK, with a move to a 'business manager' model which can be called HRM. HRM is now in the forefront of managing change. In the cases that follow three typical changes are descibed: the impact of the new employee relations policies in Coats Viyella, the value of management development as a part of equal opportunity policies at BT and the integration of European companies in the Square D case. Some of these strategic issues are, as in the case of changing bargaining structures, largely domestic. There are other changes, however, typified by new approaches to the development of women managers, which are common throughout the European Community. Perhaps the most exciting issue is the extent to which HRM is becoming, of necessity as in the Square D case, European.

Appendix: Main trade unions in the UK
(with over 100,000 members)

Union name and initials	No of members 1990
Transport and General Workers Union (T&GWU)	1,223,891
GMB	865,360
National and Local Government Officers Association (NALGO)	744,453
Amalgamated Engineering Union (AEU)	702,228
Manufacturing, Science and Finance Union	653,000
National Union of Public Employees (NUPE)	578,992
Union of Shop Distributive and Allied Workers (USDAW)	361,789
Electrical Electronic Telecommunications and Plumbing Union (EETPU)	366,650
Royal College of Nursing of the United Kingdom	288,924
Union of Construction Allied Trades and Technicians	207,232
National Union of Teachers (NUT)	218,194
Confederation of Health Service Employees (CoHSE)	203,311
Union of Communication Workers	202,500
Society of Graphical and Allied Trades 1982 (SOGAT)	168,753
Banking Insurance and Finance Union (BIFU)	171,101
National Association of Schoolmasters and Union of Women Teachers (NASUWT)	168,539
National Communications Union (Engineering and Clerical Groups)	154,783
Assistant Masters and Mistresses Association	138,571
National Graphical Association (1982) (NGA)	129,575
Civil and Public Services Association (CPSA)	122,677
National Union of Mineworkers (NUM)	116,252
National Union of Civil and Public Servants	113,488
National Union of Railwaymen (NUR)	101,311

Sources: Annual Report of Certification Officer 1991
Central Office of Information 1992

15

Coats Viyella: Decentralisation of Collective Bargaining

Godfrey Smith

Introduction

Within the United Kingdom collective bargaining with trade unions on pay and benefits has become more decentralised, away from national employer federations. By the mid 1980s single employer agreements had largely replaced multi-employer agreements as the major influence, particularly on the pay and conditions of manual workers. In 1986 the UK Government highlighted national collective bargaining as a cause of restricting labour mobility because of the common minimum pay rates which were set. The minister for employment stated in February 1987 'We must move away from the belief that national pay bargaining is the right way to determine wages. It is remote and destroys jobs; it takes insufficient account of the different circumstances of individual enterprises or of variations in the demand for workers and the cost of living in different parts of the country'. Those employers who have been proactive in restructuring have done so for a variety of reasons, none more important than looking for greater flexibility, productivity and other initiatives restricted previously by national agreements, while attempting to develop closer links between themselves and their employees.

Background

This study is based on the Apparel Division of Coats Viyella plc, a multinational textile company with sales turnover of approximately £2 billion, formed in 1986 as a result of the merger of three separate firms, Nottingham Manufacturing plc, Vantona Viyella plc and Coats Patons plc. The company is now organised operationally into a number of divisions, within which local management boards run subsidiaries or profit centres with responsibility and authority for the achievement of financial and other key targets. Collective bargaining arrangements mainly consisted of five national agreements, covering 22,000 manual workers in the UK on over 100 sites, within 65 profit centres. Following the formation of Coats Viyella plc a management task group was established to examine the relevance of national collective agreements to the bargaining process. A number of major disadvantages were identified:

- Participation in national bargaining restricted local management's ability to act independently within profit centres. It conflicted with the 'decentralised' culture of the company when, in a labour intensive industry, pay awards and benefits were negotiated within a national forum.
- Traditionally national bargaining produced only improvements in pay and benefits without any return to employers via improvements in productivity.
- New concepts, for example profit-related pay, could not be implemented nationally.
- Opportunities to develop a wider 'raft' of benefits necessary to recruit and retain employees were far too frequently constrained by opposition from other employers in the national forum.
- The company's key strategy to develop closer relationships with all its employees was fettered when issues of primary importance to them were dealt with away from their work-place.

It was these disadvantages which led the main board of the company to conclude in late 1987 that its participation in the five national agreements should be progressively terminated. The first step in this process centred on the knitting industry agreement, where the trade union involved was the National Union of Hosiery and Knitwear Workers and the subsidiary companies were those within the Apparel Division.

302

The preparatory process – management

With the company's culture of 'decentralisation', the first step towards achieving a successful reorganisation was to gain the commitment of senior line management within the 'profit centres' of the division. This discussion process with each managing director, of which 16 were involved, was led by the company's employee relations executive. None of them had any experience of conducting bargaining on pay and benefits. During discussions two major schools of thought emerged. Some welcomed the opportunity to establish a proactive role, believing that national arrangements did not reflect a company's 'ability to pay'. Pay awards and benefits negotiated did not emanate from the specific performance of each profit centre. Others supported national arrangements, (a) because they removed from them significant additional work and (b) because only personnel staff had the necessary experience and skills to conduct collective bargaining. Those who held this opinion argued strongly for extensive training for managing directors and senior line management in the techniques of collective bargaining. All held the view that discontinuing support for national arrangements would lead to the trade union 'picking off' a particularly profitable 'profit centre', achieving a settlement and then using that as the basis to achieve similar settlements in other less profitable units. Added to this was the concern that future national agreements within the knitting industry would set the 'going rate' and locally bargained arrangements would be unable to break this mould.

However, while some disagreement continued, the general consensus from managing directors was to support the restructuring process. Those who were more reticent were influenced progressively, particularly by the training established for them in collective bargaining. A series of training programmes were organised with Ashridge Management College, structured so that those 'managing directors and supportive line management who would be the negotiating teams in each 'profit centre' acted as such during the training process. The contribution that this training made to the attitude of the more recalcitrant cannot be over-emphasised.

The preparatory process – the trade union

While achieving support from line management was relatively easy, support from the National Union of Hosiery and Knitwear Workers was likely to be more difficult to achieve. As the sole trade union in the knitting industry it had a long and established involvement at very senior level within the national bargaining process, from which had emanated a comprehensive national agreement covering not only the annual pay award but a wide range of other benefits and terms and conditions of employment. National and other senior full-time officers were involved, with a very limited amount of authority and responsibility given to local shop stewards even where this covered local issues, eg piece rates, working conditions, work-loads. The national agreement set the 'going rate' for many companies not party to the national agreement who often did not recognise the trade union. As a result the union with its limited full-time officer resources, used the 'going rate' as the 'catch-all' for all those companies. Additionally the union was concerned about its reducing membership and believed any attempt to reduce the standing of the national agreement would put an even greater strain on retaining membership.

The company was anxious at a very early stage to gain the commitment of the union to its decision, seeking to work jointly towards an alternative bargaining structure acceptable to both sides. The company's employee relations executive held a series of meetings with the union's general president and its national officer and from the outset made it clear that there was no intention of withdrawing its recognition as the sole trade union, even though collective bargaining would take place outside the national agreement. In addition the company recognised that, with its move away from the national agreement, the union feared that existing terms which formed part of the contracts of employment of its members would be altered unilaterally prior to the alternative bargaining structure being established. Consequently at a very early stage in the discussions the company gave a positive assurance that this would not occur. These two assurances were key to the union and, having been given, were circulated in writing to all employees, before discussions proceeded towards the concept of 'profit centre' bargaining. The company had accepted in the early stages of the process that some flexibility was necessary and that its preferred structure might not automatically be acceptable. As it transpired only some minor variations were necessary. The timescale established by the company to achieve the restructuring aimed to ensure that by the end of September 1988 the new arrangements would come into effect and local bargaining commence.

The pre-bargaining phase – the trade union

Given acceptance by the trade union in March 1988 of the company's decision and its commitment supporting the union's position within the 16 profit centres, the discussions then moved into a negotiating phase to establish (a) the procedures for conducting bargaining at local level and (b) the existing substantive terms from which negotiations would commence. These negotiations were conducted centrally for the Apparel Division between the company's employee relations executive and the union's national official. They were structured at the centre in order to arrive at two model agreements, one on procedure and one on substantive issues, which could then be amended at the local 'profit centre' bargaining unit to incorporate only any current local variations.

Both model agreements were concluded by the end of June 1988. The procedure agreement covered union recognition, facilities for local representatives, internal and external negotiating machinery, joint works committees, disciplinary procedures, safety representatives and committees. The substantive agreement incorporated all the terms of the current national agreement, to reinforce the commitment made by the company to honouring all existing terms.

Armed with these documents, the general president of the union conducted a line by line examination with all shop stewards to gain their commitment. From there, the two model agreements were examined by both sides within each profit centre via the local joint negotiating committee, amended as necessary and then signed. During this phase from March to the end of July 1988, the company and the union issued a series of joint statements to all employees to ensure that everyone knew the amount of progress being made. This was an extremely vital part of the process. Communication was extremely thorough and detailed in content, essential to avoiding doubt and apprehension among all employees.

The local bargaining phase

By September 1988 the national agreement for the knitting industry had been finalised for the period January to December 1989. This gave a 5.5 per cent increase in pay and additional improvements in holiday pay, holiday entitlement and minimum pay rates. The cost of implementing this, had Coats Viyella been party to it, was estimated at between 6 and 6.5 per cent. The 'going rate' had therefore been established before local 'profit centre' negotiations commenced within the company. It should be of no surprise, therefore, that claims tabled by local union representatives followed the national claim with the objective of achieving at least the 'going rate'.

The negotiations were conducted against a background of difficult market conditions as customers sought to stabilise or lower their costs in the face of intense overseas competition. Each trade union team consisted of a maximum of six representatives plus a union full-time officer, while in many the managing director led on behalf of the company, supported by his production director and personnel executive.

The union's written claim was supported by detailed argument during the first meeting. Management responded with their estimates of the overall cost of the claim, moving then to an offer being tabled. Each trade union side concentrated very much on the level of pay award and other benefit improvements, many of which, for example sick pay schemes, were new to the negotiations, while management sought to achieve concessions in terms of new working arrangements and practices to reduce the cost of any settlement. Initially no one, recognising the close geographical proximity of the profit centres, wanted to settle early and therefore establish the 'going rate'. While the trade union negotiators pressed for concessions equivalent overall to the value of the national agreement, management were operating under the general financial constraints of forward budgets for 1989, including increases in labour costs. They were in a position within this constraint to operate flexibly in terms of the elements in any settlement which made up the total cost of the package.

While in those profit centres undergoing very difficult trading conditions negotiations were conducted under the threat of redundancy and closure, in others management wished to avoid disruption because that could lead to loss of market and of threats to their business viability in the long term. Some management would have preferred a nil cost settlement in the light of trading difficulties, whereas others who were performing profitably recognised that they would have to offer reasonable levels of settlement if agreements were to be achieved.

The results

Following on average 5 negotiating sessions, out of the 16 'profit centres' all but 2 had concluded agreements during December 1988. The rest were concluded after ballots of the labour force early in January 1989. However, there was no disruption in any profit centre in terms of lost hours or strikes, neither was there any need to involve external parties provided for in the procedure agreement to assist in concluding agreements. The following points emerged:

- Each agreement was different from the others and none was the same as the national agreement. Pay awards varied from 3 per cent to 7 per cent, but additional costs were less because of concessions achieved. All were less than the cost of the national agreement had that been implemented.
- Throughout, there was no evidence of the trade union 'playing off' one negotiation against another by targeting a particularly profitable company in order to set the 'going rate'. A 'going rate' was never achieved.
- Since the performance of each profit centre was key to the level of settlement, while one or two loss-making companies did concede pay awards, levels of awards were lower in less profitable areas than others.
- Every agreement achieved changes in existing practices from the trade union side, eg the implementation of cashless pay, increased flexibility, new working methods. In addition a number of principles were established for both sides to build on to improve future business performance.
- Management were able to concede improvements in benefits which had been anathema to those involved in national pay bargaining, for example, sick pay schemes, trading these off against the level of the pay award in order to produce a package which was more competitive in the external labour market.

Early in February 1989 all the management negotiators from each profit centre met to review their experiences. The clear message which emerged was that none wanted to return to the national structure. They still had some reservations as to whether they had broken the concept of going rates. As a footnote, the negotiations for 1990 agreements took place against a national agreement which gave a flat rate increase of 22p per hour. None of the local agreements settled on a flat rate increase.

Case analysis

1. If collective bargaining is to be restructured, all alternatives to the existing structure should be examined and a choice made which best suits the objectives of the company's strategy. 'Profit centre' structures may not suit those companies where, for example, manufacturing processes between sites are interdependent on each other. This heightens management's vulnerability to being 'picked off' in the negotiating process.

2. Management who will negotiate locally must be committed to their roles within the bargaining structures and to the objectives of the revised arrangements. Without that, any plans will fail.

3. The programme to achieve change must be planned in greater detail, before any new structures are discussed with trade unions. Timescales must be set clearly.

4. Revised bargaining arrangements require management to exercise new skills and understand new techniques. Training in these is critical to achieving success in handling local negotiations.

5. Trade unions will be concerned about any proposals to change traditional bargaining structures. The commitments made in this case to maintaining sole recognition of the union and to the existing substantive terms of the national agreement, which could not be altered unilaterally by the company, were fundamental to establishing the platform for support for the change.

6. In this case the trade union's full time resources were strained to cope with the additional workload arising from 16 negotiations. This has established a need for the company to offer assistance to the union to develop training in collective bargaining for local shop stewards, as well as knowledge of the operations of the company, so that they are better equipped to develop as negotiators for their membership within each profit centre.

7. During the planning process, a key area identified was the need for a detailed communication programme. In the major change illustrated in this case study, it was absolutely essential that everyone affected was kept informed of progress being made at each stage to maintain, on the one hand, management commit-

ment and trade union understanding and, on the other, to avoid rumour and fear of the implications of the change among all other employees. It was also important that the union was afforded full facilities to report back to their shop stewards at all stages of the process.

8. Given that one of the objectives was to develop a closer identification of shop stewards and employees with the performance and development of their employing 'profit centre', management need to recognise that communication with employees should be geared towards this objective, in a structured manner. To leave presentations on performance just to the negotiating round on a 'one-off' basis will not achieve this objective.

9. This same objective also requires a recognition by management that traditional pay and reward systems need to be carefully reviewed and geared towards linking at least some element to profit performance. Such change may be difficult to achieve, but if the maximum benefit is to be gained for both management and manual employees, then it is in this area that the real challenge lies for the future.

16

British Telecom: Establishing Training for Women Managers

Donna Burnett

In 1986 British Telecom (BT) launched its Management Development Programme for Women (MDPW). Although other companies in the UK (such as British Gas and ScotRail) offered similar programmes to their women managers, the BT programme was unique in a number of ways. This case examines how the programme was initiated, what its objectives were and how it was evaluated. The case sets out the process for implementing such a programme, noting the sorts of inputs which were required in this instance and commenting on whether it is possible to generalise from the way it was launched.

British Telecom: the organisation

BT is the largest private employer in the United Kingdom, with a staff of over 200,000 in occupations as varied as engineers, computer technicians, caterers and medical practitioners. It is the provider of 99 per cent of the UK's telecommunications and network systems and establishes and maintains these services throughout the country, covering an area ranging from the northern marshes of the Hebrides to the City of London itself.

The company was originally a division of the UK Post Office and, as such, was a monopoly under government control. Still within the scope of the government, it was established as a separate identity in 1980 when it became British Telecom. In 1984 the company became a public limited company (plc) and now has share capital of £6 billion, with the government still holding 48.7 per cent of total shares.

BT, then, has experienced enormous structural changes within the last ten years to accommodate the changes of ownership and, in the late 1980s, the emergence of a competitor in the telecommunications market. Along with these internal changes, this mammoth company has also had to respond to an external environment which is increasingly complex and fast-moving, in an industry sector which is on the leading edge of technological advance.

The workforce

Traditionally British Telecom has been an organisation which people joined soon after leaving school and where they advanced through to maturity and retirement. Personnel have entered the company on certain 'tracks' (eg management or engineering) and, most commonly, have advanced through the levels of each track until reaching the top of a pay scale. Jumping between tracks was relatively uncommon, although possible. People were promoted up through the company, with relatively few senior posts ever being filled by 'outsiders'. Due to the huge scale of the operation and the varying opportunities within it, employees did tend to remain in BT 'for life'.

Management structure

There are five management levels below the main board of BT. Generally speaking, each level is comprised of three 'bands'. Managers can be promoted through each level within the same division and they can also take sideways moves to other divisions.

Women

In looking at the numbers of women and their positions in the company, BT resembles many British companies with the largest numbers of women concentrated in the clerical and secretarial ranks, significant numbers of them within the first two management levels and very few found at more senior levels within the hierarchy.

Management development within BT

In the early 1980s management development had been handled centrally by corporate personnel. This branch within corporate headquarters held information on all BT managers, charted managers' progress within the company, suggested training and handled training requests. With decentralisation of the company in 1985, manager development came under the control of divisional personnel. Corporate's role became largely one of 'information broker', both inside the company and to the outside world (liaising with outside providers of training, establishing links with educational institutions). Divisions decided themselves how training funds should be apportioned and who should be trained. In reality training became the responsibility of line managers as part of the company's appraisal system.

The management development programme for women

Organisations are often reluctant to train women managers. Those who make decisions about who is trained often still harbour prejudices about the 'value for money' of training women. 'Why should we spend resources on training our women managers when they will undoubtedly leave the company when they decide to have a family, or to follow their husband's career?' is a commonly heard justification for this stance.

Apart from questions about whether or not women warrant training, a debate exists about what sort of training women should receive. Should it be identical to that experienced by their male colleagues, or do women have needs which are different and which training should address?

In the mid 1980s, factors both internal and external to BT encouraged scrutiny of the career paths of its women managers and consideration of ways in which women might be encouraged to stay with the company and reach more senior levels of management. Internally, in the 1980s BT found itself with an unexpected skills shortage. No longer government-owned, the business required an entirely new range of management and functional skills, such as accounting and marketing. As a monopoly under government ownership these functions had not been needed. When exploring where these skills might be found within the company, an internal human resources audit indicated that although women comprised nearly a third of the firm's workforce, their numbers were concentrated within clerical, secretarial and lower management ranks. Perhaps here was an untapped resource within the company itself to fill some of the necessary skill and managerial gaps.

In 1985 the external environment in which BT operated began to demand that something should be done about developing women managers. Baroness Platt addressed the board of BT demanding to know what the UK's largest private employer was doing for its 70,000 female employees. The answer was 'very little'. It seemed that the company was a clear target for investigation by the UK Equal Opportunities Commission. Therefore a number of different factors, both internal and external to the business, made the time ripe for an initiative to be taken on women's management development.

The team

There were three people who were most involved with the launch of the MDPW, Sue Lewis, Alec Thomas and Dick Greensmith. Each played an important role in the launch of the project both because of the energy each contributed, but also because of the position each held within BT.

Sue Lewis was the project champion. In 1985 Sue worked as a level 1 manager in corporate personnel. Very involved in women's issues of her own volition, she brought this interest to her work-place and wrote the initial document which highlighted the plight of women within BT. Her statistics showed the appallingly low number of women at management positions above level 2 and she made a case for the waste of human resources that was occurring. She lobbied senior managers with this information, explained what positive action was and prepared a report with recommendations of what should be done. One of the recommendations was for a training course for women. Sue saw the objectives of the course as providing a leg-up for women to make the leap from level 2 management upward. The success of the course, she felt, would be reflected by increasing numbers of women at management levels higher than level 2.

Although Sue's document offered several options for developing BT's women managers, a course was seen as the most feasible to 'get off the ground' while interest was high in the area of women's development. Sue's manager, Alec Thomas, was head of the management development group within corporate personnel at the time the programme was launched.

If Sue provided the 'fire' behind the project, Alec provided the logic and political skills to sell the idea to higher levels of management within BT. He toned down the paper which Sue had prepared in order to make it readable and acceptable to those who would, in the end, have to finance the programme.

Together Sue and Alec decided on the objectives of a training course which would be offered to women managers. They were adamant that they did not want to offer a 'general management' type course, as they felt this would be inappropriate. They reasoned that there were plenty of courses available which could provide a 'quick fix' of general management knowledge. Instead, they wanted a course that would specifically address issues faced by women in management.

At BT (like many traditional British companies) the most visible symptom of the fact that there were differing issues for men and women in management was the dearth of women at senior levels of management. Perhaps one explanation is the dilemma many women face of how to balance work and home life. This can especially be demonstrated at BT, where at managerial levels 1 and 2 there exists a substantial number of women, but thereafter the number rapidly decreases. Typically managers at level 2 have reached their late twenties or early thirties: critical years for women who wish to have children. Once outside main promotion streams, women often find it difficult to re-enter at the same level, especially in a high-tech business such as BT where change is rapid.

Misunderstanding of and aversion to company politics can also deter women from advancing in management. Even for women who are politically astute, exclusion from the 'old boy network' can leave them ignorant of crucial bits of organisational information.

Furthermore, although personal effectiveness is vital for both male and female managers and fundamental for grounding in other functional skills, Alec and Sue saw it as especially important for women managers who might not have experienced general management training before. They saw it as an enabling force to help women deal more effectively with their jobs as managers.

Once the objectives of the programme were formulated, the next step was to sell it to those in higher levels of management who could actually make it happen. The third person without whose help the programme would not have been launched was Dick Greensmith. Dick was head of corporate management development when the programme was initiated. He had recently seen his role change from one in a centralised function, in which he exercised total control, to that of an advisory function to the now decentralised divisions which were encouraged to be autonomous, even in terms of management training and development. When presented with Sue Lewis's report, Dick saw the programme as an opportunity to 'own' a programme of importance to the company. He envisaged the role of corporate personnel as one of innovator in the field of training programmes, and launching this programme would support that view. Additionally, as a policy for women's management development did not exist within the BT portfolio, such a programme would take a step towards remedying that gap.

Forces affecting both the internal BT environment (the shortage of skills required by the business) and the advent of external demographic changes, which could make the labour market even more competitive, further aided the attractiveness of the project. Dick hoped the programme would help BT resource itself internally. He thought the programme should have two primary objectives: firstly, that of developing talented women within the company and enabling and encouraging them to reach for more senior levels of management and secondly, providing them with a structure in which to consider options available to them in terms of their career and family.

Once Dick's support for the project had been won, Sue and Alec considered who the provider of the course should be. They realised that there would be resistance to the programme from throughout the organisation and managers would question the necessity for and relevance of a programme for women only. In order to gain credibility from within the organisation, it was vital that the provider be recognised as a sound broker of 'traditional' management training. As the programme was to have a high 'personal development' content, they had to have a favourable reputation in supplying this element as well. Sue and Alec presumed that since the course would come under a degree of scrutiny to which other training programmes would not be subjected, the pressure to find a provider who would 'come up with the goods' was further increased. After approaching several UK business schools, BT decided to place the MDPW with Cranfield School of Management, under the direction of Dr Susan Vinnicombe, Dr Kim James and Ms Sandy Cotter.

Women only?

The decision was taken to make the programme for women only because of several factors. One of the recurring problems for women once they reach higher levels of management within an organisation is that of isolation. By having women experience the programme together, it was hoped that they would feel less isolated and more supported. Furthermore the assumption was made that women managers do face different problems from their male colleagues and by having all women on the programme, these issues could be explored within a supportive environment.

Although a course which focused on general management issues could perhaps have been handled within a mixed group, it was acknowledged that issues of personal development, balancing career and family and politics within organisations were considered to be best handled within a single-sex group.

Whether or not one believes that women managers do in fact have different training needs, they often have different pressures on their lives which can make attending training programmes difficult for them. Even with the arrival of the 'new man', women in the UK still do the lion's share of the home making. Residential programmes can therefore be very difficult for them to attend without the necessary support at home. Even at this logistical level, it is important to recognise the different pressures facing many women which can affect whether or not they are able to attend training.

Funding

The programme was financed by corporate personnel, rather than by individual BT divisions. This has certainly made the programme more accessible to all the women who work for the company. There is a question as to whether individual divisions would actually pay for their women to attend – as women are so often given such low priority for training programmes. By making it corporately sponsored every women who works in BT has the potential opportunity to attend.

Women who attend

As the programme was seen as one way of encouraging women to climb higher within the BT hierarchy, the decision was taken to accept women for the programme who had the potential of attaining higher levels of management. It was expressly not seen to be for the so-called 'high flyers' within the company, as it was expected that these women would 'make it' without additional breaks. The MDPW was seen to be best suited to women who clearly had potential, but who needed a bit of encouragement to reach that potential. One of the criteria for being accepted on to the programme was that the woman should have been promoted once or twice and should in some way have demonstrated that she had the potential to move upwards through the organisation. Line managers nominated candidates to take part in the course. There were potential problems with this, such as the importance of the line manager and how she (or usually he) saw the programme. One response was also that line managers saw the course as something for women who needed remedial help and that participants should not make it known that they had attended as this might actually hurt their promotion prospects.

Educating the organisation

There was considerable resistance to the programme's establishment from throughout BT. Women themselves were at first reluctant to take part. Although senior management expressed support for the programme, most resistance was felt from middle managers. These were often precisely the people who decided what training their subordinates would do and which subordinates would do it.

However, reports following the pilot programme were favourable and soon applications began to flood in from all parts of the organisation as potential participants learned of the programme's existence.

The programme design

The programme was built in two one-week modules. This design was chosen for a number of reasons. By taking place for two one-week sessions a month or two apart, women's absence from work would be more amenable to line management, who might be reluctant to 'lose their managers continuously for two weeks'. Additionally, it was hoped that the participants could gain more from the course by being able to practise what was learnt in the first week and then come back to discuss it during the second. Participants were also encouraged to undertake project work during the time between the two modules. Also it was hoped that by designing it in two separate week-long modules rather than two continuous weeks, women would find it easier to be away from their home and family.

Programme focus

All along, the course was not to be a general management 'fix'. Instead it was to focus on personal effectiveness and broader issues such as organisational politics and time management. To this end, Sandy Cotter introduced a strong element of bioenergetics into the programme. Bioenergetics is a particular type of management development approach which concentrates on a mind/body perspective. This move is reflected in other management development practices as managers prepare for the 1990s and the need for personal effectiveness rather than specific skills.

Follow-up work

After taking part in the first course in 1986, the 20 participants approached British Telecom to secure funding for the establishment of a women's network within the organisation. Although the thought of establishing such a formal network had not been envisaged at the onset of the programme, its creation fulfilled one of the objectives of the programme: to encourage support and networking for women within the organisation. Today the network boasts many members, both men and women, and has regular monthly meetings.

Survey results

A survey about the programme was carried out in 1989 to assess its long-term impact. The evaluation was undertaken by the Cranfield School of Management in an effort to gain information on two areas:

- the long-term impact of the programme on course participants;
- the impact of the programme on British Telecom as perceived by line managers and subordinates of those participants.

The sample population was all sixty-one women who had taken part in the first three programmes, July/September 1986, March/May 1987 and May/June 1987. Questionnaires were also distributed to a role set for each participant, comprising their partner, line manager and two subordinates at the time of the programme. The response rate for participants was exceptionally high at 82 per cent. The overall response rate was 42.5 per cent. The response rate itself speaks of the high level of interest in and commitment to the programme.

The results demonstrated overwhelmingly the high impact of the programme both as reported by participants and as by partners, line managers and subordinates. Perhaps the result which most clearly articulates this view is that to the question: *'Which statement most accurately reflects how you perceived the participant reacted to the programme?'* 68.4 per cent of line managers and 46.4 per cent of partners answered: *'The programme had made a profound impact on her as evidenced by lasting behavioural changes.'*

As to whether or not the MDPW had in fact aided women climbing up the BT hierarchy, more than a third of participants had been promoted up one or more levels since taking part. Additionally, a significant number of women who had started families in that time had decided to stay with the company, successfully combining their career and their family. As one participant stated, 'Once you hold a job of reasonable responsibility, it seems more worthwhile to stay with the company. The programme demonstrated to me that it could be done.'

Conclusions

This case proposes to achieve two objectives: firstly, to present a prototype for project development and secondly, to examine how a programme for women managers was conceptualised, implemented and evaluated. Both are interesting in that both present problems with which personnel managers are constantly faced: broadly, how to launch such a training programme; what decisions have to be made concerning design, structure, target participants and training objectives; how decisions about funding are taken; how decisions about design are taken.

Also, as the demographic shift reduces the labour market, the importance of making the most of the entire workforce, including women and minorities, increasingly preoccupies employers. The problem then becomes how to train; who is best to train; should training be done in single sex or mixed sex groups; and how should decisions be made about who is trained.

Case analysis

Project conceptualisation, implementation and follow-up

It can be seen from this case that there were three distinct roles required in establishing the programme. A project champion, the person closest to the grass roots level, who understands the problem intimately. This person spots the problem and has the creativity and drive to pursue a solution. Often because of this person's emotional involvement, they may not be in the best position to sell their idea to those less interested and more concerned with bureaucracy and the *status quo*. But it is their emotionalism and commitment which drives the project.

In this case, there was also a 'tactical expert'. This person, though sympathetic to the cause, is not as emotionally involved and can present the case in a way that can be sold to senior levels in the organisation. This person is the bridge person, she or he speaks both 'languages' and knows the organisation well enough to put the project on the agenda.

Finally, there was the person near the top of the organisation with the political clout to push the project through. The idea has to be sold to him or her in a palatable manner and in a way in which he/she is also gaining something. These roles could well be embodied in fewer than three people, but each role is still necessary.

Women's development training

The area of women's management development training is a fraught one. Questions abound as to whether or not women managers actually have different needs in terms of training; whether, even if they do, they should be trained separately from men; whether or not such training should focus on catching up on technical and functional management techniques, rather than personal development. This case does not presume to answer these questions. It does, however, present one possible solution and way of going about resolving some of these dilemmas. Most of all, it presents some questions which organisations can ask themselves before embarking on the trail of training their women managers.

These questions might include:

- What is the objective we hope to achieve by training women? Are the women managers in our organisations not achieving higher levels of management because they lack functional knowledge, in which case would it be more beneficial to train them on standard functional courses, or are there other issues to be addressed?

- If a course for women only is decided on, who should teach the course? If it were taught by outside contractors, would it be held in higher or lower regard by both those undertaking the training and by others in the organisation?

- Does such training raise expectations – if so, how will these be resolved? How should the training be sold to the organisation as a whole and to participants? A problem often encountered by women's training is that it may be seen as remedial or 'because women can't achieve promotion on their own'. How will such objections be tackled? Who will decide who gets on to the training? If it is line managers, how do you get around managers not making it possible for their women to take part?

- How should the training be designed. Since organisations can often be reluctant to train their women managers, sometimes making it 'easier' for line managers to do without their women managers, how can it be made more possible for women to be trained? Further questions arise. Women, too, can be reluctant to attend training which is away from home as they are often primarily responsible for the home, and getting away for extended periods can be difficult, if not impossible, for women with young children. This should again be considered when thinking of the target group of participants.

- Finally, how should the training be evaluated? It is interesting to note that of all of the training programmes run by British Telecom, the MDPW is one of the only courses to be formally evaluated. This is primarily because of funding decisions, but perhaps it is also symptomatic of the fact that such training comes under harder scrutiny than traditional manager training.

Historically, training for women managers has been of low priority to organisations. As the labour market tightens, firms must look to the largest possible pool from which to choose and develop good managers. In order to establish effective training for women managers, organisations must consider the special demands inherent in providing such training.

17

Square D in Europe

Carol Ward

History

As an electrical equipment manufacturer in the USA since 1903, Square D has contributed to the success of the industry and has shared in its growth. Square D is one of the biggest manufacturers of electrical distribution and control equipment and a major supplier of electronic materials, components and systems, and rates as a Fortune 500 company. Square D operates more than 70 manufacturing and distribution facilities with 160 sales offices across the US and 18,000 employees worldwide. The company has been profitable for 50 years, markets more than 18,000 products and has annual sales in excess of US $1.5 billion.

In 1905, the company name was The Detroit Fuse and Manufacturing Company and its flagship product, an enclosed safety switch, was embossed with a capital letter 'D' in a square. The product became known in the industry as 'the Square D switch' and was so successful that other products were dropped, the fuse business was sold and the company's name changed to the Square D Company. A series of acquisitions followed which gave Square D its vast product range.

In the 1950s and 1960s, Square D expanded its operations into the international market place and at this time had manufacturing and sales centres in Canada, Latin America, Europe, the Middle East and the Asia Pacific area.

Competitive environment

Square D's major competitors are:

- Allen Bradley;
- ASEA Brown Boveri;
- Cutler-Hammer;
- General Electric;
- Siemens;
- The Schneider Group (Merlin Gerin, Télémecanique, April);
- Westinghouse.

Of these companies, only Allen Bradley and possibly General Electric have a more dominant market position than Square D in the USA. In Europe the position is considerably different, with markets dominated strongly by Siemens and The Schneider Group, of which Télémecanique is the most significant competitor. General Electric is also a significant player in some of the European market sectors. The Square D Company is operating in what are essentially mature markets in the developed world.

Formation of Square D in Europe

Square D has only relatively recently entered the European markets by a series of modest acquisitions in West Germany, Spain and Italy in the 1950s and 1960s. The company opened a sales organisation in England in the 1950s and subsequently established a significant manufacturing and distribution centre in Wiltshire. More recently sales and distribution centres were established in France and the Benelux countries. In 1987/88 these companies were integrated into a European profit centre under the direction of a European vice president who reported into a senior VP international operations in the USA.

Prior to this integration these six businesses ran very autonomously and reported direct to the US organisation their monthly, quarterly and annual results against planned performance. Up to 1988, several of the European businesses were managed by the previous owners from whom Square D had acquired the small family businesses.

There had been minimal investment by the parent company in these European businesses, real growth in earnings had been negligible and modest growth achieved in overall market share. With the exception of the UK business, in which some investment was made in 1986/87 (mainly in plant, equipment and sales infra-structure, which has paid off and turned in a profit on sales which have grown by up to 50 per cent year on year since 1987), none of the European businesses plays a significant role in the markets which, with the exception of one or two specialist niches, are dominated by two or three of the competitors already mentioned. The business strategy in 1987/88 with the formation of the European headquarters organisation (Square D Europe) was to integrate the six operations to achieve:

- integration of management structures and decision making to optimise the 1992 single market in Europe;
- pan-European product marketing strategies;
- rationalisation of manufacturing to create centres of excellence and achieve economies of scale;
- cost reduction;
- pan-European customer service;
- rationalisation *and* expansion of the product portfolio;
- professionalism of operations in all disciplines and functions;
- increased market share;
- profitable growth.

To achieve these objectives, a European business team was formed, comprising VPs of finance, manufacturing operations (including customer service/product distribution and R & D), corporate planning and Management Information Systems (MIS), marketing and human resources (see Figure 17.1).

It was decided to leave the six country operations under the control of six locally recruited general managers, reporting to the European president, and to create a European matrix organisation with strong functional direction being provided to each of the six businesses from the VPs at the European HQ.

The human resource challenge

At this point in late 1988, human resource management and support

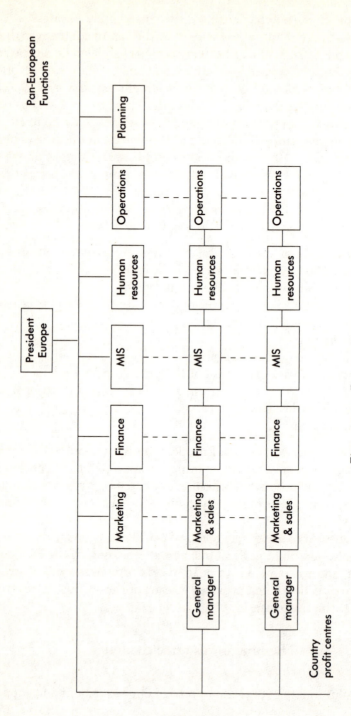

Figure 17.1 *European organisation structure*

to the European organisation had been focused on record keeping, administration and some filtering of initiatives from the corporate human resource function. The formation of the business team at the European headquarters (which was UK-based) meant that, for the first time, there was a position created which was both pan-European and strategic in orientation.

The emphasis of the role was to assist the European businesses to grow and become profitable by improving current practices, recommending initiatives for the future, providing support to the president and the evolving European team and interfacing with the corporate human resource group to establish functional philosophies and synergies. In practice, the priorities emerged as follows:

- Assist the president to attract and select suitable candidates to head up each of the European operations and hire Euro-VPs to complete the HQ team.
- Evaluate the competitiveness and relevance of the compensation and benefit practices in each of the six European operations and recommend actions as necessary, assisting the operations to design policies and procedures for future remuneration strategies.
- Evaluate the professionalism and effectiveness of the HR staff in the countries (only the UK and Germany had 'personnel managers' and a personnel department) and recommend actions to establish high-calibre HR resources in the businesses.
- Assist the newly appointed GMs to evaluate the organisational structures and competences of key managers in the six European businesses.
- Establish human resource policies, standards and practices in the European businesses to enable those units to grow and achieve long-term business objectives.
- Assist the president, Europe to build the top team* matrix relationships and interdependencies.
- Initiate human resource development programmes and processes to upgrade the professionalism of managers in the businesses.
- Assist the president to develop the competences and career development of the top team.

---

*Six general managers and five vice presidents.

Corporate culture change process

In 1988 the Square D Company, under the leadership of a new president, initiated a world-wide total quality programme and process. They called it 'Vision-Mission' and created a 'college' and a 'faculty' to spread the messages.

The principal messages conveyed by this process were those of:

- ownership by every employee of the company's service to its customers;
- permission given to every employee to escalate and resolve perceived inefficiencies/blockages;
- encouragement of risk taking;
- delegation of accountability down into the organisation.

The vehicle chosen to be the agent of change was a two-day, off-site programme facilitated by volunteer trainers from all parts of the organisation. The trainers, or facilitators as they were called, were trained by external consultants provided by corporate headquarters and who conducted train-the-trainer sessions all over the USA, in Europe and in Australasia. Training materials were provided centrally and translated locally and the target was to 'train' 20,000 employees over a two to three year timeframe. At the time of writing this case, this process was 75 per cent completed in Europe.

European organisation analysis

An analysis of organisation and human resource issues in each country revealed:

UK

800 personnel in manufacturing, product development and sales/marketing. Manufacturing processes employing both skilled and semi-skilled personnel. Features:

- a largely reactive and administratively orientated personnel department;
- salary levels somewhat below market averages in an area being infiltrated by the newer industries;

- mediocre benefit package (ie modest use of company cars and difficulty therefore in attracting high-calibre staff in critical jobs);
- no profit- or performance-related pay, except for sales personnel;
- ageing workforce but higher labour turnover at the lower end of the age spectrum resulting in a lack of solid competence in the middle of the age range;
- supply market for labour creating more and more shortages as the birth rate drops;
- a profitable business but in mature markets and in a time of economic 'softening' facing severe pressure on margins in the near term;
- a low profile, cooperative trade union representation;
- some management training had been provided as well as the US total quality programme.

West Germany

600 personnel in manufacturing, product development, sales/marketing, using the same skills as the UK company. The company is split into two units, sales and manufacturing. This is a historical phenomenon created by the establishment of a Square D sales organisation and the purchase of a privately owned manufacturing operation. The two companies had separate structural status for many years and the different cultures exacerbate a real 'them and us' syndrome. Features:

- a personnel department which had as its prime focus the interface with the works council;
- a management team which had been leaderless for 12 months;
- robust pay rates against market averages (this would be expected as the company was a member of an employers' federation and pay levels established according to tariffs);
- no history of performance-related pay or managing by individual performance objectives;
- very little training done other than with traditional engineering apprentices and with the exception of the US total quality programme;
- a strong but apparently cooperative works council;
- a workforce who expressed fears that the US parent would withdraw from the German market which is a tough one, dominated by Siemens and difficult to penetrate by a non-German supplier.

Spain

200 personnel in manufacturing, product development, sales/marketing, using same skills as UK and Germany. Features:

- an antiquated plant into which it was difficult to attract and motivate staff and in which it was difficult to produce high-quality (dust-free) product;
- no HR department;
- recent recognition of the Communist Union with which the company dealt exclusively;
- a cooperative relationship with the work-force in general who were loyal and stable;
- no training and development had been done, with the exception of the US-initiated total quality process;
- poor pay levels and benefits against market averages;
- with its cost structure and manufacturing processes the company would have difficulty in growing profitably.

Italy

200 personnel in manufacturing, product development, sales/marketing, using same skills as UK, Germany and Spain.

- no human resources department;
- a mainly cooperative work-force with some evidence of pockets of militancy;
- a legacy of difficult relationships with the union representatives;
- high absenteeism amongst blue collar employees (ie 10–15 per cent);
- high unit costs and issues of poor product quality and customer service;
- no training and HRD had been done with the exception of the US total quality programme;
- low pay levels and poor benefits;
- under-investment in sales and marketing with resultant poor sales growth;
- a strong market position in a niche market but barriers to gaining greater market share for other products in a very fragmented market.

France

20 personnel in sales, distribution and administration.

- no HR function;
- no training and development had been done in the company's history with the exception of the US total quality process;
- markets in France dominated by Télémecanique, therefore significant barriers to entry for smaller competitors;
- difficulties of attracting high-calibre personnel to a small operation with apparently limited growth potential.

Benelux

30 personnel in sales, distribution, product support and administration working in both Holland and Belgium with a distribution and sales centre in Holland.

- no HR function;
- very little training and development had been done other than some product training and the US total quality process;
- some opportunities for growth in markets which are not totally dominated by a national supplier (as are France and Germany);
- difficulties in attracting and retaining high-calibre personnel in a small operation with limited career development opportunities in Benelux.

The way forward

At the time of writing the European business team was in place. The six country general managers had been selected for their business skills and industry know-how and the headquarters function heads were chosen for their specialist skills and expertise gained in large, well-run organisations. Only the president and one general manager in the group had been with Square D for more than one year.

As with most North American-based organisations, Square D was essentially profit-driven and the expectations will be for Europe to continue to contribute to corporate profitability while reinvesting in its organisation.

It was clearly articulated policy that the European headquarters organisation will remain small and that all of the infra-structure to drive programmes and processes to improve organisational effectiveness will be resourced and implemented by the operating companies in Europe.

In the six to twelve months following the appointment of the country GMs and the headquarters VPs, an exhaustive analysis of the six businesses was undertaken by the GMs with assistance and specialist intervention by the VPs. This process was complemented by days of discussion as a full team on a more strategic level. These discussions evaluated and reviewed the European company's strengths and weaknesses in its markets as well as considering how those markets were changing, the impact of 1992 on markets and competitors and how Square D Europe should structure its business over the next three to five year period to effect the changes necessary to take advantage of the evolving markets.

This dual process of operational analysis and future planning produced a five-year strategic business plan which was presented to the corporate senior management in mid 1989. The plan was characterised by requirements for:

- rationalisation of manufacturing processes including automation, JIT (just in time) manufacturing, production cell introduction, transfer of processes to effect economies of scale and take advantage of know-how;
- rationalisation of products including cessation of non-profitable lines, development of new products, brand labelling/joint marketing arrangements;
- reinvestment in sales and marketing personnel including an aggressive hiring programme and retraining of existing sales personnel;
- development of new channels to market with implications of 'doing business a different way', involving new skills, new understanding and differently experienced sales and marketing resources;
- centrally driven, pan-European direction of customer service and inventory logistics;
- externally sourced professional services to plan and implement a pan-European MIS strategy;
- investment in organisation and human resource development

including management and supervisory training, sales and marketing training and team building.

The organisation therefore was poised to move itself into a new phase of development. There was a good collective understanding among the European management team about what needed to be done. The challenge was how to achieve it.

Questions

The reader is asked to assume the position of a vice president human resources, Europe. What strategies would you recommend to assist the senior team to achieve its business goals? What two-year programme would you establish to achieve your recommendations? You will need to consider resources, budgets and returns on investment in HRD to the company. You will have to sell your objectives, the programme and the benefits to corporate senior management who will be looking for outputs and value added. Please give consideration to these specific issues:

1. What assistance will be needed to help the 'top team' establish their matrix role interdependencies?

2. How would you assist the six European businesses to formulate and execute HR programmes and processes?

3. How would you drive pan-European management development?

4. What contribution from the human resource function is going to be most valuable to Square D Europe in the next two to three years?

Case analysis

At the time of writing this case and in the subsequent two years, the European OD plan was characterised by the following elements:

1. Construction of new bonus schemes which were based, for general managers, 80 per cent on total Europe pre-tax contribu-

tion and 20 per cent local country pre-tax contribution, and for the level below GMs on a 50–50 split between total Europe and country PTC.

2. An internal accounting process which removed the 'who takes the profit' debate from the process of one country selling product manufactured elsewhere within the European 'family'. The same system identified some significant pan-European programme costs, such as product development/product management, high-potential management development programmes, college/university hiring programmes, career planning and so on. All these programme costs were expressed 'below the line' and removed from the country performance measures.

3. A strong focus on the cascading of performance objectives based on business plan and strategic plan objectives and training at all levels in the skills of objective setting, performance tracking and counselling.

4. Introduction of performance-related reward programmes based on both individual and group achievement with elements of both salary range penetration methodology and group profit sharing.

5. Introduction of cost identification by 'readiness to serve' costs (ie the fixed cost element attributable to doing today's business) and future costs (ie the costs associated with future investment in organisation, product, process) and a rigorous analysis and review of ways in which to take cash out of the RTS element in order to invest in the future.

6. An analysis of human resources and structures associated with both RTS and future costs and an introduction of programmes to move resources from the former into the latter activities, while eliminating supervisory and management roles and overall flattening organisation structures. Alongside this process was one of work redesign to optimise human resources, reskill as many jobs as possible to improve productivity, quality and disinvest in unskilled resources.

7. A new approach to the construction of a European business plan which was a horizontal product line build-up, rather than an add-up of six country profit and loss accounts.

8. The formation of several pan-European teams, centrally managed but with distributed resources, the budgets for which (for those teams which were permanent in structure or semi-permanent in project duration) were taken as a 'below the line' cost and not

counted in the results for which the countries were accountable. These teams covered manufacturing rationalisation, product rationalisation and development, customer service and logistics, management information systems, marketing communications and corporate image. There was also linkage established into world-wide R & D programmes to leverage corporate budgets for the benefit of Europe.

9. The introduction of a European-wide organisation audit featuring high and low potential managers, career development planning and tracking and key job-holder action planning. This was a centrally driven process executed by the countries but monitored centrally and which linked into a world wide process.

This entire process was orchestrated under the umbrella of a group consultative and decision-making body comprising all the European general managers and European functional vice presidents which met monthly to review not only historic operational results but to discuss and plan longer-term strategies and programmes. There was considerable resource sharing and involvement in specific projects by the country general managers and those reporting to them. By this process, the organisation made the transition from being a six-country business towards a European business using its collective strengths to optimise market opportunities and organisation resources.

Commentary on the UK cases

The cases from the United Kingdom presented here offer a surprisingly constant set of issues for consideration. Whatever the changes to collective bargaining we have seen, whether it be the Japanese influence or the changes reflected by the new occupational structure, the need to create productive relationships at the work-place is paramount. Similarly, management development remains the most potent instrument for changing organisations. The need to develop women managers also at this time coincides with a shift in values among employees and raises important questions about the balance between work and home life which are of significance in career development and life planning.

The new opportunities which stem from pan-European operations offer an opening to human resource managers to become involved in the serious strategy and structure debates which are current in European companies. Competitive advantage is gained by corporations which have discovered how to be flexible and accountable across Europe and to use their multicultural and multifunctional top teams effectively.

Throughout Europe, companies are adapting and changing. Most of the cases described in this book have taken the practical and often urgent need for change as a focus for a debate on strategic human resource issues. That there are similarities between countries, such as the move to better quality, the shift in trade union relationships and the move to more responsive, market driven structures, should not prevent us from seeing that organisations and employees are also strongly influenced by national culture. To describe the 'French' or the 'German' approaches to management may invite accusations of stereotyping, but although they involve generalisation, such descriptions help to remind us that the issues we face as managers are embedded both in an organisation and in a national culture. We hope this book has illustrated through its descriptions and cases the relationship between the organisational and the cultural context.

Index

Michael J. Schott, MA, MLS

Medical Library
Downsizing
Administrative, Professional,
and Personal Strategies
for Coping with Change

Pre-publication
REVIEW

"**M**ichael Schott is fresh, funny, and fearless in this take-no-prisoners guide to dealing with corporate takeovers, mergers, and downsizing that threaten and challenge the survival of hospital libraries. Learn from the mistakes and triumphs of other librarians who have survived budget cuts, layoffs, organizational restructuring, and pension buyouts.

Schott's wry and insightful work includes case histories, practical tips, and hints for anticipating and dealing with these organizational threats and opportunities. Highlights include warning signs that every library manager should heed; the importance of crafting a well-written résumé, library mission statement, and library vision statement; metrics, benchmarks, and organizational studies that prove the worth and value of the library under fire; and strategies for surviving layoffs and negotiating deals.

I wish this book was in print when I was a hospital librarian. Recommended reading for entry-level, mid-career, and seasoned hospital librarians alike."

Elizabeth Connor, MLS, AHIP
Assistant Professor of Library Science,
The Citadel,
Charleston, South Carolina